DEBBIE GIBSON

Eternally Electric

Number 100 of 2499

Eternally Electric

Eternally Electric

THE MESSAGE IN MY MUSIC

DEBBIE GIBSON

with Richard Buskin

Gallery Books
New York   Amsterdam/Antwerp   London
Toronto   Sydney/Melbourne   New Delhi

This publication is a memoir. It reflects the author's present recollections of her experiences over a period of years. Some dialogue has been re-created from memory.

Gallery Books
An Imprint of Simon & Schuster, LLC
1230 Avenue of the Americas
New York, NY 10020

For more than 100 years, Simon & Schuster has championed authors and the stories they create. By respecting the copyright of an author's intellectual property, you enable Simon & Schuster and the author to continue publishing exceptional books for years to come. We thank you for supporting the author's copyright by purchasing an authorized edition of this book.

No amount of this book may be reproduced or stored in any format, nor may it be uploaded to any website, database, language-learning model, or other repository, retrieval, or artificial intelligence system without express permission. All rights reserved. Inquiries may be directed to Simon & Schuster, 1230 Avenue of the Americas, New York, NY 10020 or permissions@simonandschuster.com.

Copyright © 2025 by GibsonGirl Productions, Inc.

All rights reserved, including the right to reproduce this book or portions thereof in any form whatsoever. For information, address Gallery Books Subsidiary Rights Department, 1230 Avenue of the Americas, New York, NY 10020.

First Gallery Books hardcover edition September 2025

GALLERY BOOKS and colophon are registered trademarks of Simon & Schuster, LLC

Simon & Schuster strongly believes in freedom of expression and stands against censorship in all its forms. For more information, visit BooksBelong.com.

For information about special discounts for bulk purchases, please contact Simon & Schuster Special Sales at 1-866-506-1949 or business@simonandschuster.com.

The Simon & Schuster Speakers Bureau can bring authors to your live event. For more information or to book an event, contact the Simon & Schuster Speakers Bureau at 1-866-248-3049 or visit our website at www.simonspeakers.com.

Manufactured in the United States of America

10 9 8 7 6 5 4 3 2 1

Library of Congress Control Number: 2025939672

ISBN 978-1-6680-5676-9
ISBN 978-1-6680-5678-3 (ebook)

Dedicated to Diane Gibson
Proud Mother and the original Momager
She filled the room

CONTENTS

Foreword by Joey McIntyre	1
Introduction	5
Chapter One: My Way	11
Chapter Two: Bitchy, Not Pitchy	31
Chapter Three: Setting the Stage	49
Chapter Four: Only in My American Dream	69
Chapter Five: Pretty Little Veneer	91
Chapter Six: Pop-Bullseye Girl	111
Chapter Seven: Shock Your Mama	133
Chapter Eight: Bobbies in the Lobby	155
Chapter Nine: Sing Out, Louise!	179
Chapter Ten: Ms. Naked Vocalist	201
Chapter Eleven: Stuck	221
Chapter Twelve: All Good Things Discontinued	241
Chapter Thirteen: The Gift	261
Chapter Fourteen: Anything Is Possible	285
Acknowledgments	303
Photo Credits	309

FOREWORD
by Joey McIntyre

I've seen Debbie Gibson naked.
 Actually. But more on that later.

Metaphorically, I've had the privilege of watching Debbie bare her soul, up close now, for about the last six years. She is my teacher, my friend, my sister, my pop soulmate. To sit with Debbie for more than five minutes is to know her—present, caring, unselfish, curious. Funny! Loves a good laugh—looks for them on a consistent basis and applauds any joke, even if that joke wasn't very good.

So, yeah, if you asked me if I knew who Deb was, I'd say confidently that I do. But after reading this book, I might have to be placed in the "you think you know, but you have no idea" pile.

I knew she was tough—Long Island–bred Italian, not a stretch. Sure, she had the DNA to weather a nor'easter from time to time, but the toughness, the grit, the drive that she imbues came from a journey that quite simply most girls/humans would not survive. She is a force of nature. And she walks hand in hand with Mother Nature herself.

FOREWORD

Knowing when to let the sunshine in. When to stop and look up into the heavens and smile. And breathe. She also knows when to shut it down, even when she doesn't want to. She learned to do so by listening to her body. Because yes, indeed, the body sure 'nough remembers. You, the reader, will now see and hear what Deborah Gibson's body remembers:

For starters, being the youngest person to write, perform, and produce a #1 record, all while . . . wait for it! . . . going to high school. Literally. Teenage-butt-in-seat-in-a-Long-Island-New-York-classroom. Who does that? Is it normal? No. Is it healthy? Not sure. As you hear this story, you might find yourself hollering: "Stop the world, Deb needs a nap! No, she can't take another picture. No, she can't do that seventeenth interview of the day. And no, she can't kiss another radio station boss's ass for a few more spins! She doesn't want to get off, she just wants to pull over." The thing is, we have to learn as we go. There is no handbook for being a massive star at seventeen. If there were, she might have handed down hers to me, scribbled with notes and ideas. Knowing Debbie, it would have been jammed with pitfalls to avoid and also the best places to stop for soft serve. Or a massage! Or some crazy guru who can cure frozen shoulder. But, alas, we didn't have the tools back then.

She did have her mom, a maverick. She did have her dad, who gave her the love of song. She had her sisters. She had her "fur babies." And she had you. Yes, she weathered the storms, but I don't see Debbie as a survivor—that term connotes a "before and after." Deb is so very much in the *here and now*. She's a fellow traveler. Curious as ever. Always digging for the next treasure. And after all she has experienced, it somehow feels like it's only the beginning.

She's a singer. She's a songwriter. She's a musician. She's an actor. And now an author. And like everything else she does, a damn good

FOREWORD

one. This book is a living, breathing thing. I related in such a visceral way. It's like she did all the heavy lifting: going back into our childhood, our teens, and our young adulthood, so graciously laying out the good, the bad, and the beautiful.

Because Deb shares with such humility, I know you will relate as well, regardless of the circumstances. I know there will be moments here when, like me, you are going to want to go back in time and take her away from the pain and struggles of such an exhausting, exhilarating journey, but odds are she would turn to you and say, "Thank you. I so appreciate you, but I got this."

Introduction

ELECTRIC YOUTH TURNS 35

"Extra! Extra! Read all about it!"

BACK IN NEW YORK CITY, WHERE IT ALL BEGAN...

It's July 26, 2024, a perfectly sunny summer's day, and I'm celebrating the thirty-fifth anniversary of my #1 album with a live performance at The Town Hall. I know this city by heart and I feel at home in the middle of its chaotic, colorful streets. One of my favorite things about NYC is I can think of a friend, send a text, and within ten minutes we're walking toward each other, meeting up for a coffee.

It's great to be back after performing all year, creating an updated version of the 1989 concert with many of my original band members, singers, and dancers. And I'm brimming with anticipation as my team and I found the perfect venue for this special event that will also be live-streamed around the world. It is intimate enough to be able to really commune with my audience, but it also has a built-in excitement and energy reminiscent of my days selling out venues like Radio City Music Hall.

I see the faces of my die-hard fans as they post their travel day in real time while flying in from all over the world. Tears immediately surface and I take a beat to take this in. We've been on this journey together for over three and a half decades, and now more than ever, it is about them as much as me. This latest pop-music resurgence has enabled me to see the kindhearted, beautifully authentic, empowered people they have grown to become. And yes, my audiences look to me, but they are a constant source of energy and inspiration.

I arrive at the venue in a bit of a heightened state, as I always am on a show day. You'd think after all these years I would be like, *Yeah, another show tonight.* But it is always special and therefore brings on all the feels, including my old pal, anxiety. Though I'm a thousand times more stable than I was in my teens, it comes as a relief to find myself in the presence of my manager, Heather Moore, a blonde, badass, quick-witted gal who always has my back. I tend to wear many hats, but being the leader 24/7 is exhausting, and she knows how to allow me to be the artist and take my director hat off for a bit.

All at once, I'm transported back in time by the sound of Stepp Stewart singing "Love Under My Pillow," which he and I will later duet on. This sweet sound pulls me from the door into the wings, and the first face I see coming toward me, arms open to share a celebratory hug, is a familiar one. My OG dancer/choreographer Buddy Casimano, my bestie, with his megawatt smile, bald head, and en pointe backflips that he still nails in performance, has been a joyful force in my life since our days together at Calhoun High School in Merrick, Long Island.

"Hi, Bahhh!"

A nickname we share.

"Hi, Bahhh!"

Buddy is one half of the Bookend Baldies. The other is Eddie Bennett, who, wise beyond his years with his grounding energy and insights, is also one of my BFFs who I met in 2002 during a production of *Chicago*. Running through some of the songs with Adam and

Kirk, from my original band, as well as with my new onstage team of Joey, Ariel, and Ronda, my energy is lifted even higher and I know I'll be ready to rock—after I've had an hour to myself to quietly doll up, warm up, and get my preshow game on.

Makeup artists often hit me up to help me get my glam on for concerts, but this is my sacred time when I get to revel in the reality that my dreams have come true—hard-earned dreams my team and I relentlessly pour ourselves into. I allow very few interruptions, but family is different, so when my sister Denise comes bounding up the backstage stairwell with her brood in tow, I welcome them with a smile.

It occurs to me that I've been in thousands of dressing rooms, and this one—with its stark, old-school NYC vibe, long makeup table, simple gray couch, and warm lighting—feels like an old friend. I am suddenly thankful for waterproof mascara. No stranger to being vulnerable these days, feelings kind of sneak up on me, and I cannot help but wish my mom, Diane, was here. She and I were a dynamic duo—two girls taking on the big, bad music business. Without her tenacity and singular vision as one of the world's first and greatest momagers, we probably wouldn't be here tonight celebrating songs like "Lost in Your Eyes" and "We Could Be Together."

Nobody would be living for this moment more than her, and though my spiritual side knows she is presiding, oh, how I wish I could give her a preshow hug.

I glance at my phone upon hearing the text tone pierce through the song "Our House" by Crosby, Stills, Nash, and Young, which is appropriate because the text is from a certain boy who's held my attention for quite some time. Maybe since childhood, maybe from another life—I'm not quite sure. Though we've had a bit of a journey that is currently at a romantic standstill and might not play out fully in this lifetime, we are indeed super close, texting and voice-noting daily. And this boyish man shows up virtually to let me know the universe has told him this is going to be the best show of my entire life.

I wish this boy and my mom could be here today. They knew each other once upon a time and long ago. Occupying very different spaces in my heart, they each tie to a time and a place that connect to this music. They remind me of who I was and who I've become. It is all otherworldly. And, though I'm beyond grateful for all the people who *are* here for me in this moment—including dear friends Orfeh and John Lloyd Young, who will both be gracing the stage tonight—I remind my recovering people-pleaser side that I'm allowed to have an array of extreme feelings, from gratitude to loss to euphoria, at the same time. It's all valid. Longing for that feeling provided by Mama Di, and by my dad, who can't travel because of age and health, and by this boy who reappeared in my life last year—instantly making me feel cozy and seen—is why "Our House" is top of my playlist these days. I'm big on manifesting through the message in the music.

The fact is, in addition to my past career victories and glorious present touring-and-recording rebuild moment, I still dream of that be-all end-all love. Some may say it's "Only in My Dreams" to finally figure out how to have it all—and at the same time. That being said, there's no reason why that can't happen at any point . . . should it choose *me*.

It's nice to know I can feel so fulfilled on my own. But I'm also not cynical about partnering up by any means. So I constantly look at it all. I've designed my life in a way to always have options that aren't defined by age or by anyone else's projections or perceptions of who and where I should be. In fact, I've lived my entire life out of conventional order and not ticking anyone else's boxes. No matter how others perceive what I do, you better believe I'm always being authentically me. *That* is what being *eternally electric* is all about.

Now is the time to do something I've done throughout my life: put my emotions aside until the appropriate time in the show—maybe during "Foolish Beat," where feelings of loss and longing can be channeled into my art, taking the audience on an emotional journey. First, however, I'm tapping into the vibration in the crowd... which ignites my happy—and I do so with intention because happy is my emotional starting place as I prepare to take the stage for "Who Loves Ya Baby?"

This is when I get to do something completely unique: take a roomful of wonderfully diverse people back in time while simultaneously inspiring them to move forward. I call this feeling *newstalgic*, as I don't believe everything good was done in the past, but I do know we can harness all the feels from our youth, bring them into the present, and leave at the end of the night full of renewed vitality, having been moved to laugh, dance, cry, reflect, sing, and hang on to hope in a world that threatens to dim our shine. That message in my music that paints a visceral picture of reality is layered with ways you can flip the script to lean into joy every chance you get.

I feel my lungs expand... that rush I get when I'm ready to roll. It is a core feeling that connects me to that little girl walking into the first day of kindergarten, ready to play my first original song for the class. It's a feeling I have whether performing for millions of people on a live television broadcast or for three hundred in an intimate acoustic setting. I take every single person's time and energy and money spent to be here seriously. I also take a moment to remind myself that I've been endowed with the power to make each one of my people's lives brighter and richer; some may get an energy shift tonight that creates a ripple effect in their own lives and in the world, and that profound impact is never wasted on me.

It's easy for cynics to downplay the power of pop music, but tonight we get to celebrate, transcending the gatekeepers and naysayers. We did it! What a triumph! Nearly four decades later, we got past the music-business politics to forge and sustain this pure, enduring connection. This is our night to lose ourselves in the music, the universal language that keeps us united and ignited.

As my 1989 *Electric Youth* concert production manager Omar says into his walkie-talkie up on the big screen, in a throwback movie-montage moment that sets the stage for what is about to unfold in the present: "It's *showtime*!"

Chapter One

MY WAY

7:15 a.m., October 3, 1968. My mom, Diane Gibson, hears a knock at the door. Expecting to welcome my dad, Joe, home from TWA, where he works the night shift, she's instead greeted by two police officers taking their hats off: every wife's and mother's worst nightmare.

"Mrs. Gibson, there's been an accident."

My father, Joseph, ever the nice guy, had decided to swing by the neighborhood bakery on West 86th Street in Bensonhurst, Brooklyn, and was just two blocks away when an elderly couple ran a stop sign. The outcome: nearly deadly. Rushed to the hospital, Dad was read his last rites. Miraculously, he survived, but at home he then experienced complications that required a blood transfusion. Turns out "Bad Blood" is not only a Taylor Swift song. Having contracted serum hepatitis, he was read his last rites yet again. In a theme that would recur his entire life, Joe Gibson had nine lives and pulled through once more! Mom would tell the tale of how they decided to have baby number three. That miracle baby, who was nearly not here, would one day change the world with her music. That baby was me. However, before I take you back to my electric youth growing up in a New York suburb, let's rewind to set the stage for my grand entrance.

Mom's parents were both second-generation Sicilian: Albert Pustizzi, a hardworking blue-collar farm boy with movie-star good looks, and Josephine Sicuso, a feisty gal whose dyed jet-black hair made her look like a starlet who'd just stepped out of a 1950s movie musical.

Diane was born in 1946. Three years later, shortly after her sister Linda's birth, their parents lost the farmhouse and business due to a hailstorm ruining their tomato crop. So in 1950, they relocated to Brooklyn, where Albert began working as an auto mechanic and Josephine became a bank teller, which was unusual for a woman back then. Breaking from stereotypes was always in our lineage. They moved to Hollywood, Florida, in 1955, and even though the namesake Diane Motel (now the Diane Oceanfront Suites) built by my great-grandpa stood proudly, that wasn't enough to keep the family there. So in the early 1960s, they packed up and returned to Brooklyn.

As kids, my mom and Linda would come home from school and dance to *American Bandstand*. Music was an outlet for my mom, who was self-conscious about her weight and appearance as a young girl. In her eyes, Linda was the prettier and more popular one, but their shared love of Dick Clark was the great equalizer. Even at family gatherings in later years, the two of them would do the Lindy. It was so cute!

Whereas Mom loved doo-wop and Motown, during his teens Dad sang in a barbershop quartet called The Peanuts that he formed with three other boys who, like him, were in the foster-care system. My dad had been given up by his mother as a baby, and his father wouldn't appear in the picture until fifty years down the road.

The original family name had been Schultz, but upon his mom marrying a guy named Gibson, she returned to the group home to have his name legally changed to Joseph Gibson . . . though he remained living in foster care. Weirdly, my grandmother is responsible for my great stage name! Can you imagine the announcer at Madison Square Garden: "Ladies and gentlemen, please welcome to the stage *Debbie Schultz*!"

Doesn't have quite the same ring . . .

My dad was twenty and stocking boxes when Diane, eighteen, caught his eye. He proposed and they were married in April 1964. My sister Karen was born on September 6, 1965, followed by Michele on June 15, 1967, and it's lucky our father was a natural girl-dad because I was then born, on August 31, 1970, at Victory Memorial Hospital in Bensonhurst, Brooklyn.

We all lived in our grandparents' townhome attic, and although it was a bit crowded for a family of five, we never noticed. There was always a festive vibe with Daddy Joe serenading his girls, holidays featuring Grandma's famous "football-meatballs," and block parties. Still, our parents longed for a better life, so in the summer of '72, they used their savings as a down payment on our first house in Merrick, Long Island.

On moving day, Aunt Linda and Uncle Carl—her tall, quick-witted, classically Italian husband—took us girls to Jones Beach on Long Island. Uncle Carl tried to carry my metal lounge chair for me because I was only a toddler, but I insisted on dragging it the whole way along a concrete path myself, wearing a fabric toilet-paper cover on my head that I'd decided was a hat. Cue everybody on the beach cringing while my aunt and uncle apologized for the screeching of the metal. I couldn't have cared less—which was why I also wouldn't let anyone wash off the fruit punch that was all over my mouth.

"It's part of my charm"—a phrase Mom instilled in me from birth, reminding me to be my unique self. Even though I hadn't yet spoken that sentence, I was already living it at the precious age of two.

It's funny looking back at that carefree, defiant two-year-old on the beach who did things her way while, right now writing about it, looking at a different beach, I'm waiting for my besties Buddy and Eddie to hop into my vintage Fleetwood Flair here at the Malibu RV park. We all need some coffee and boy talk before venturing out to the bluff overlooking the Pacific Ocean, which will serve as our stage to rehearse for my 2024 concerts.

Giggling hysterically because Buddy does a spit take with his hot coffee after seeing my hot shirtless RV park neighbor, I am suddenly preoccupied with my phone because *The Boy* has just sent another voice note.

"I love him for you," Buddy says, "but is he going to really show up?"

Eddie continues with his tough-love perspective. They know when I love, I love hard.

I was happily solo until the reappearance of this person in my life. These days, I cannot hear a song in three-quarter time without flashing back to when he pulled me in close for a little waltz at his house. The guests had left the party and his daughter looked on adoringly from the couch, loving how lovingly I was looking at her dad. This is a moment that's stuck on repeat like any timeless love song.

But . . . enough about *The Boy*. It's time to get to work. So we venture out to a grassy area with a breathtaking ocean view—a far cry from the four walls of a dance studio with its mirrors and worn hardwood floors—to begin learning some new choreography the boys have come up with.

"Oh, guys, before we start, can one of you spot me for a cartwheel? I'm so scared doing them these days . . ."

Buddy quickly steps in to spot me, and by the third rotation, I'm shouting, "Let go, I got it!"

"*I got it!*" I say as I defiantly shoo my Uncle Carl's hand away in his final attempt to get the chair from me. And, just like that, we're back in 1972.

Then and now, the only thing that mattered was doing things my way and enjoying myself.

Mom and Dad were the same way. He loved singing around the new house; she played records nonstop; and they bought a piano before they bought a couch. He initially commandeered that piano, playing and singing by ear, much to the delight of his little girls—especially me, as we shared a passion for music. Eventually, Karen and Michele got into the act and my parents signed them up for piano lessons. Taking it all in, I waited my turn, and though my feet were dangling off the bench, still unable to reach the pedals, I discovered what would become my happy place throughout my life: the feeling of the ivories beneath my fingertips. That's when I realized channeling music was actually my first language and first love.

"Play 'My Way'!" my dad would shout like he was making a request in a piano bar, and I'd play it perfectly by ear. Lazy about reading music, I got away with it for a long time with my first piano teacher, Miss D'Alto. While my sisters took their lessons, I'd sit cross-legged to the right of the piano bench on Miss D'Alto's '70s shag carpet, look up longingly, and take in every note, impressing on my brain whatever I could. Full of mischief, I would also cartwheel from one side of that bench to the other even though my little-girl body wouldn't quite clear Miss D'Alto's larger one in her chair or my sister's on the bench.

Sticking the landing, I'd look up to see our teacher—who'd felt a small gust of wind behind her—do a double take. *Wait . . . wasn't Deborah on thisss side?* To this day, I'm not a good liar, but playing little pranks like that does make me giggle.

My childhood was really happy. I was five years old when my little sister, Denise, entered the world, and I remember how, upon first seeing her, I ran to our neighbors, who we called Aunt Tot and Uncle Bart, shouting, "Baby Denise is home! Baby Denise is home!"

We lived at 1684 Sterling Avenue, a dead-end street that formed a T with another dead-end street, and our house was four blocks from the elementary school, a five-minute drive from the junior high, and a walk away from the high school. So, although there were no other kids on the street, it was a really sweet spot, with tennis courts down at the end and bleachers that my big sisters and I would ride up to on our bikes. Once, trying to get my bike up the ramp, a testament to my tenacity, I couldn't make it all the way and got badly banged up when it rolled backward with me on it.

At that time, my siblings and I were a little gang of girls who started doing community theater and talent contests. Not because our mother pushed us into it—I know everyone wants that to be the story, but the truth is we all just gravitated toward performing, and everything revolved around the piano in our high-ranch-style house.

For much of my childhood, I shared a bedroom with Denise that was so tiny, we also shared a pullout bed. Evenings in that little room after watching *The Muppet Show*, I'd teach her the Catholic prayers we recited in church every Sunday. Meanwhile, Karen and Michele, who had the bigger bedroom, were probably figuring out how to spin things in the confessional booth.

Downstairs in our house, a den and a playroom were rented out for a time to my second cousin Lisa and occasionally to random tenants so my parents could make extra money. We all loved that room, with its brown carpet, brown leather couch, and Dad's reclining chair—also brown—because that's where the record player was. During my childhood, Dad would stand in the middle of Denise's and my bedroom and sing us to sleep, crooning songs by the likes of Ronnie Milsap while swaying back and forth. I cry just thinking about that.

What a way to grow up, right? Our father played piano by ear, and I learned from him what it meant to play and sing for the pure enjoyment of it. He was so carefree in his delivery. This served as inspiration for the way I'd want to connect with my audience later in life. To this day, I still call music a glorified hobby and constantly reflect on those years of making music just for fun.

My first day of kindergarten, when I was five years old, I wrote my first song:

Make sure you know your classroom
Make sure you know your seat
I'll help you find your teacher
I hope she looks so sweet
Make sure you know your classroom
Make sure you know your seat
I'll help you find your teacher
Or you'll have to wait in the street.[*]

The message in the music indeed! It was like, *Better know your way around, kid, or we're kicking you to the curb!*

See why I have a therapist on speed dial? My mind was always going to the worst-case scenario. Soon after, when I was visiting my grandpa's brothers on their farm, I wrote a song about ducks and geese and sheep called "Lovely Day on the Farm." I'd literally just sing my thoughts—as I still do to this day. Even just walking around my house, the musical ticker tape is always going.

I loved to play Tony Orlando and Dawn's "Say, Has Anybody Seen My Sweet Gypsy Rose" and "Tie a Yellow Ribbon Round the Ole Oak Tree" on the piano. I used to sing, dance, and play, kicking the bench aside so I could move around freely. Another crazy thing I used to do

---

[*] *"Make Sure You Know" by Deborah Ann Gibson. Copyright © 1975 by Birdsong Publishing (ASCAP). Used by permission. All rights reserved.*

was play blindfolded and upside down because I'd heard that's what Mozart did! A bit precocious, I know.

Songwriting comes more naturally to me than singing, and even now, whenever I write a new song, it feels like I'm keeping this secret: a song that nobody's heard. And that's because I'm about to unleash it on them for the first time. Whether it comes from me or through me is hard to say. Hearing it is like tuning a radio dial—it's singing to me inside my head. *Wait, is this meant to be mine to claim as my own or is it something I heard along the way?*

Playing piano by ear was a fun party trick. When I was six, Miss D'Alto pulled away the sheet music and I just kept playing.

"Okay, we have to go back to square one," she said, baffled and frustrated. "I've got to teach you how to read music."

She thought she already had.

By now, I was playing Beethoven's "Für Elise," which, although it isn't technically that difficult, is quite an emotionally mature piece of music. I was very lucky because I had teachers who taught me to use the feeling part of my artistry, which, by the way, is still important because the life experience and the emotion make all the difference in the world to my performances.

While teachers were demanding my best, being this kindergarten virtuoso was creating a divide between me and my classmates. Apparently, nobody wanted to talk about Mozart at the crafts table. Didn't they know I was into Mozart *and* macramé?

I was yearning to be one of the gang—which would be a recurring theme in my life: how to blend in and be "normal" without downplaying the things I was passionate about. I also never wanted my intense love of all things performance to drive a wedge between my sisters and me. I hoped they knew how much I looked up to them for all the reasons a little sister looks up to her big sisters.

ETERNALLY ELECTRIC

When our church advertised a Catholic Youth Organization talent contest, Karen, Michele, and I wanted in. Preliminaries, semifinals, finals . . . every round was another show and another chance to sell tickets to our families and friends. So there I was, a six-year-old competing with eighteen-year-olds. Uncle Carl always says he paid his dues by sitting through hours and hours of ballerinas, Irish cloggers, ventriloquists, Raggedy Andy . . . you name it!

Many parents out there know how beautifully torturous the talent-competition scene can be. My older sisters and I all played the piano, and I got to debut my "Für Elise." Little did I know two other kids would be performing the same exact piece. What were the odds? When they played, my inner critic came out.

I always rooted for everyone to do their best, but I vividly recall saying to Mom, "Wow, they played really choppy." So when the announcer began, "First prize goes to . . ." I stood up, in the floor-length yellow gown that Mom had helped me pick out at Macy's and my Dorothy Hamill haircut, before my name was even called. I knew by the process of elimination that I'd won. Precocious? Maybe. But . . . I just *knew*.

If it's down to who played "Für Elise" the best, come on!

That confidence would carry me far. But I also knew when I sucked, and I still do.

One really important thing that we grew up with in our house was a beautiful blend of humility and confidence. We were allowed to say, "I'm proud of myself."

Whenever I was asked, "What do you want to be when you grow up?" I would reply, "I *am* a musician."

I knew I was an artist through and through. And if I didn't turn out to be a successful artist, well, then, by now you'd have found me busking in the subways.

Music was *in* me. It was always what I was going to do with my life. No plan B. That was rare for a little girl, but I never thought that made me better than anyone else. I remember a classmate saying, "I don't know what I want to be," and me replying, "You love animals. Maybe you can be a veterinarian!"

I was always looking at what made other people shine.

And you take each victory as it comes
And you don't look down on those who are down
No, you're not that one
You see the good in everyone
Sayin' look at how far you have come![*]

I played the cast recording of *Annie* nonstop and sang "Tomorrow" in the living room for my grandfather, trying to emulate that oh-so-special tone of Andrea McArdle's voice. I was nearly seven when my parents got word that the producers of the Broadway show were holding auditions. The only other time I'd been on a stage was for that church contest, but now here I was, dreaming about what it would be like to walk onto the stage of a Broadway theater.

Mom and I picked out a frilly, pale pink, knee-length dress and off I went. We were keeping Macy's in business. Thousands of little girls showed up at the theater and the streets were closed for several blocks. My grandfather and my dad created a system—which they'd use for years to come—where they'd hold a place in line and wait for Mom and me to show up. That meant I could go to school and still get in.

Everybody was resourcefully making these things happen even

---

[*] "Legendary" by Deborah Ann Gibson. Copyright © 2021 by Birdsong Publishing (ASCAP). Used by permission. All rights reserved.

back then. My mother parked the car several blocks away and I remember thinking, *Oh my God, where did all these kids come from? Do they sing better than me? Why aren't they dressed up? Don't they know it's a special occasion?*

I felt my palms start to sweat as we saw Dad and Grandpa frantically wave their arms above the crowd. We were met with glares from mothers and daughters who'd been standing in line since the wee hours, and this wasn't the first time I'd apologized for being ahead of the game while elbowing my way through the crowd.

"Sorry, sorry, excuse me," I murmured while Mom dryly said, "Don't apologize, keep walking."

Which I did, all the way into the Alvin Theatre, with its breathtaking chandeliers and velvet seats. Welcome to the big-time!

Each of us girls was asked to sing "Happy Birthday." It was quick, quick, quick—and the show's conceiver, director, and lyricist, Martin Charnin, was totally intimidating. Looking like a mountain man with his bushy beard, he got right in my face. And although I was shaking on the inside, I looked him dead in the eye, determined to show him he didn't scare me. That's just who I was.

I don't know if it was the frilly dress or my lack of experience that he detected, but I was cut immediately—and I felt short-changed because I hadn't gotten to perform "Tomorrow," the song I'd worked so hard to prepare. Clearly, he didn't want to take the time to get to know me; this was how I learned that the showbiz higher-ups were not there to coddle you. After such a big buildup, it was all over so quick. But, as with every audition that ended in disappointment for me, my parents were upbeat.

"All righty, then, let's go out for a burger and fries to celebrate how *well* you did." It was never dramatic: "There's always next time. You did great."

We made a fun day of it, and when we got home, I was greeted with congratulatory flowers from Grandma's cousin Rose before retreating to my room to share my *Annie* adventure with my crew of stuffed animals. They all had names. There was Emily the elephant and Bartholomew the monkey, and when I lined them up on the bed, I promise you, they listened attentively. My vivid imagination kept me very much a little girl in the midst of the adult world of showbiz.

Our neighbor Bart, who was the head of the local Kiwanis Club and wore the Grand Poobah hat, arranged for my big sisters and me to perform at old-age homes, using our talents for good. Although our parents couldn't afford to send us to summer camp, they discovered the Long Island town of Hempstead teen repertory theater, which staged traveling shows on a flatbed truck and required daily eight-hour rehearsals. It was like a free camp. Karen and Michele wanted to audition for it—and as the tagalong younger sister, I did too.

When they pointed out I was six years shy of being a teenager, Mom pushed back: "Let's take her anyway."

So the three of us auditioned for *The Elves and the Shoemaker*, taking turns accompanying each other on the piano.

"Oh, the Gibson girls are here. We can give the accompanist a coffee break."

My sisters landed roles, and I was cast as the littlest elf with a small featured solo. That part hadn't existed at first; the team created it specifically for me.

A church, a temple—we didn't care about the venue so long as there was a show. When I went to an audition at the Bellmore Jewish Center, the girl who usually got the lead role in every show was not so happy to see me, as I was clearly not a member of the synagogue.

"Wait a minute, who let *her* in?"

I was promptly cast in the plum role of Baby June and immediately began working on my baton twirling, splits, and banana-curl hair game.

We were up for everything—and though baby Denise didn't love it, we dragged her along. She had the most gorgeous childlike soprano voice and was always perfection.

Denise had the perfect pout, in direct contradiction to our happy home life, a pout that even landed her the role of an abused child in a print ad. Our sister crew ended up portraying four of the seven von Trapp children in Merrick's Curé of Ars church production of *The Sound of Music*: Karen as Louisa, Michele as Brigitta, me as Marta, and Denise as Gretl.

Playing Friedrich in that same cast was one Tommy Williams, who didn't love that there was now this little girl getting singled out for having perfect pitch like he did. Not only did we work things out—despite him popping my birthday balloons on a wire fence—but I'd hire him as my guitarist for my first two major tours.

When the church wasn't available for rehearsals, my parents were always like, "You can use our backyard." We didn't have one of those big fancy homes with a housekeeper, but our house became a gathering place, as my parents set the welcoming tone with a "come one, come all" attitude. I didn't know what a mortgage was, let alone that they'd taken three of them out on the house. In what was essentially a lower-middle-class existence, I didn't notice any material things we might have been lacking, but what I did know was how full of life, friends, and music our home invariably was.

We always had the choir in the yard or in the playroom—and I'll never forget lining up outside as the von Trapps and being joined at the end by our dachshund, Sam. Maybe he was looking out for the Nazis! What with the music, the harmonizing, and accompanying each other on the piano, there was plenty of joy and sisterly bonding without much rivalry. That is, except for that time I felt left out of swinging from the high bar of the swing set and my competitive spirit got the best of me, resulting in my little-sister self being airborne, then flat on my back with the wind knocked out of me and a fractured vertebra.

Whereas Karen and I were the most alike—very outgoing and the closest at that time—Michele and Denise were a little quieter and more sophisticated, although Michele was also kind of rebellious.

She was the one drinking beer and sneaking off to Eisenhower Park with the boys. Karen and I were a bit boisterous and would sing and dance while we were washing the dishes. Always disliking chores, I had to sing to make them fun, and that started with Karen performing numbers from *Mary Poppins* while handing off the dishes in rhythm and prepping Sam's bowl.

"Feed the dog, tuppence a bag."

Our spin on "Feed the Birds."

"Mom, make them *stop*."

Michele and Denise couldn't stand it. But that was Karen and me when I was eight. And it's still me, speaking in song and posting videos on social media of me singing and dancing while taking out the trash. Life's a musical, I always say. Yet it wasn't all singing and dancing, especially for Michele when she was diagnosed with viral meningitis and encephalitis in December 1978.

This preceded optic neuritis and put her in the hospital for a month. The recovery process was slow and she missed the rest of the school year, which was traumatic for a sixth grader in her final year of elementary school. While my family banded together, with our parents and grandparents taking shifts at the hospital, there were regular sleepovers at Aunt Linda and Uncle Carl's house, ice-skating outings with Denise and our cousins Monica and Albert, and shopping to add Smurfs to our collections—including the baker Smurf with a chef's hat I simply had to buy for Michele because she was such a good child cook! My big sis took all of this on with grace, and things eventually went back to normal in the Gibson household.

Mom and I loved to go dress shopping with money she didn't have, like we had for the *Annie* audition, because if life's a musical, you have to dress the part. I'm laughing as I write this because Buddy, Eddie, and I are about to go dress shopping post–beach rehearsal for two big music events I'm attending this weekend: the MusiCares gala and Clive Davis's pre-Grammy party.

Although I could hire a stylist, nobody captures exactly where I am fashion-wise in a life moment better than I do. So, for Clive's party, I've tracked down the perfect sexy yet elegant classic pink-and-white gown from a girl on Poshmark who seemingly had my taste in low-cut alterations.

For MusiCares, the boys and I venture out to Rodeo Drive, blasting "Pretty Woman" through the sunroof of my Kia, arriving at Neiman's all high hopes. However, after being shown dresses that are over my budget by fourteen thousand dollars, Buddy sashays toward the elevator, giving personal shopper Carl a wink and a smile.

"Yeah . . . thanks, Carl. Good times!"

We take to the streets for a quick bite and a scan of the boutiques. And suddenly, right there in the window on the corner, I spot my dream dress. What's more, it's a cute three hundred and fifty dollars that will allow me to channel a sort of fairy-tale-vixen vibe. I'll pair it with my crystal Louboutins. I love playing characters when I dress up; I do now and I did then.

In fact, I remember wearing my *Sound of Music* costume to Camp Avenue Elementary School on a regular ol' Tuesday because I thought the crisscrossed vest with the skirt and apron looked cool. Resembling the Swiss Miss girl, I wanted to live in a musical. Maybe that's why I became so fiercely aligned with the concept of "Why can't a boy wear a dress in class?"

I was an individual who didn't care what people thought and felt puzzled when they didn't celebrate whatever *I* wanted to celebrate. I feel like the LGBTQIA+ community senses this in people, hence our strong alignment and unbreakable bond today.

I would show up for auditions, and as there weren't enough theater-loving boys in town, I'd often end up playing a boy role. They'd turn a boy part into a girl part—it happened to me all the time. There was a gag where, still totally flat-chested, I put keys down my dress and they fell right out because I had nothing to hold them. That worked for a boy . . . and for me as "Little Jenny"—formerly "Little Jake"—in *Annie Get Your Gun*. You'd think I would have been mortified, but I was happy not to have developed at an early age, and I enjoyed making the audience laugh at my expense! What's more, if anyone out there ever doubted my range, I even played a Polynesian girl in a church production of *South Pacific*, with dark tan pancake makeup and charcoal-rimmed eyes. A bit of a stretch and a sign of the times!

For me, the best thing about Camp Avenue Elementary School was a gifted and creative program called WINGS: Widening Interests Through New Experiences for Gifted Students. Fourth-, fifth-, and sixth-graders. A handful of us from my class were accepted into the program, and every week we left our regular classroom for a day and a half. The teacher, Sheila Berman—a short, impeccably dressed lady with feathered-back salt-and-pepper hair, manicured nails, and a put-together look—had a big impact on my life.

Mrs. Berman was pragmatic, down-to-earth, and a true champion of out-of-the-box thinking. I can hear her voice in my head now: it had a *ping*, a certain timbre indigenous to the region—that is, the region of Long Island—and I loved her. At a time when I didn't know about brainstorming, she encouraged it.

I chose "The History of Rock 'n' Roll" for my final project, and I was like, *This is* my *kind of history!* Talk about a great big excuse to study popular music since the mid-1950s. I loved it. And now I was into discovering pop records big-time: Marie Osmond's "Paper Roses," Elton John's "Crocodile Rock," and that single's B-side, "Elderberry Wine."

I was so fired up, I spent all the money I'd earned selling greeting cards door to door on Billy Joel's *52nd Street* album. Once I had it, I would lose myself in the music, dancing around in the brown-themed room, and was obsessed with trying to play "My Life" on the piano.

"Billy Joel grew up on Long Island," I remember Mom saying. "Let's find out who his piano teacher was."

She and Dad found Morton Estrin. His piano studio was attached to his house in Hicksville, Long Island, where my mother was working as a secretary in a plastic surgeon's office. It was about a half hour from Merrick and from JFK Airport, where my father was working rotating shifts for TWA both behind the scenes in crew scheduling and at the ticket counter, often defusing ornery travelers' attitudes with his dad jokes.

Once, he even tried one of them out on Bill Murray, who, upon reading his name tag, good-naturedly replied, "Joe, leave the jokes to *me*!"

Mom and Dad would take turns driving me to and from Hicksville after we decided to up our piano game. To this day, I can't smell a cigar without being transported back to Morty's studio, but I'd suck it up all over again for the caliber of technique I was getting.

I always felt intimidated playing one of his two grand pianos while he sat fifteen feet away in a reclining chair. Morty knew every piece inside and out, so when I made a mistake, he'd call out: "Fourth bar, third note, supposed to be a G-sharp, not a G natural. Try it again."

Intimidation was part of his strategy and I ultimately wanted to be the best version of myself, even if he had me shaking in my shoes a bit with one of the lowest human voices I'd ever heard. It was kind of scary, especially as, through my eyes, he looked like a cross between Gene Wilder and the devil with his long kinky red hair. In truth, he was a pussycat, but he also meant business.

As far as he was concerned, a student didn't know a piece unless it was memorized. I was a great sight reader and I could play complex pieces by ear, but no, everything had to be meticulous and memorized. There was no fooling him or phoning it in. So, after starting off by seeing him once a week, I soon began attending his three-hour Saturday-morning theory classes with my three sisters and a few other students, including Seth Rudetsky, who's now a big Broadway actor, writer, producer, musician, and host.

Morty would play a passage and we'd have to write it out with the notes and the time signature and everything. Treble clef, bass clef, right hand, left hand.

"Mr. Estrin, listen to what I did," I'd say and then play him a rocked-up version of some classical piece.

I had so much adrenaline, I'd practice classical for an hour and then play pop or theater music for three hours just for my own enjoyment.

"I had one other student who did that," my piano teacher told me, "and his name is Billy Joel."

"Oh, he's my *favorite*." I feigned surprise, not letting on that Billy was the reason I was there.

With me monopolizing the piano so much, my parents decided to buy a second one: a brown Kimball baby grand. I was eight years old when Mr. Estrin sent me for an evaluation at Juilliard. I played Chopin's Minute Waltz, a college-level piece. I vividly recall walking into that stark and serious atmosphere, talking to myself to calm my nerves as this was not the land of "Sweet Gypsy Rose."

I must have harnessed my energy pretty well because my audition earned me *a*'s across the board, so my teacher was heartbroken when, fanatical about show tunes and pop music, I said I couldn't picture myself studying there. Weren't there enough classical pianists in the world? Those judgy professors were in direct opposition to my rock 'n' roll spirit that was ignited when I imagined seeing Billy Joel on the concert stage.

How can you place a score on art anyway?

Even though I wasn't going to be Mr. Estrin's dream classical protégée, he would miss me. And I missed him when, struggling with the thirty-minute car ride every week as well as the cost of his classes, Mom and Dad replaced him for a bit with a teacher closer to home named Cecilia Brauer. Any parents out there who perform a juggling act with multiple kids participating in assorted lessons, team sports, and other activities *know* how valuable that drive time is.

In hindsight, it was an understandable move, but back then I was thinking, *I would drive myself to Hicksville or the ends of the earth to study with the best . . . if only I were old enough to get my license.*

Chapter Two

BITCHY, NOT PITCHY

I'm going to be alert, I'm going to ace this test, and I'm going to be type A attentive all the way.

That was my attitude in fifth grade, but I knew my teacher would still find something negative to say. It was never fun walking into class, bracing myself for her comments. I was always in the hot seat because of my extracurricular showbiz activities and my time spent out of the classroom, doing my stint in the gifted and creative program. Even seeing that word *gifted* now makes me cringe. It's a recipe for being picked on, which one might expect from fellow students, but not from the teacher.

I can remember the feeling of sitting in class, never able to fully relax because I didn't know when the next mean remark was coming my way. You have to remember, in 1981, nobody was calling out bullies. Having signed on for showbiz, I felt that meant I'd also signed on for jealous people's abuse. I was afraid if I complained, people would think I was an ungrateful brat. This is how people-pleasers are born and where anxiety begins.

Why is this woman picking on me? Is this what I have to look forward to as an adult? Don't sign me up!

This went on all year and really put a damper on my eleven-year-old spirit. That's why I was blown away when, nearly a decade later, after fame hit, my old teacher wrote me a letter making amends. She said she really didn't understand at the time how serious I was about my career. I took a lot away from that, and to this day, I never shy away from a chance to apologize to someone and admit I was wrong. I wonder if it's any coincidence that I love mentoring kids and helping to nurture what's unique about all people. Life is not about a one-size-fits-all cookie-cutter model and I don't think school should be either.

Ultimately, my teacher and I taught each other some beautiful lessons that weren't in the curriculum.

Meanwhile, the kids were equally brutal, singing, "Figaro, Figaro, Figaro," and making fun of me for my perfect pitch in my purple puffy coat with a pin that said I LOVE OPERA. Was it snobby to be wearing my musicianship on my sleeve? Oh, well . . . I'd rather be bitchy than pitchy! But little did my schoolmates know that although I outwardly exuded this confidence, I also stayed awake nights if I told the tiniest white lie to my parents, and couldn't sleep 'til I came clean. Standing in the hallway outside their bedroom, I would literally be shaking.

So, although I knew I had to say something to the bullies at school, the direct approach back then was too overwhelming for sensitive me. Instead, as my therapeutic revenge, I sat at the piano and wrote *Alice in Operaland* to give them the *Reader's Digest* version of the opera world. I wanted to show them who Figaro was—a relatable, comical barber—and how cool this art form was, with its colorful characters and beautiful music.

So how did Deborah end up in Operaland?

Well, though my chops suffered a bit while not under the watchful eye of Mr. Estrin, switching to Ms. Brauer was the best thing that ever happened because it turned out she was playing in the pit at the Metropolitan Opera.

Hello, universe?!?

"You need to audition for the Children's Chorus at the Met," she told me.

My parents and I didn't even know about any children's chorus and had never been to the opera. But all that was about to change. Tagging along little-sister style, Denise auditioned too—and we both got in!

Showing up at Lincoln Center for a rehearsal, we'd each sign in and receive a ten-dollar bill that would usually go toward tolls and parking. Every now and then, Denise and I were allowed to keep the money. To this day, my heart skips a beat when I see the outside of the Met and those five glorious arched windows. Back then, I had a sweatshirt with that image that I'd wear to school. When I got into something, I was *into* it. And I loved the Met with its red carpets, velvet chairs, and crystal chandeliers.

I was immediately cast in three operas. I didn't intend to become an opera singer like my Met cohort Jennifer Hines. But I still wanted to have that experience with a bunch of city kids who did what *I* did, including one Sarah Jessica Parker, who was in the cooler teenage set. Much to her amusement, I had all the kids sign a raggedy piece of loose-leaf paper just to slyly get her autograph. Sitting with our music in a classroom with choral mistress Mildred Hohner, we'd learn around ten arias in different languages, because we'd inevitably sing at least one of them when auditioning for a particular opera.

Able to absorb melodies easier than most other people, I could visualize and learn them, just like I could with languages. Phonetically, languages are music to me, but it was also very important to know the meaning of the lyrics that we were acting out, which was why English translations were printed beneath them. I wanted to meet the crew members and watch the artists, so it was amazing to see Teresa Stratas, Renata Scotto, José Carreras, and Plácido Domingo. Mr. Domingo was in his dressing room, and upon seeing me sneaking around backstage, he started waving his arms and, in his thick Spanish accent, called out, "Come in, come in!"

Taking it all in, I was shocked that such a big star had such a tiny dressing room and such a warm, welcoming vibe. Even Luciano Pavarotti was down-to-earth, vocalizing in the hallway with that glorious resonant tenor, smiling as I walked by. I was in awe.

Cast in the operas *Le Rossignol*, *La Bohème*, and *Hansel and Gretel*, I loved the grandeur. And I also loved the costume fittings, which led to me rocking pigtails and a gingerbread outfit in *Hansel and Gretel*, a bonnet and a big hoop skirt in *La Bohème*, directed by Franco Zeffirelli, and a column dress with a white mask in *Le Rossignol*. In awe of James Levine, who was often conducting, I was always super focused, eager to impress the high-caliber creatives.

After my part in the performance was done, I'd stay for the remaining acts and curtain call, a privilege that wasn't wasted on me. I wanted to see it snow onstage; I wanted to watch the death scene so I could re-create it with my stuffed animals. Even though I prioritized that world over the one at school, I still needed to be that little girl at play to counteract all my adult responsibilities.

As if I wasn't busy enough singing at the Met, I could never resist the urge to audition for a musical, and Long Island had a great community-theater scene. I played the Fairy Godmother's helper—another role created especially for me—in *Cinderella*, Baby June in *Gypsy*, Darlene in a Mickey Mouse Club musical, and, as mentioned before, Ngana in *South*

Pacific as well as Little Jenny (gender-bent from Little Jake) in *Annie Get Your Gun* at Eisenhower Park... So many fun shows!

A couple of years later, I'd play Baby Louise in *Gypsy* and hate it because, unlike Baby June, I didn't get to do the high kicks and sing "Let Me Entertain You." Never mind that it was the better acting role; I wanted to show off! I also appeared in another production of *South Pacific*, this time as Janette (formerly Jerome) while Dad played one of the sailors after I'd ribbed him, "I dare you to get up and audition."

I remember him fumbling his words, smirking and blushing at the *Gypsy* audition, and ultimately getting up there and landing five different parts, including the photographer and Uncle Jocko's assistant. He'd practice this one line in the car on the way to rehearsals, which was hysterical as he would repeat, "Hey, Gyps, what do you say?" by experimenting with placing the emphasis on a different word each time.

"Hey, *Gyps*, what do you say... *Hey*, Gyps..."

You get the point. He was just so cute in those shows.

Singing, dancing, and playing the magician's assistant in *Canterbury Cantata* at Nassau Community College alongside Denise, I became fascinated with magic. To this day, I can juggle because of how I soaked in circus-type skills while doing that show.

I always knew I wasn't the classically pretty girl; I wasn't the best singer; and I wasn't the most graceful dancer. So I used resourcefulness, stick-to-it-ness, personality, and a tough backbone to make it through. Don't get me wrong: I cried when I didn't land the role of *Annie* at eleven after making it down to the final ten girls. I wouldn't have a chance to try again because I was too tall.*

I found solace in my dog Sam, who'd burrow under my covers as

---

I'd later play one of the orphans, July, at the Broadhollow Theatre.

I cried myself to sleep every night for a week. Nothing like a wet nose on your foot to quell your grief! He couldn't care less whether or not I was going to play Annie. In fact, he much preferred that I stay home with him. I finally retired the red curly wig I'd dreamed of wearing on Broadway to a box in the back of the closet.

My *Annie* dream now behind me, I got on with my life, which was all piano lessons, talent contests, musical theater, and auditioning for television commercials. I auditioned constantly and, at age eleven, did a voiceover for Daisy Bicycles. Enamored with recording and being in a proper studio, I knew that was where I was truly meant to be. And in that studio owned by my dad's friend Sandy, I also recorded a three-song demo to showcase my vocal skills: "I Sing the Body Electric" and "Out Here on My Own" from *Fame*, and Judy Garland's "The Trolley Song."

I was captivated by singer-songwriters like Billy Joel and Elton John, who each had their own unique style. And I wanted to be that Barbra Streisand/Liza Minnelli/Bette Midler–type vocalist, but I hadn't yet done a deep dive into all of that. Instead, fascinated with the recording process, I kept thinking, *If I knew what those buttons and faders did, I could do my own thing. I don't like how it sounds. It doesn't sound like me!*

I felt like I was cooler than this demo tape that had just been produced. I always was a little spicier. Quirky and unique. The man behind the console didn't capture that.

While dabbling in songwriting, I still had my foot firmly planted in the theater and wanted to be considered a professional in that world. So I auditioned for Equity shows because getting my union card was very important to me. Once I had it, instead of standing in line with everyone else for the cattle calls, I could audition more privately in the Actors' Equity Building on West 46th Street.

ETERNALLY ELECTRIC

This all happened when I landed the role of Tiny Tim's sister Belinda Cratchit in a musical adaptation of *A Christmas Carol* at the Hartman Theatre in Stamford, Connecticut, written by Sheldon Harnick and Michel Legrand. There's no better sentence to hear than "You've got the part." I loved getting to know Mr. Harnick, who'd written the lyrics to *Fiddler on the Roof*. My résumé mentioned that I wrote songs, and he was interested, curious, and supportive right off the bat.

"Play me something you're working on," he said one day during a break when the actors left the rehearsal room.

I had a song called "So Sweet the Music":

Everybody sing that music, everybody sing that song
If we all sing together, everybody will sing along.*

Not destined for the pop charts, this spoke to the joy of music and puppy love, as did cute age-appropriate originals like "Doo Wop Rock," "Rock and Roll Baby Doll," and "Never Stop Loving You."

Little did I know that my new BFF was about to introduce me to a new way of musically expressing myself. My best girlfriend in junior high was Iris Eplan, who came bounding down the hall on the first day of seventh grade at Brookside Junior High all smiles and long, flowy, thick brown hair. Though I wouldn't be caught dead wearing Birkenstocks, I envied how Iris was able to rock her bohemian style. I also became obsessed with the rinky-dink Casio synthesizer her parents bought her for her twelfth birthday. It didn't have eighty-eight keys, like a regular piano, and the keys it did have weren't weighted, but I loved that it had auto-accompaniment.

---

* *"So Sweet the Music" by Deborah Gibson. Copyright © 1983 by Music Sales Corporation (ASCAP). International Copyright Secured. Used by permission. All rights reserved.*

With all the beats that were generated, I gained endless inspiration. So when it came time for my confirmation, I told my parents that, instead of the usual jewelry, I wanted my own two-hundred-dollar Casio keyboard.

That's what I used to write a song called "I Come from America," inspired by the stock samba beat and by all six of us flying on standby for our annual family vacations because Dad worked for TWA. We'd watch planes take off from morning until night—which often found me entertaining fellow standby folks with dance routines—before boarding the last one, so the lyrics combined the places we traveled to with the countries people living in America came from:

> *I may look like I'm from Korea*
> *I may speak like I'm from Africa*
> *I may have an Italian accent*
> *But I come from America.*

America the melting pot. I was always celebrating different cultures...

> *I did the hula in Hawaii*
> *I went swimming in Peoria*
> *Although I may visit Spain and Portugal*
> *I come from America.**

I gave the *r* in *America* a little *West Side Story* flair, and I was feeling pretty good about this quirky yet poignant composition when my

---

* "I Come from America" by Deborah Gibson. Copyright © 1983 by Music Sales Corporation (ASCAP). International Copyright Secured. Used by permission. All rights reserved.

ETERNALLY ELECTRIC

seventh-grade English teacher, Dr. Deck—a great man who also ran a creative arts program—shared something with me that would change my life. Aware I wrote songs, he said, "Deb, WOR Radio is staging a songwriting contest. The theme is America."

"Are you kidding? I just happen to already have a song about America!"

Again . . . Hello, universe?!?

The contest was split into two groups: eighteen and under, and nineteen and over. I was twelve when I handed Mom the basic demo that I'd recently recorded for free at Sandy's studio. Talk about synchronicity. The only caveat: the deadline was in two days. Mom was gonna kill me! She would have to hustle to get it to them in time.

She'd secretly use the messenger service of the high-end surgeons she worked for in New York City. It was a risky move, seeing as she'd worked her way up to the position of office manager after fudging her way through her first secretarial job interview out of high school. But, in true Diane Gibson fashion, she got my demo to WOR Radio just before the deadline.

"I'm going to get fired for doing this," I remember her saying.

She claimed that she almost threw it away and I never would have known. But I think there was a big wink-wink behind that story, which she always told with a bit of bravado. We all knew she would never have thrown it away. She believed in me and it was absolutely thrilling when we received a call informing us that I'd won first prize: $1,000. Competing against eighteen-year-olds? We were all pretty shocked. That's a lot of money today—and it was even more back then. But the bigger deal to me was that, after being handed the check, I did a little interview and had my song played on the radio.

Oh. My. God. People are actually going to hear it! Ahhhmazing!

I felt like I had arrived when I performed "I Come from America" on a float in a parade wearing a red beret, a blue vest, and a white leather miniskirt. The funky-little-girl vibe with my energy poking through was starting to come together for this scrawny all-American girly-girl-next-door; I had graduated from sundresses in elementary school to plaid Benetton vests and rolled-up Guess jeans in junior high. There were also the blue Gloria Vanderbilt corduroy jeans with bohemian brown platform clogs handed down from Michele. I would rock that vibe today!

Around that same time, I also won a spot on *The Joe Franklin Show*, which aired on WOR-TV at three in the morning. Fortunately, Aunt Linda and Uncle Carl were ahead of the curve with their VHS recorder. And the coolest thing about the whole experience was that Dad had appeared on the same show decades earlier as a member of his barbershop quartet of orphan boys called The Peanuts.

Getting out and about, performing, I appeared at a street fair in Brooklyn. And the beret-vest-miniskirt outfit I wore in the parade also came in handy for a little club gig that I did with Laura Branigan when I was thirteen. Laura, who'd later become a label mate at Atlantic, had already enjoyed chart success with her 1982 single "Gloria," so sharing a restroom mirror with her, I was like, *Holy crap, it's Laura Branigan!* I hoped that I'd soon share not only a mirror with her but also a spot on the charts!

Had I been asked at the age of six what I wanted to be, I would have said Annie. I wanted to be a big Broadway star . . . until I started writing music, at which point I wanted to be the female Billy Joel. Then again, aware I wasn't going to be glued to a piano, I was also determined to dance and act. So as I got older, I fine-tuned my answer: I wanted to be an all-around entertainer.

The songs I'd already written came into play at Something Different, which was essentially a dessert nightclub for kids on the Upper East Side. There I'd perform one of my originals along with "Rinka Tinka Man," "I Love a Piano," or a Billy Joel medley that involved me duetting on the piano with Bob Marks. As the resident musical director, Bob loved giving me a showcase for my chops in this professional environment that made Sundays a highlight of my week.

Hustle and bustle surrounded the singing servers, like my friend Holly Robinson Peete, who was also managed by her mother. I'd cross paths with her my entire career, through Hallmark movies and beyond. There was also Daniel Guzman, who I would later get to star opposite in *The King and I* out in LA, and a guy named Bobby Lee, who we'd lose to AIDS. At Something Different, Bobby performed a comedic number from the musical *Barnum*, complete with a red clown nose, and all the kids noticed he had only one thumb, leading to the rumor it had been chopped off in the meat slicer that lived in the little holding room with an ice machine and a small card table.

Walking down the rickety steps to the basement with the dripping pipes, I'd see an occasional rat running by all the restaurant supplies. That's where we went to rehearse the finale with the assigned solo parts. Cue the grumbling moms: "My kid only got two solo lines and she got three."

She wasn't always me, but it was invariably that feeling—and it wasn't fun.

What parts am I going to get this week? Do I get to open the finale? I hope the moms aren't mad at me if I do . . .

There was a drummer named Marcus Pickett who had just a kick, a snare, and a hi-hat off to the side of the stage, right where the doors swung open from the kitchen. The venue was *crammed*, mainly with the kids and friends of wealthy Upper East Side parents who'd throw very pricey, elaborate birthday parties there. To them, we were celebrities—many of the young performers had been in *Annie* and in movies—and they all wanted our autographs after the show. As this was a showcase, there was no money to be made. But I was happy to be paid in dessert.

I always chose hot pecan pie with chocolate ice cream, not vanilla, because I wanted all the rich, most decadent stuff in one dish. Kind of a metaphor for how I've lived my entire life.

A rush invariably came over me when Bob, perched on the three-foot-long awkwardly shaped stage (one wrong move and you'd fall off because of the weird angle on one side), announced, "Here, singing an original song that she wrote . . ."

Original song. How cool. I was the only one, and I remember how special that felt. I also recall getting the audience clapping along to "So Sweet the Music."

Oh my God, people are clapping along to my song*!*

Was there anything better? No. That was a big deal back then and still is today.

I loved how we all got along so well, and I have such fond memories of the kids who performed there. Many of them went on to do great things, like Ricki Lake, Brad Kane, and Scott Grimes. Scott also visited my house in Merrick with his sister Heather and their parents, Pam and Rick.

We kids played tennis down the street, and Scott marveled at my drum machine, with programmed beats and sounds reminiscent of Michael Jackson's "Beat It." I might have had a little crush on him back then, as I can remember that feeling of my face flushing while Scott, Heather, Denise, and I stood awkwardly on the curb, chatting when the tennis game was over. I'm not sure if he liked me too or was just enamored with that drum machine.

ETERNALLY ELECTRIC

I thought he was cute and vividly remember a mischievous red-headed boy with boundless energy and a lisp like mine, a prodigy with perfect pitch and an ownership of himself far beyond his years. Some crushes never die. Such delicious memories of an innocent time.

Maybe that's why I wanted a redheaded Cabbage Patch doll for Christmas, and Grandma braved the stampede. Christmas Eve was a blast. We kids would wait in the car impatiently as my parents oversaw the stocking stuffing, so when we arrived back home that night we'd see Santa had dropped by. Then it was off to Grandma and Grandpa's, where we'd sing, play games, and eat more Italian food than you can imagine. One of the men in the family, like Uncle Sal or Sal Jr., would not so conspicuously disappear, and Santa would make a ruckus on the roof and come down the walkway to squeals and screams. He'd then unload his sack, first handing gag gifts to the adults, all pillaged from the basement.

"Ho! Ho! Ho! A spool of thread for Martha, a jar of red peppers for Josephine..."

These are precious memories of our tight-knit family. And that family loved seeing me on the small and big screens as my show-biz adventures led me to the 1983 drama *Daniel*, starring Timothy Hutton. Another all-time-favorite moment came when I got the call to dance on a car and in the streets on the TV series *Fame*, starring Debbie Allen in the Janet Jackson era. Being a day player (as we were called back then) in the energy space of those high-caliber professionals, I felt like some fairy dust was going to rub off on me; I racked up credits and experiences while learning whatever I could from whomever I could.

All the agents and managers who represented me pointed out that my lisp and unconventional nose might limit my booking potential. They never talked about star quality, the virtue I held dear. The more people focused on my *s*'s, the worse my lisp became. Couldn't they just get over the fact that some of us speak differently and chalk it up to character? It was starting to make me angry that powerful creatives were so shallow and easily distracted from the things that really mattered.

Unwilling to change my appearance to fit their ideal of beauty, I had to work really hard to find my own center. I made some really great friends professionally and also had my circle that I ran with in school. However, off doing my performer engagements, I wasn't a part of things as much as the other kids were.

In a business that liked to put you in a box, I didn't know where I fit in. I was a little edgier than the ski-slope-nosed California girls who were snagging all the lead parts, but I wasn't quite edgy enough to play the troublemaker-friend-type roles. Nor was I the woe-is-me loser underdog who everyone rooted for. So in terms of casting, I often fell between the cracks.

"Where should we put her?"

In my theater career, I played the Beauty and the Funny Girl who's funny *and* funny-*looking*. Depending on which way my nose was shaded with makeup, which way my hair was parted, and how my body shape was featured, I could go either way—which I always loved. I could pretty up or I could character-girl it based on which role I was gravitating toward. I would learn to embrace this versatility as a secret weapon and my superpower, proving that, kids, you don't have to change for *anybody*!

Children's talent managers back then were primarily women, and because of that, they weren't dismissive of the mother-managers like the music business was. Moms were not just tolerated, they were embraced and encouraged to be immersed in the business. Parents had to understand the contracts as well as the on-set protocols, and I had to learn independence when Mom or Dad dropped me off to work on a movie or a commercial. Even if I didn't know where I was going, they weren't hanging around: "Check your kid at the door and leave."

I even got stuck in an elevator once at twelve years old, inciting a panic in my dad, who was waiting for me to come out of a rehearsal. But thrust into this business where kids grow up fast, I learned to adopt a new way of looking at the world, a great training ground for my music career, which was way more hardcore.

When we went into the city for auditions or my work at the Met, the newsstands carried *Show Business* and *Backstage* with casting calls listed toward the back. My heart still skips a beat when I recall circling those ads with a red pen: *Student film needs girl aged 12 to 14*. I'd rip them out and leave them on the kitchen table with a note asking one of my parents to take me to an audition, submit a headshot, or call the relevant agent. I was doing my own detective work.

This led to me appearing in an educational anti-drinking film that cast me and—at my urging—the garage band with whom I was playing keyboards. Then there was my big 1984 uncredited role in the blockbuster comedy *Ghostbusters*. When the call came, my younger sister, Denise, and I thought *Ghostbusters* was such a cool, weird kind of title. We kept saying it over and over, wondering what the heck this movie could be about: "Ghooooostbusters?!?"

I had no idea what I was going to be asked to do. I just knew it was a night shoot with Rick Moranis, a scene where, during a game of Twister, he's chased outside his apartment by a monster, runs across the street, and stands outside Tavern on the Green, banging on the window. The monster was, of course, added later in post-production and I recall marveling at how incredible his acting was, reacting to nothing as he cowered and slid down the glass window to the ground.

Well, lo and behold, once I was there with all these other background actors, they picked me to be featured as the birthday girl. And that's probably because I always had an energy that conveyed I wasn't just a girl here to have fun. This was my *life* and I was *the* girl. Got it?

It was so great being on a film set. I loved meeting and being corralled together with all these new people throughout the night, while Dad, who accompanied me because he could work rotating shifts, was thrown in with the other parents and got to tell his jokes to a captive audience. And I got to be up all night.

Back from the bright lights of the film set and into the fluorescent lights of the classroom, I immediately shifted my focus to boys. It wasn't unusual for me to be writing future hit songs in my notebooks with hearts drawn around my favorite boys' initials on the front cover. I'd often preview my new songs for my friend crew. I knew I was safe and free to get excited over creative and career victories with my core group who were privy to how much work I was putting in.

In the eighth grade, Adam Sheinken, a nice, preppy boy who I thought was really cute, bought me a flower in the carnation fundraising sale and invited me to go roller-skating at United Skates of America, the hot rink in Massapequa. I can still remember Foreigner's "I Want to Know What Love Is" providing the perfect soundtrack on my stereo as I was getting ready for the date that would lead to my first grape Bubble Yum–flavored kiss.

When I told my parents I was going out with Adam, Dad said, "You mean going steady?"

"Oh, *Daaaad*, this isn't the 1950s and it's not called going steady. It's called going *out*."

This inevitably led to a Who's on First–type comedy skit, with Dad repeatedly asking, "But where are you going?"

"No, Dad. Not *out* as in going out somewhere. Just going *out*!"

"Like going steady?"

"Oh, it's useless. Forget it. Parents just don't understand."

So, yes: all of this meant we were going steady . . . 'til we weren't.

Chapter Three

SETTING THE STAGE

So I put on my 45s and started to come alive
Felt the rhythm, moved my feet
Ever since then I never, never missed a beat.[*]

Boys might come and go, but music was my constant. That's why I was tormented by the fact I couldn't yet rely on my voice. I still hadn't found my "sound." So I started emulating my favorite singers in an attempt to be more pop to suit the style of songs I was starting to write.

I'd break out my 45s and listen to the singers whose voices I admired, like Marie Osmond, Linda Ronstadt, and Vic Damone, whose single "My World Is You" was a favorite. The music was made sweeter because, through marriage, he was actually my crooner uncle: the brother of Theresa, who married my grandma's brother Sal. Though

---

[*] "You Make Me Wanna Dance" by Deborah Gibson. Copyright © 1989 by Music Sales Corporation (ASCAP). International Copyright Secured. Used by permission. All rights reserved.

my pop-loving preteen friends didn't think Vic was cool, I always had respect for the generations that came before me. So Mom and I decided to play him my demo after dinner one night at the Westbury, Long Island, house of Aunt Terry and Uncle Sal in the hopes that he would open some doors.

Vic nodded politely as the cassette went 'round and 'round in the player. And I could feel my heart get speedy as it always does when playing people my original songs. Oddly, he didn't say much, and the grown-ups resumed their conversation. It was an awkward moment, so I went outside to join Denise and my cousins Monica and Albert for a game of Old Maid on the side porch. Later, during the car ride home, my mom just couldn't keep it in and blurted out that Uncle Vic was overly critical of my demo.

"I cannot believe he said your vibrato's too wide and the songs aren't radio-friendly."

I could feel the tension among my sisters as the conversation turned to me and my career. And Diane wasn't finished venting quite yet.

"Not only that, he said girls don't belong in the music business. What does *he* know? We'll show him!"

A sign of the Rat Pack times? Was Vic just trying to protect me? All I knew was that the joke was always "Did you make it because you have an uncle in the music business?" and here I was, with an uncle in the music business . . . and I'd have to go it alone. Not only that, but I had a complex about my voice—my vibrato at that time *was* kind of wide and his criticism didn't help.

From that moment on, there was a bittersweet feeling whenever I heard "My World Is You." It was hard to separate the man from the music. Having someone I'd admired discourage my dreams gave me a knot in my stomach and an ache in my heart. I lost sleep. I guess you could say my world was not him—and vice versa. That night, Vic inadvertently taught me this: people teach you who you want to be and who you don't want to be. Encouraging young people would become my mission.

There is always room to grow as an artist, and grow I would. But not before I got turned down no fewer than eleven times by one of the biggest television talent competitions of the 1980s, *Star Search*. It's ironic they didn't think I had potential, but champion Sam Harris would become a friend and my duet partner on an '80s symphony tour in 2013.

There were critics not only of my songwriting and vibrato but also of my *s*'s, which, I was told, were a problem. Although it wasn't a Cindy Brady lisp, where the tongue is between the teeth, I was determined to avoid letting this so-called impediment get in my way and dove headfirst into speech therapy. This time it was of my own accord, as opposed to when I was involuntarily thrown into speech therapy in kindergarten. Mr. Buongiorno had me lift a small lightweight button attached to a little rope that I tied around my tongue to strengthen what were perceived as sloppy *s*'s.

"Tongue out! Tongue on the roof of your mouth!"

We would drill over and over. Mr. "Good Day" indeed!

In school or on an audition, I dreaded having to read a sentence with a lot of *s*'s. It was this weird thing of almost trying to change my physical structure and I was thinking, *Why am I spending all my time trying to talk like everybody else?*

With songwriting, your gift is the uniqueness. You think Billy Joel took a class to learn how to write "Scenes from an Italian Restaurant"? That was a very nonformulaic, out-of-the-box song. Somewhere along the way, someone must have said to him, "It's okay to be you, to be unique." One of the things I've always loved about him is he's never lost that edge in his tone that speaks to people on a human level. You hear the Long Island punk, you hear the scrappy guy who was a Golden Gloves boxer and had to work his way up in the piano bars. Hence me embracing my lisp as a recognizable part of my sound.

I continued honing that sound under the guidance of one of the most important figures and instrumental voice teachers in my life, Guen Omeron, whom I began studying with in New York City at age fourteen. An elegant soprano with a tell-it-like-it-is New York candor, Guen lived and taught on West 54th Street. And she knew how dedicated I was. We began our journey with three-hour lessons that incorporated breath work and a Pilates-style core-and-connection kind of process that found me strapping scuba weights to my body.

Guen, I now realize, was my foundation for singing and ahead of her time. She would have me hold ten-pound weights, strap on a twenty-pound scuba belt, and wear five-pound ankle weights, which, for my little fourteen-year-old body, inexperienced in the workout world, was pretty extreme. But I loved it. And I got it. A form of Pilates before Pilates was big, this unique technique jump-started the feeling of opposition and grounding and inner connection she was trying to get me to achieve, as my legs and core had to take over and provide the support for my sound. My family fondly referred to me as Robo Singer!

My hard work and the long treks to Manhattan for this new caliber of training started paying off when I was offered a part in an opera called *Harrison Loved His Umbrella*. But Mom wasn't feeling it: "You get five hundred dollars for four weeks of rehearsal and maybe a two-week run?!? That is too low for someone who's just done three years at the Met!" Kind of demanding? Maybe. Ballsy? Yes, but Diane knew my value: "You sight-sing, you've done professional opera, you are worth more."

This was the moment when, although she didn't officially become my manager, Mom started giving me managerial advice. She had an awareness, she was a mama bear, and she had street smarts like any good tough Sicilian woman does. So although she left the decision to me, I turned the opera down.

Shortly before opening night, she received a call from the producer:

"We've been trying to make it work with this girl we cast, but she isn't delivering. Can Deborah come in and learn the whole thing in three days? We'll pay her the same five hundred dollars for a lot less work."

That was fine with us. And it was a big lesson for me: know your worth and be okay to walk away; it'll come back if it's meant to be.

In this case it was, and I delivered exactly what the director wanted. You get what you pay for. I thrive when my feet are being held to the fire. That's my idea of a good time. And that's who I've always been: the go-to girl.

My versatility was helping me set the stage for all the things I wanted to do. Being open enough to try all these things was an advantage, and right now I wanted to make multitrack recordings of my own pop compositions. So lining up all my sisters' cassette recorders on the ironing board, I would play my Casio keyboard and the Sam Ash music-show drum machines that I'd managed to buy with the money I was earning from commercials. Drum beats, bass lines, string lines; I was experimenting with multitrack recording by playing beats and melodies into one recorder, playing that back while playing another part with it into another recorder, and on and on, overdubbing until all I could hear was static with a faint arrangement in the background.

When Mom walked in and saw my makeshift setup, she said, "This is ridiculous. We must get you some proper equipment. I'm going to talk to Uncle Joe. He might be able to help."

Joe was her successful cousin. She drove three hours to Vineland, New Jersey, to ask if he'd loan us ten thousand dollars for me to set up a home studio. What an investment of faith in me and my dreams. When people would say, "You must really believe in Deborah," she'd reply, "I don't just believe, I *know*. I know what she can do." And apparently, so did Uncle Joe.

My mother was gone all day, but she returned triumphant: "I got the loan!"

Cue hugs and cheers. I was so grateful.

"You're going to do this with or without me," Mom said. "So I may as well help."

That's precisely what she did. We were on a dual mission with a singular vision.

There is an art to being a great manager. It's a craft and it's a learned craft. "A great manager is so many things," Mom always said. "A manager is like a parent, a therapist, a vision facilitator."

I think a good manager works backward from goals. My momager and I had big goals, but we were also really green, and our naïveté worked in our favor because if we had known the hurdles that were ahead, we wouldn't have gotten out of bed in the morning. Instead, it was "What do we need to do next?"

Managers need to be intuitive and resourceful. If they can't do something, they must figure out who can. My mom never had any problem making cold calls. She had to learn about contracts, royalties, sync licenses, and publishing. And she also needed to know when it was time to give something away to get what we wanted in return.

"The money isn't great, but you'll get exposure," we'd frequently hear.

And, yeah, sometimes the mother-manager gets a bad rap because if she refuses to sell her daughter, it's like, *Oh, the mother's tough.*

Nobody would ever have said that about Roger Davies refusing to sell Tina Turner up the river she was rollin' on.

In a business full of sharks, my mom learned as she went along. Something we both learned was that there's knowing the business and there's knowing the business of *you*. Nobody knew the business, the artistic side, and the nuances of me better than she did. Like any relationship, you have to be aware of the needs of your partner, and a manager must be plugged in to the needs of the client—the emotional needs, health requirements, pacing, you name it. Your manager's got to be passionate about your music and always focused on what's best for *you*. If you're being treated like a commodity, forget it.

Mom loved my music, and even if I weren't her daughter, she would have listened to those songs. She knew there was a place for them in this world, she knew there were people who needed that music at that time, and she knew I was a good entertainer. I don't know *how* she knew I could hold a crowd, but she had watched me perform in front of several thousand people in Eisenhower Park at the age of twelve in the teen talent contest.

I recall that eve before the audition 'round the kitchen table, figuring out how to best alter a Xerox of my birth certificate to make it look like I was thirteen, thinking, *My family is nuts . . . in the best possible way.*

Newsday ran a lead picture of me performing in my wide-brimmed, off-white hat and frilly little polka-dot dress. And Mom saw me hold that crowd for four whole minutes while I sang "Nothing Can Stop Me Now," a big belty tune with a showstopping sustained high C at the end. But based on that brief stand-alone performance, how did any of us know I could hold an audience for an hour and a half?

I had noticed that my voice felt a little edgier than usual in front of all those people as my adrenaline was kicking in. To this day, it still has a roughness to it on a high C. It's right on the edge and you can hear that edge when I'm nervous. It's not warm and buttery like the quintessential theater diva sound. I remember clocking that back then. But I never wondered, *What do I do onstage?* I instinctively knew I could just be me and project my personality while connecting with the audience.

The entertainer who taught me that as a child was Liberace. When I was seven, what I wanted more than anything in the world was to see him in concert at the Westbury Music Fair. I'd watched him on *The Lawrence Welk Show*, *Donny and Marie*, and *The Merv Griffin Show*, and it always stuck with me that Liberace was the first entertainer to look directly at the camera during a live broadcast. Until then, other performers had largely ignored it, but "Mr. Showmanship" wanted to connect with his audience.

I remember watching him play the Minute Waltz—which I was already learning and would play for my Juilliard evaluation at age eight—and thinking, *That's not a very difficult piece, but look what he's making of it.*

Wearing a flamboyantly bedazzled costume, he spoke about his brother George, cracked jokes, and engaged viewers with his charm as well as his musical talent.

My musical talent caught the attention of an entertainment attorney in his thirties named Doug Breitbart whom my mom found while relentlessly looking for contacts in the industry who might facilitate things for us. He helped liaise the intro with Atlantic's dance department, and Mom, in turn, introduced Doug to a gorgeous, leggy blonde au pair named Cheryl who worked for one of her doctor bosses, Mark Reiner . . . and who Doug eventually married! He was knowledgeable and definitely believed in me, though I'll never forget him playing me a song called "Spin" written by somebody else and saying, "I think you should record this."

"But we have all of my original songs that I've already demoed," I replied, shaking my head. "Why are we looking at random outside material?"

Doug and I definitely weren't always on the same page, but he did introduce me to the musician-producer Leslie Ming around the same time my voice teacher Guen put me in touch with a recording engineer named Phil Castellano. Those two tech guys gave me advice regarding what gear I should get for my home studio with the ten thousand dollars borrowed from Uncle Joe. Both provided a basic overview of how everything would be wired up in the laundry room/playroom–turned–studio, but essentially they told me I needed to learn and figure things out for myself to best understand the craft of producing and engineering.

Picture me looking like a telephone operator from the 1950s, plugging and unplugging wires into and out of the patch bay to connect the reverbs and mics and keyboards . . . Oh my!

In those days, there was a general assumption that little girls couldn't keep keys or mix records. From Little Jenny to Little Debbie, I couldn't care less what people thought. So after acquiring the recommended equipment—a Tascam four-track with a built-in cassette, reverbs, delays, compressor-limiters, and a reel-to-reel tape recorder to bounce the mix to—I used common sense and trial and error to hook everything up and create my own system.

At first, without a sequencer, I played everything by hand. Some of it would be terribly out of time, and because I was playing in one take, there would inevitably be wrong notes. But this was all about sketching the arrangements and getting my ideas down on tape. To that end, I recruited local musicians, and Phil brought over the great jazz saxophonist Najee to perform solos on my four-track demos, which I still have.

Writing at least a song per day, I was also demoing daily. I was very prolific, and one of the beauties of doing this as a teenager was that I had no bills to pay and nothing on the line. It was all for the love of it and I enjoyed the creative freedom. It wasn't about the money, then or now. Though I was earning and saving from my blossoming theater and commercial career, I felt torn because music was the biggest pull: *I can't demo this new song because I'm auditioning to sell yogurt.*

Of course, the daily demoing interfered a bit with the normal playroom and laundry needs of my sisters, but they were great sports. Only a stinky load or two per week had to be redone because I'd inadvertently shut down the machine to cut a vocal. I was in love with demoing my own songs, but I was also in love with a cute boy in my biology class, Pete Ragone. Nervous on the inside when I said, "Here! Listen to this," I handed him the headphones and popped a cassette into the Walkman in the school hallway. The fact that he was about to hear something he'd never heard before because I had written it was the coolest thing to me, absolutely glorious.

I was no dummy. This was a love note... in a song! And I knew it would pretty much blow him away. It was a typical male thing for a boy to join a band to impress a girl, so me sending him a love note by way of an original song was pretty darn cool! We never could get our timing right and didn't end up dating, but we are friends today.

Pete is now a public affairs expert, entrepreneur, and political advisor. He has a teenager, Rye, who makes music, and he says, "I can't tell you how much I'm imparting to them because of what I learned from seeing how you did it at fifteen."

People talk about the craft, the craft, the craft. There *is* a craft to it, but it's mystical and magical. And the biggest part, in my opinion, is getting out of the way so that the universe can drop something into the channel. That's how I approach it. Of course you need to know structure, but I also picked up a lot from my classical piano days.

I loved Mozart and the movie *Amadeus* because I love his creative genius. Mozart, to me, makes such musical sense—whether it's a piano line or a string line, something's going up, resolving, and taking you on different journeys before coming back around to the hook. I think Mozart would approve of Chappell Roan's "Pink Pony Club," which, to me, is that masterful. I learned a lot from classical, as well as from being around a full symphony at the opera. I adore string arranging and I hear string parts in my head.

During this time, I discovered doubling and layering vocals. I love matching a vocal, panning things left and right. You'll hear a current pop performance that is, let's say, three lead vocals very closely matched, sounding thick and cool and ambient. Subtle, not meant to be identified as layers, this is a part of modern music. I learned all of that back then by experimenting. And, as playing all the synth parts by hand created a big cacophony, I eventually got a Linn rack-mount sequencer and graduated from the four-track tape machine to a twelve-track. Having twelve tracks to play with and the ability to bounce them was like having forty-eight tracks in my hands.

Early on, I'd drag my family into the studio for the annual Gibson family Christmas tape: Denise singing "Silent Night"; Dad, my sisters, and me performing "One Family" from *A Christmas Carol*. My friends also got immortalized on cassette one day after school for a song called "Rappin' on a Snowy Day," which we wrote out of boredom and because I'd become obsessed with the sampler. I was using Carvel ice cream sprinkles as my shaker, and to this day still prefer live percussion to programmed. It has a vibe!

Aware I wasn't going to be on pop radio with "So Sweet the Music," "I Come from America," and "Rock and Roll Baby Doll," I let my new

LinnDrum machine lead the way on one of the first real pop songs that I wrote: "Only in My Dreams." Some of the sounds that machine made inspired me to create a beat. I didn't know what the title or the hook was going to be; I looped my LinnDrum pattern, played a little synth riff, and, with no idea where this was taking me, kept going until it led me to the opening line and then the beloved hook, a section all about stacked harmonies and this long, sustained note. It just formulated itself. And even Mariah Carey recognized that drum sound. We'd have a lovefest about the Sam Ash music expo in the Instagram DMs, with her voice-noting an exquisite a cappella version of "Only in My Dreams."

Songwriting was always a quick process for me. As fast as my pen would move, those hits were written literally within ten minutes. To this day, I sing my thoughts; back then, any little phrase that entered my brain would usually, within seconds, turn into a song. That's just how it works. I wasn't going to write a song about social studies class, but inspired by my falling asleep in that class, I'd write about how some guy needed to open his eyes and wake up to the fact that we'd been in love for all this time. Imploring myself to "Wake up, wake up, wake up," the song "Wake Up to Love" was born!

Weirdly, a lot of my lyrics didn't come from personal experience. They came from my love of pop music, and *shake your love* was a catchphrase that was part of my inner monologue: *I can't shake this love I have* for someone or something. So much of my creativity is an awareness of that inner monologue and not dismissing those ideas as just voices in my head. I'm always writing these things down because, to me, those random drop-ins are the gems. And with this song, my inner monologue was probably about some boy I liked.

ETERNALLY ELECTRIC

I'm under a spell again
Boy, I'm wondering why
This is not a game of love
But an emotional tie*

The words would just transform into a hook. I was always a pop-hook fan and that's really how those songs came about. My sister Denise, whose bedroom was right above the studio, paints this cartoon-like picture of her bed vibrating as she bounced up and down in her sleep while I was demoing "Shake Your Love" late into the night, prompting her to leap off her bed after being woken up.

"All I heard was you singing 'shake your love' over and over and over. It's the most repetitive song in *history*!"

There's nothing more grounding than a disgruntled sister. Thanks to her good-natured mocking, I knew my song was a hit.

Of course, I had feelings too. My muses were boys like my elementary school friend Anthony Valenti, who showed up on my doorstep *out of the blue*, and *red-hot* lifeguard Rick Lunger, who surprised me at the Newbridge pool with a red rose and Paul Young tickets.

Back in the seventh grade, before I was even dating, if I had a crush on someone who didn't reciprocate, I would feel like my world was completely over. I therefore wrote about it, basically saying, "I could never love again the way I loved you"—an idea also inspired by Mom putting a bug in my ear to write the American-girl version of "Careless Whisper." I took those assignments seriously. So, with a mix of emotional inspiration and wanting to throw my hat in the ring of unreciprocated-love ballads, "Foolish Beat" was born.

---

* *"Shake Your Love" by Deborah Gibson. Copyright © 1986 by Music Sales Corporation (ASCAP). International Copyright Secured. Used by permission. All rights reserved.*

At one point, I had nothing to write about. I was staring at a blank page and looking at the lines in a looseleaf notebook, and that became "Between the Lines." Everything is a song inspiration to me.

Lines, lines . . . between the lines . . .

As my friend Tony Robbins says, "It's not the lack of resources, it's your lack of resourcefulness that stops you."

Creativity is readily available to everyone who chooses to tap into it.

I knew I loved belting B-flats—which, weirdly, would become the note I belted in *Cabaret*. It's a whole step away from that edgy C, which makes all the difference in the world. So I intentionally wrote "Between the Lines" based on the empty page, the lines, and my love of belting B-flats.

Lyrics would become more important to me later on, but for now they were my own quirky brand, imitating my pop idols at the time, influenced by songs such as Whitney Houston's "How Will I Know" and Madonna's "Borderline."

A big fan of simplicity, I didn't really take note of lyricists back then. I paid attention to melodies and composers while approaching the words like a little girl telling a simple story: *Here's my diary entry set to music!*

I didn't start that trend, mind you. There were a lot of people who came before me, like Carole King. But for that generation and that era of music, I was certainly at the forefront. It was important to me to sing like I felt and like I spoke.

Whenever people ask about the meaning of the opening line to "Only in My Dreams"—"Every time I'm telling secrets"[*]—I say,

---

[*] *"Only in My Dreams"* by Deborah Gibson. Copyright © 1985 by Music Sales Corporation (ASCAP). International Copyright Secured. Used by permission. All rights reserved.

"What does it mean to *you*?" Everything's interpretation; some things just sing well.

The best songs I've written haven't been crafted; they've flowed out and, at the age of fifteen, I was constantly writing in notebooks at school and, at night, with a flashlight under the covers. "Tomorrow I'm going to demo 'Out of the Blue.'"

I had my little system. Once a demo of my best songs was done, I'd sit at the kitchen table with Mom and combine all my worlds, putting a theatrical headshot, a résumé, and a cassette in an envelope along with a letter addressed to the heads of A&R—Artists and Repertoire—at all the labels, big and small.

Even though I was delving deeper into my writing and recording, I still had a love of theater and was auditioning for shows that appealed to me. I always got close to getting parts. It was between Elisa Fiorillo and me to play Brigitta in *The Sound of Music* at the Westbury Music Fair, which was a big show, and she got it. I remember looking up to her as being so pretty, better than me vocally, and way cooler in general. But then I got the role she usually played in *A Christmas Carol*, and while I was happy, I also felt like I'd taken something from her. Letting go of being apologetic in that way is something I still work on.

I heard about an audition for a Beach Boys musical that put a lot of pieces together for me. Pop and theater . . . *fun*! It was called *Surf City*, I auditioned . . . and got a total of *fourteen* callbacks. I must have sung "Surf City, here we come" fifty thousand times. When I started getting paid for the callbacks, I realized those people had no idea what they wanted.

I had to audition in a bathing suit, so I wore a turquoise one-piece with little green pinstripes to go with my twelve-year-old-boy body and blonde ponytail. I was paired with a young guy—who still was way older than me—and we ended up losing the roles to a couple who were an older, sexier version of us. I remember being in awe of the beautiful, curvaceous redhead who got the role. I heard the show closed in previews. And then I heard about *Les Miz* opening in London's West End.

It seemed like every theater girl immediately gravitated toward Éponine and the song "On My Own." Totally obsessed, I arranged and demoed that track just in case "they" ever needed to hear me sing it on repeat. When I heard Frances Ruffelle perform it with her modern edge and raw vocal inflections, I thought, *Wow, this is like a pop girl doing Broadway*. Next: the announcement that *Les Miz* was coming to Broadway.

After securing an audition through an agent, I got a callback. Associate director/executive producer Richard Jay-Alexander was running the audition. He would go on to direct bona fide divas like Barbra Streisand, Bette Midler, and Deborah Cox, and I knew he got a kick out of me. Still, vocally I wasn't quite where I needed to be to do that show eight times a week. I didn't have the sustaining of the high notes down. And maybe I wasn't quite gritty and scrappy enough yet to play the role. That would come a little later. Five years in pop music would prove to be the thing I needed to toughen me up.

I could tell Richard knew I had it in me because at the callback, he tried to guide me on hitting those high notes while giving me other directives. I was the underdog, eager to please. But I also knew what I was on the verge of—and I owned it. I don't know what made me do it, but I said over my shoulder on my way out, "If you're gonna cast me, you better cast me now cuz next year I'm gonna be a *big pop star*!"

Richard gave a little nod, as if to say, *Yeah, right, kid*. But I think he knew it too.

"I kept tabs on your career," he'd tell me many years later. "I knew there was something going on with you."

He also recently told me he vividly remembers reading about my graduation in *People* magazine. Still, I meant what I told him. I'd decided beforehand that this was going to be my last audition.

If I don't get this, that's it. I'm literally going to end my audition chapter on this high note.

I didn't get the part, so Mom told the agents and managers, "She's putting her theater career on hold and the same with commercials. We're going full throttle on the music."

They thought we were nuts because we'd built up to this place that every showbiz kid wants to reach. So it was kind of a ballsy move and a gamble, but also a sign of having extreme focus and a knowing beyond my years.

My obsession with having my music played on the radio came from a passionate place. I was the biggest fan of pop radio. Knowing all the DJs' names by heart, I'd call in to the countdown shows, and after a year of persevering on the prize hotline—much to the dismay of my sisters, who couldn't receive calls from boys from seven to ten p.m.—I began to win contests on WPLJ. I'd rattle off thirty records in ten seconds flat in the album rapper contest; I remember a bit of it today because I practiced so much: *Arena, Like a Virgin, Big Bam Boom, Reckless, 17, Crazy from the Heat, Chinese Wall, Flashdance, Footloose, Thriller, Private Dancer, Can't Slow Down* . . . and the rap went on.

I even disguised my voice and gave a phony name a time or two because I was winning too much, which led to me breaking out in a sweat because I've always been the worst liar in the world. But Fast Jimi Roberts let it slide, even though he asked suspiciously, "Don't I know you? Didn't you just win last week?"

"No-o-o-o!"

I fibbed my way to walking off with the entire Chicago catalog, rattling off *Chicago V*, *VI*, *VII*, *VIII*, et cetera, as their albums were all numbered (clever, I know), and I won not one but two pairs of Madonna tickets for her Radio City show. Karen and I were all aboard the *Whamtrak* to Philly.

So you see, pop radio stole my heart—and before long my own songs would be on those countdowns and my tickets the coveted prize. From now on, I wouldn't leave my studio, I'd just demo day and night. And that wasn't because I had grown tired of the theater. I'd simply discovered within me the purest expression of myself and was going to find the most gratification. Everything else could wait.

Musically, there was nobody speaking to an audience my age; Madonna was a bit older and sexier. Something in my songs convinced my mom and me they needed to be heard and that people would be affected by them. I don't know how we knew this, but it was a calling. There's a difference between a career goal and a calling; I was living and breathing music. And MTV was just becoming the big thing and beckoning. It's all about the timing.

Halfway through my fifteenth year on the planet, Doug introduced me and Mom to Larry Yasgar, Bruce Carbone, and Anthony Sanfilippo in the dance music department at Atlantic Records. Those three goombahs reminded me of all my Italian relatives. In their windowless back office, they had stacks of twelve-inch vinyl dance singles, and their energy resonated with me because they were real music lovers, getting stuff done grassroots-style with Nu Shooz, Stacey Q, and all those great dance artists of the era.

It was a definitive time for dance music and I wanted to be a part of it. I left that first meeting with stacks of records just like I had left only months before from Tower Records as a contest winner. Soon,

ETERNALLY ELECTRIC

The boys in the back office! Eternally indebted to Anthony Sanfilippo, the late Larry Yasgar, and Bruce Carbone.

contest winners would be able to leave with *my* record. Isn't that mind-blowing?

After we played the boys in the back office my songs, they invested five thousand dollars to do a twelve-inch dance single because I was young and female and everyone's vision of where my career could go was limited. They were kind of like, *Even if we get in bed with you for this one song, we want to know that, should this catch fire, you have a catalog. Otherwise, where are the other songs coming from?*

"I have them," I replied. "I have about a hundred demoed. And I have notebooks with loads more."

It didn't faze me that they weren't investing millions or committing to a full album. I knew if I could get a foot in the door and prove myself, the bigger payoff would come.

I'd vowed to get a deal by my sixteenth birthday, and I missed that deadline by just three days, signing with Atlantic on September 3, 1986, while we collectively decided "Only in My Dreams" should be the first single.

The all-American girl was living the all-American dream.

Living the all-American dream in my Electric Blue *home studio.*

Chapter Four

ONLY IN MY AMERICAN DREAM

The label's dance department boys assigned an up-and-coming producer named Fred Zarr, who'd worked on Madonna's first album, to produce my debut single, "Only in My Dreams." Fred was a hot keyboard programmer, which was everything in the dance world, and I loved his beautifully built basement studio in Brooklyn. Its vocal booth was his laundry room with an orange curtain in front of the washer and dryer. We all know I'm at home singing with a washing machine nearby! It was really cozy.

Fred's an unbelievable sweetheart of a guy who, instead of seeing himself as some sort of Svengali figure, really just wanted to empower me and help me with my vision, which is quite the opposite of what one might have expected. But remember, at that time, the acting world's casting couch was more commonly talked about; young girls who wanted to be in the movies often fell prey to older male producers. Being that there weren't any teen-girl singer-songwriter prototypes, I really didn't know how fortunate I was to be working with male creatives who looked at me with a deep appreciation for my talents without ever acting in any ways that could be considered creepy.

Solely focused on the music, Fred studied my demos and got inside my head, even keeping many of my original keyboard parts to capture my vibe. Hearing an original two-bar pattern, he'd say, "Let's repeat and quantize it [which means putting it in perfect time] and make a really cool part that loops over and over."

That's what a producer should do, in my opinion: elevate the vision. Fred did that so brilliantly on "Only in My Dreams," even though I felt weird not being the one pushing the buttons and sliding the faders. Back in Merrick, sitting with my AKG 414[*] microphone in its stand between my legs and wearing headphones, I didn't have to talk to anybody if I wanted to go back and redo a line while recording in my home studio. From my head to my fingers and out the speakers—no time was wasted. So it was definitely different to have to direct the engineer or producer and say, "Hey, go back two lines. I want to grab that one again." But it was really nice when they pushed and stretched *me* a little too.

I am a pitch fanatic; Fred is a pitch fanatic. So although there was no auto-tune back then, on the recordings we made together you'd be hard-pressed to find notes that make you cringe because we ensured they weren't there. The bad notes would have haunted us the rest of our lives. We were real perfectionists that way. And my producer picked some great musicians to lend their talents to my records, including guitarist Ira Siegel, Bashiri Johnson on percussion, and Jeff Smith on saxophone. Jeff's a hardcore, seasoned player, but I always wanted him to play grittier.

"Oooh, lean into that B-flat, Jeff. *Dirtier!*"

---

[*] *Officially the AKG C414 (for techies!)*

A little suburban white girl telling Jeff Smith to play dirtier? My mom would wince and shrug apologetically while her inner monologue was saying, *Attagirl.* Thankfully, Jeff and the other band members were really warm toward me. Ira handed me a Sharpie to draw a Snoopy on his prized guitar because he loved working with me so much and wanted the session immortalized. It was a mutual admiration society with these guys, who were total pros and mensches. They were fascinated by this young girl who wrote songs and could communicate: "No, that's an E-flat seventh chord not a straight-up E-flat."

It was so awesome to be able to speak that language and have it spoken back to me. These were Fred's guys, and we had a system where we'd cut a vocal and do a rough mix. I always got married to rough mixes; even today, I'm like, *Oh God, don't listen to the demo too much because you will get demo love and you won't be able to make any changes.* I'd take a rough mix home, live with a vocal performance, hear things, go back, and do a round two, then sometimes a round three. A round three might find me fine-tuning a word here or there.

I've got my own unique balance of being very in the moment, surprising myself with a take, not pre-shaping anything with some outside perspective, as if the artist and producer in me are two different people. Every now and again, as spontaneous as I am, there's a thought of, *I want to scoop that note and push the air at the end. There shouldn't be vibrato on the last note, I should straight-tone it.* A blend of being present and open to surprises with a pencil sketch of how I want it to sound in the end as a producer. That's the craft of recording.

A stickler for those details—I wasn't this little chick singer who just showed up, cranked out six takes, and said, "Hey, guys, take it from here!"—I've always tried to be objective while making the final vocal compilation, so as not to perfect the soul out of the music. Being hands-on while remaining objective about your own performance is a delicate balance.

On "Only in My Dreams," I purposely performed the chorus vocals a little more straight-toned, almost like a horn section instead of a vibrato-ish, Broadway kind of sound. I always wanted my personality in the singing, so I think I had a pretty good blend of slickness and dynamics. Working alongside someone like Ira, I would start by describing my vision, and he instinctively played something that I then helped shape. That splashy, clean rhythmic guitar became a signature sound on my hit songs.

Enjoying the luxury of having a live musician play a part, I wanted to see what he was going to bring. I'm not an electric guitarist, but, like Fred, I was specific about the sound: *How distorted, gritty, or clean is it going to be? How bright is it going to be? Is there a frequency in the range he's playing that's competing with something else?*

A Quincy Jones production, for instance, is like a Tetris puzzle: everything has a place, yet it's spacious at the same time, simple and impactful. I never want a bunch of clutter. Fred taught me to do as much as possible up front rather than wait for the mix. Taking care of the arrangement out of the gate, leaving spaces for where things weave in and out, is easier and more refined than the alternative: throwing in everything plus the kitchen sink and making decisions later to fix it in the mix. Kind of like measuring out your ingredients first when baking a cake, the cake being the record.

"Only in My Dreams" was perky, packed a punch, had a cool syncopated rhythm, and was spacious in the verses, while the choruses had a fuller, four-on-the-floor dance rhythm that really drove the track. There was respect and joy among the musicians working with this self-contained sixteen-year-old artist, and they wanted to bring everything to life for me. Yet during that era, the music industry had no idea what to do with a teenage girl:

Maybe we can groom you for when you're twenty-one.

Today it's the complete opposite: *Let's sign you when you're eight so that when you're thirteen, we've got some product in the can.*

Sure, before I came along, Brenda Lee was twelve when she had her first hit, Marie Osmond was fourteen, Lulu was fifteen, and Lesley Gore was sixteen, but none of them were writing their own hits and there was nobody I modeled myself on. Carole King was eighteen when she cowrote her first hit nearly three decades earlier, but that's a lifetime in music-biz terms, and the big machinery wasn't yet oiled up for my generation. With the dance-single deal on board, I saw this as an opportunity to kick down a door and prove to the powers that be as well as to the music fans out there that I was worthy of a chance to record a full album.

"What do we have to do to make noise in the clubs?" Mom asked.

"Debbie has to perform live. As in, do a club tour."

I immediately began doing club dates with Buddy, a rotating second backup dancer, and my sister Karen, who, age twenty-one at the time, took care of the sound and lights. "Little" Louie Vega did a twelve-inch remix of "Only in My Dreams," which, right from the intro, took listeners on a gorgeous, ethereal journey with percussion and vocals weaving in and out. It was exciting; it had drama and a musical structure that made sense to me; and that's the version I performed in the clubs, along with an extended version of "Shake Your Love" and a twelve-inch dance arrangement of "Fallen Angel." That song, even though it was never a single, became a fan favorite with its edgier, minor-key, Madonna-type feel. Spending half an hour performing ten-minute versions of those three songs, I did so with an all-new look.

My sister Michele was always design-oriented and she could sew. So, away at college, she made me satin jackets and miniskirts. Even then, I loved showing my legs. This look featured them and covered my little-girl squishy middle section while incorporating layered hair, cutoff lace gloves from a teen-trash store, and lace-up Peter Fox granny boots that made me look approachable and accessible to young girls but with a bit of couture class.

Madonna was one of my heroes back then, and it was like, *I'm not creating anything totally original here fashion-wise; I'm a young school-girl emulating my idols.*

The great thing was that, having splashed out five thousand dollars, the Atlantic guys weren't micromanaging me and nobody was saying *You have to dress like a slut* either, although I had to age up a bit to be accepted by the club crowd. My very first performance was at the Limelight in New York, and the invitations for that promotional event billed me as *Deborah Gibson*. I was *Deborah* in the theater and on the demos I'd submitted, but the label guys didn't think that was catchy enough and suggested just my first name or *Debbie G*.

"No way!" I remember telling Mom. "*Debbie G* sounds like a throwaway for a one-hit dance artist."

As did just *Deborah*. *Debbie Gibson* was the obvious front-runner. But the first time I shook someone's hand and said, "Hi, I'm Debbie," it felt so weird. Which was why, wanting to return to my roots, I'd go back to Deborah for a spell—and always chuckled when I'd hear people remark, "Oh, it's *Deborah* now," as if I were trying to be more sophisticated. No, that was actually my childhood name. Who was sophisticated? Not me! That was just how I identified.

My first real paid booking following the Limelight show was at a club called Joey's Place in Clifton, New Jersey—and it was a memorable one. Buddy and I would giggle about it for years to come. He had competed against me in our high-school talent contest a year earlier, and I'd performed a song I'd written called "Somebody Loves You," first to a backing track I created in my home studio and then a cappella at the front of the stage, by default, after the microphone went out. One of my strengths has always been rolling with mishaps, and Buddy recognized this.

"Oh, she just won," he told his dance partner, Linda, feeling defeated.

The two of them had been on before me, doing backflips and lifts, and I was amazed: *Oh my God*. The football team also got together and did something called the "Calhoun Colts Shuffle" because the "Super Bowl Shuffle" was out. It was spectacular to watch those hot boys doing a rap song, but it was Buddy and Linda who took first place. And I was the one who caught Buddy's attention. So, seeing my photo on the wall of talent agent Scott Sedita a few weeks later, he said, "She goes to my high school," to which Scott replied, "Well, she's signing a record deal and looking for dancers. You should call her."

Buddy did indeed call me and left a message on the answering machine that lived in my parents' bedroom. That was the first and last time he ever called me Debbie. He auditioned in the kitchen, we hired him on the spot, and he's been along for the ride ever since. At Joey's, his dance partner was a guy named Rocco, and the three of us thought we were just the divas of all divas. I'm not really a *dancer*-dancer, but we planned this big lift without considering how low the ceiling was, and the result was me being lifted right through it; stucco was cascading down, creating an effect we never could have paid for! Hysterical—though maybe not back then.

Oh my God, I'm so fired, I'm so fired, I'm so fired, Buddy was thinking while trying not to slip on the flakes on the stage as Karen kept the backing tracks rolling. Always one to flip the script, I chalked it up to making a memory... One for the books indeed!

We performed all over the country, on the bill with hardcore dance groups and freestyle acts of the era like the Cover Girls, TKA, and Exposé. I was definitely the youngest on the scene and performed everywhere, from a club called Escapes in my hometown of Merrick to a church in East LA. Doug was still managing me, and my mom questioned it: "East LA? That could be a little rough."

It had been booked through the priest, so how bad could it be? Bad enough that it was the last event they were staging there because of a shooting just the weekend before. Six armed guards walked me in, there were metal detectors, and rings were stolen off my fingers by members of the church audience. Welcome to the modern version of vaudeville, folks! Mom, as tough as she was, was totally freaking out.

"Kids, wait in the car, I'm gonna get the money," she deadpanned in the back seat of the limo before the show. She always collected the cash up front. "If I'm not out in twenty minutes, somebody come in and get me."

This was Mama Rose on steroids. In East LA. She had to be tough. And although Gypsy Rose Lee and her infamous stage mother had to work with farm animals and in burlesque, I don't recall any concealed weapons! I'm not a parent. But to those of you who are: Can you *imagine*?

We sat in the car while Buddy kept chanting under his breath, "I came to LA to die, I came to LA to die..."

His conviction grew stronger when, post-gig, we went for a late-night bite at Ben Frank's on Sunset. Burgers, fries, shakes—I was a kid in perpetual motion, so I was hungry all the time. Outside, we saw people being egged in the parking lot. When we walked inside, a biker with a shaved head took one look at Buddy and said, "Sit down."

Buddy obeyed.

"Stand up."

What was going on here?

"Now spin around in circles!"

The guy laughed. He was just taking the mickey out of him, as my British friends would say. But we felt terrorized in this late-night world: a sixteen-year-old girl, her twenty-one-year-old sister, and a couple of dancers, plus her mom, who was forty and, as she put it, "straight out of the kitchen with roots and a bad perm." I'd later come to learn that all of this fish-out-of-water stuff kept me in a constant state of fight or flight.

I didn't get heckled at the clubs. Actually, I was kind of ignored. So, to get everyone's attention, I decided to start "Only in My Dreams" a cappella and hold the big high C for as long as I could: "It was only in myyy . . ." Not my favorite note, as you might recall, but I tackled it to make it known I was singing live. I always felt a vibe in the regular middle-of-the-night mainstream clubs: straight guys drinking, trying to pick up women, and wondering, *Who's this little powder puff interrupting our night?*

Powder puff was a favorite moniker of Mom's. She was aware of how tough I was on the inside juxtaposed with how I looked. We had wild, far-fetched dreams and a solid grasp on reality, both of which were needed.

A huge benefit of playing clubs that young was that it completely turned me off the idea of sneaking out with a fake ID to drink. I had a front-row seat to the nightlife scene and was like, *No, thank you . . . not for me!*

Then there was the time we got booked at this beach-themed radio event. The stage was a sandpit and Buddy had to remove his shoes to perform backflips. We constantly had to adapt: small stage, big stage, good sound, crappy sound, great audience, lousy audience... sandpit.

It's all right, I'm just going to keep doing my thing, honing my craft, building my audience.

Female sound engineers were a rarity back then, and some of the DJs resented watching my tomboy sister Karen climb ladders in her sneakers and jeans to fire up my wireless mic and run the backing tracks. At a teen club, one of them wouldn't let her put the tape on— and that freaking DJ then played it backward just to mess me up. I had friends there that night, and rather than announce, "Okay, we have a technical mishap," and risk losing everyone's attention, I kept my cool and pivoted.

Nobody knows or cares, so I'm just gonna sing and dance to the backward beat and get outta here as fast as I can.

I performed with backward tracks for the entire show and even my friends didn't notice.

"That was *amazing*, Deb!"

"Didn't you think the music was a little strange?"

Uncle Carl decided to come to a show at the legendary Backstreet Nightclub in Fort Lauderdale, Florida, unaware his niece was on the same bill as a six-foot-eight drag queen named Belle Kincaid. At least that's how tall she looked in her high heels, towering over my uncle, who is quite tall himself. The visual of Carl, a tough Brooklyn school principal, looking up at the gorgeous Ms. Belle lives on in my mind even though I can't recall many of the names of the hundreds of clubs I played. All I know is my record started getting spins because I shook the DJs' hands. That personal touch was always important.

The thing about the dance world was that I found it and it found me. Not into hardcore remixes at the time, I wasn't frequenting discos. Unbothered by the fact I was too young to get in the front door, I also wasn't chomping at the bit to get a fake ID like many of my friends were. This was a professional engagement for me and, focused on music as the point of connection, I didn't feel the disconnect you might think I would have amid the adult faces I was singing to. When my fans and I were immersed in the power of the beats and the melodies, we were all ageless and shared a universal energy.

Those clubs were the fastest way for me to get my music directly to the people. If my song could fill a dance floor, I had something. A little-known fact is, because my age was a detriment, my picture wasn't on the original vinyl run. The music stood on its own and spoke for itself. The club DJs, many of whom initially thought I was older—and Black—gave it a shot at a time when a teenage white girl might not have gotten one.

It really was the true start of my eyes being opened to how diverse the world is. Being a teen and singing for teens at the start of the night made perfect sense; it was like being the pop queen at a sweet sixteen. Entertaining the more hardcore straight crowd and party set was a bit more challenging and where I really cut my teeth. And then there were the gay clubs. Maybe I connected with those audiences because I was the little girl with the lisp and quirky nose who didn't tick all the boxes, performing for unique, out-of-the-box authentic humans who were also being stereotyped and grappling with public perception. Or maybe it was the fact that this community was there to celebrate the music, but with a discerning taste that demanded my best. The reason doesn't really matter. All I knew was... I couldn't wait to get to the gay clubs. This was the time and place a lifelong love affair with the queer community was born.

Mom was able to run with this dance-music fan base I was building from the ground up and network with heavy hitters such as attorney-to-the-stars Paul Schindler, who signed me as a client. Famed NYC publicist David Salidor also took me under his wing.

Realizing I had an innate ability to hold my own in interviews brought many an opportunity my way, including TV shows like *Regis and Kathie Lee* as well as local press interviews and TV pieces. David really became part of the family through the years. He had a little black camera he called Snappy, and that turned into his nickname. To this day, *Snappy* comes up when he calls my cell phone; I always remember those who believed early on.

His big advice was "Don't say anything negative, because if you do, the press will take that and run with it." That's why I always kept a real, yet positive spin on things.

Not so wholesome an experience was Mom's first meeting with famed indie radio promoter Herb Rosen. When she asked him how he got records played on the radio, he opened a drawer containing a gun and a wad of cash and said, "This is how, Diane," with a wink and a smile. Was he serious? I'm sure that growing up around my Uncle Sal contributed to the fact that she didn't flinch. I was there and I'll never forget it.

Dad played his part by stuffing mailboxes at TWA with notes urging people to call and request his daughter's song on all the New York City radio stations. He even supplied the hotline numbers, and this led to my record getting spins on HOT 97 by the station's program directors Steve Ellis and Joel Salkowitz. The first time it was played, Dad and I were in the car heading back to Merrick from my voice lesson with Guen in Manhattan. As soon as I heard the opening beats of the remix super-low in the background, I turned up the volume and could hardly contain myself while Dad, head bopping up and down, began driving to the beat on the Long Island Expressway.

"You're going to drive us off the road!" I cautioned him playfully.

Hearing myself on the radio that first time was an unforgettable experience. And when the record started climbing the dance chart in February 1987, Atlantic decided to pull the trigger, releasing the "Only in My Dreams" seven-inch single along with a video that had been so much fun to shoot. To this day, that's still one of the most enjoyable parts of what I do because it's so decadent—showing up and lip-synching, hopefully after a good night's sleep and maybe even a facial, while having an array of styled clothes to try on.

Nevertheless, that video, directed by Simeon Soffer, was the first and last one on which I didn't have much creative input. The abstract elements, such as the priest on the beach in Asbury Park, the mirror shattering, and the mom waving, were, I thought, a little horror-movie creepy. But the carousel was very me, very whimsical, and I couldn't help thinking, *Oh my God, I'm getting to make a video!*

With "Only in My Dreams" now bubbling just under the *Billboard* Hot 100, Atlantic Records skipped the second top-five-hit stipulation and signed me to an eight-album deal. The powers that be could smell what was happening. And I wanted my debut album chock-full of singles. Who cared about giving listeners a break and transporting them to another realm with artistic filler? Not me. What was an *album track* anyway? Taking a page out of Michael Jackson's book, I was determined to create tracks that were all strong in their own right for what would become my debut album, *Out of the Blue*.

Everything was moving so fast. I'll never forget the day when the head honchos, Doug Morris and Ahmet Ertegun, emerged from their grand offices and made the pilgrimage down the hall to shake my hand and compliment the dance department boys. We had to churn out that full-length debut album even if it meant me stopping mid-session to get homework done. Acting as executive producer, Doug Breitbart assembled a great production team: Fred Zarr, who produced six of the tracks, half of them with me; John Morales and Sergio Munzibai, who produced "Red Hot" and "Between the Lines"; and Lewis A. Martineé, who produced "Play the Field."

That left one other Gibson composition, and it turned into a bone of contention when, during a creative meeting with the higher-ups at Atlantic, eyebrows were raised at Mom's suggestion that I should produce it by myself.

"Let's play the demo for 'Foolish Beat,'" she said. "I really feel like Deb has her finger on the pulse of what the sound of this record should be and I don't think she needs any outside influence."

Though I'd spoken briefly with Doug and Ahmet when they shook my hand, this was my first time strategizing with them in the big conference room. Of the twelve execs sitting around the table, only three were women: head of the music video department Linda Ferrando; head of publicity Patti Conte; and head of radio promotion Andrea Ganis, who recently reminded me there had been almost no female radio program directors at the time.

"Deb wants to produce this particular song on her own and she should," Mom continued.

Although not pro caliber, the demos that had secured my record deal showed how, playing and mixing everything, I knew what I wanted sonically. Never mind that I didn't have the tools; I could hire Fred Zarr as the keyboard programmer, because he was prepared to take me under his wing and was happy to support my solo production effort. I already had ideas for the keyboard sounds and the sax-solo melody. Plus I had the background vocal parts in my head. So it was a case of conveying all this to the musicians, as well as to vocalists Carrie and Libby Johnson, who I knew would bring their divine sister-blend magic along with the silky, husky tone of Tim Lawless. I trusted my instincts and knew how to get the job done. I would also guide engineers Don Feinberg and Phil Castellano on how things should be captured and mixed.

Listening to my mother's pitch, the female execs looked like they were rooting for us. The men: more like nervous giggles. This was new territory for everyone. The suit shoulders were still going up and down when Mom banged her hand on the table in frustration. I'd seen that happen before, and it would become a theme, but only when she was passionately fighting for my creative vision and needs. She never, ever asked for anything gratuitous.

"My daughter can produce this record better than anyone," she asserted.

"Okay..."

The suits stopped laughing.

"Let's see what the girl can do."

Believe me, they would. I've always loved a good challenge.

That June, "Only in My Dreams" finally climbed into the top 50 of the *Billboard* Hot 100 singles chart, thanks in part to my pounding the pavement and pulling all-nighters in the clubs. It then went Top 20 in July, Top 10 in August, and peaked at #4 on September 5. Seeing my name printed below Michael Jackson and Madonna and immediately above Whitney Houston was surreal.

Also surreal was being one of the first guests on *Club MTV*, the funky fresh showcase for dance/pop acts hosted by Downtown Julie Brown. At the taping for the episode that later aired on my birthday, I first brushed shoulders with actor and Long Island local teen heartthrob Brian Bloom on my way up to the stage. It was like in those movies where time slows down for a few seconds and there is a little whoosh of imaginary glitter. Though no words were exchanged that day, he recalls thinking, *Oh, this is the girl from Merrick who everyone's talking about.* I knew exactly who Brian was, but this was definitely more about the spark and energy of the moment being imprinted, to be continued later.

By then, *Out of the Blue* had been released to positive reviews en route to selling three million copies in the United States and five million worldwide.

"A fond remembrance of pop idols of times past," stated *Cash Box* on August 15, 1987, "this 16-year-old Long Island native has leaped into the pop/dance arena with wide eyes and a penchant for writing flowing ballads and sizzling dance grooves."

I'd hit the ground running and Atlantic's top brass were now clamoring for another single. I thought "Staying Together" should be the follow-up to "Only in My Dreams," but Doug and Ahmet insisted on "Shake Your Love," and their decision was right on the money. Released in September 1987, the track peaked at #4 that December, assisted by a video that spoke to my love of 1950s cars in a drive-through setting. The director, Jay Brown, gave it a contemporary LA vibe with bright colors, sharp lighting, and super-fast editing.

When Sean and Mackenzie Astin dropped by to visit the set, my sister Denise and I thought that was so cool! My makeup artist Paul Starr snapped his fingers at some unsuspecting PA to get them their own directors' chairs, then gave me a wink and a smile. He knew that, even though I was employing upward of a hundred people that day, I was still a teenage girl who wanted to make sure the cute boys were taken care of.

As I didn't have a lot of control over the edit, Paula Abdul's incredible choreography was cut to pieces to suit the fast-paced editing style of the time, but it was so fantastically memorable to work with her and all the talented dancers of that era. She and I are still in touch to this day, and I respect and adore her. At least I got to integrate my own style and my own wardrobe choices. My hair was growing out and everything was just a little cutesier because that's who I was and how I felt. I also loved that they kept the quirky bit where I picked up a sneaker and pretended it was a phone. I think those goofy little things are part of what connected me to my audience. But they didn't endear me to some of my classmates.

Perhaps unusually for a performer, I didn't like being singled out at school, and, always a little on edge, I didn't enjoy giving presentations. I wasn't that cool, calm, collected teen—and I'm not a cool, calm, collected adult either. I didn't go to a lot of parties as a kid because they made me nervous, and I'd feel my face get hot whenever a teacher asked me to answer a question.

There was an expectation of being cool and I didn't feel cool. I only felt cool, powerful, and confident onstage with a microphone. Playing clubs, day was night and night was day. If I was on the East Coast, I might get home at six in the morning, grab some sleep, and arrive late at school. The fatigue brought on anxiety and I'd be thinking, *I know y'all know I'm promoting a record, but nobody look at me too hard.*

Who wants to stand out in high school? Always trying to determine the common ground and the great equalizer, I didn't want to be seen as different from—or better than—anyone. But inevitably, some kids still gave me a hard time: "Oh, you think you're so great."

I was fascinated by that sentence. Certain skills I had were gifts and other things just came from hard work. I never had an elitist attitude and I never flaunted my showbiz life. But I did enjoy it. And if I sang loudly in the school choir, that was only because I *loved to sing*. I didn't think I was "great."

Some of my classmates' attitudes didn't change at all after my first single became a hit.

"This sounds like a *real record*!" exclaimed my friend Mike Provenz, who'd been privy to all my demos, when he first heard "Only in My Dreams."

Other kids who knew what I'd been doing were also taken aback: "Wait, this sounds like what we listen to on the radio."

I had no idea they'd be surprised to hear a full-on production. Some were happy for me and rooting for me. However, others who'd previously liked me suddenly hated me, while those who had never thought I was cool suddenly did:

"I've told my cousin we're at school together. He's having a big party. Wanna come?"

Until now, you've never given me the time of day, I'd think.

It was kind of ugly to see that behavior. Intellectually, I tried to understand it, but it wounded my soul.

At the Gibson family dinner table, I made sure Denise had her moment to shine and talk about her normal junior high school experiences, but I knew the dynamic was changing. Although we were all doing our best to find common ground, the reality was that Mom and Dad were going in different directions. Diane was becoming a full-fledged powerhouse manager while Joe was still in his blue-collar job, holding down the fort. Denise and I sometimes sat on the stairs and heard bickering down the hall; we rolled our eyes and shrugged it off, but it foreshadowed what was to come.

Yup, life was different, all right. My grandparents had been taking me to the East Bay Diner since I was seven, but now the managers there were falling all over themselves when I walked in—and that just made me more protective of all the patrons who *weren't* making records. *What about my sisters?* I'd think. *They're really cool, but you're only making a fuss over me.* Something about that felt bad; I didn't like it. And I didn't appreciate being allowed to cut the line and get a table ahead of everyone else. Some people might think it's a perk. I just thought, *That's so weird.* But it also would have been rude not to take them up on their offer because they were just trying to do something nice for me.

Although fame didn't change me, it changed many *around* me. And I knew that if I didn't stand up and speak up for myself, it was only going to get worse. I had to let people know I was tough and I wanted to teach them a lesson. So when I overheard kids mocking me in school as they rounded the corner, thinking I was out of earshot, I took a new approach toward their passive aggression. Face hot, heart pounding, I'd go back around the corner and hold their feet to the fire: "If you'd like to say something, say it to my face. I'm right here."

The bullying was similar to what happens now on social media. But, looking back, I realize they were just teens who didn't know how to handle my fame. Nobody does, whether you're adjacent to it or *in* it. It made more sense to me because I was putting in the work. I never thought it was about me; it was always about the music. That's what kept me grounded, even as I flew across the pond.

At the start of 1988, I traveled to the United Kingdom with Mom and Doug for some promotional appearances—and that's when the partnership with him unraveled. There were tensions during a club date right before this trip when I was on the same bill as Curiosity Killed the Cat. I thought the guys in that British pop band were incredibly cute, and as they were on after me, I told Mom I'd like to stay and watch. Doug begged to differ.

I was so triggered by that moment: *Whoa, whoa, whoa, nobody is more professional than me. I'm the most responsible kid on the planet. If anything, I have to learn to let my hair down and enjoy myself. You're not my dad!*

What I was thinking, my mother said out loud in the parking lot as we walked toward our car.

"Doug, you don't get to make that decision," she said pointedly. "When Deb says she wants to stay and enjoy the show, she gets to stay. Let the kid be a kid! She knows herself better than anyone."

I did. I was the first one to raise the white flag when I was ready for bed. I did indeed need to be a kid, which was the opposite of the discipline lesson one might have thought was suitable for an upcoming young pop diva. Discipline I knew. Being young and having fun, not so much. Though I watched the set from the wings that night, my bubble was burst. After that event and the tension-filled trip to London, my mom officially became my manager.

Although he and I have never had an adult conversation about any of this, I'm sure Doug suffered a lot of heartbreak, as he had loads of time and energy invested in me. I think about things like this now because as children, we go along with our parents, and I, for one, felt disloyal having my own thoughts and opinions at times. But now, as a fully formed adult, I pride myself on being an independent thinker and am able to see situations from everyone's point of view. Within the context of the landscape of young girl entertainers, one wrong move witnessed by a parent means the chips are gonna fall a certain way. And in the case of *this* little girl, there was a need for something specific in the way of female intuition and nuance.

Mom was tough, but she was nurturing too—and she had to be both when going to bat for me as a solo songwriter, a mission that would pay off when "Out of the Blue" climbed to #3 in April 1988. And boy, was she vindicated for all that fist-pounding when that June, while auditioning background singers for my first major tour around the piano in the living room, I got the call that I had my first #1 with the self-penned, self-produced "Foolish Beat," making me the youngest artist in history to write, perform, and produce a chart-topping US single. Now seventeen, I broke the record set by my triple-threat idol George Michael, and to date, I'm still the youngest female to accomplish this—as well as the second youngest, given that "Lost in Your Eyes" repeated the feat nine months later, making me my own runner-up.

People should have known better than to dismiss a young girl writing about her feelings and the fans who connected to it all. Yes, sixteen-year-olds write about sixteen-year-old things, including puppy love and the people we like in social studies class. I was an island, so it was easy to diminish what I was doing, but all that mattered to me was the impact those songs were having on my audience. And that's still the case with the music I make today!

Chapter Five

PRETTY LITTLE VENEER

"You've got big dreams, you want fame. Well, fame costs, and right here is where you start paying... in sweat."

—Debbie Allen, *Fame*

I function best around people with whom I resonate personally, creatively, spiritually... people I can laugh with. Getting to be the star often enough, I sometimes just want to be one of the gang because, although I'm borderline introvert, the scale tips to the extrovert side. I feed off energy and connection and community, which is why I love hanging out with people at the start of my day at Le Café de la Plage in Malibu, where the motto is "Only good vibes." This place is my *Cheers*, and apparently, everybody knows more than just my name.

"Are you Debbie Gibson?" asks a Malibu mom standing *behind* me in line with her two small children.

How did she...

"I recognized you from your speaking voice."

I hear that constantly, and I always wonder, *How much time have you actually* spent *with my speaking voice?*

"My junior high bestie was Team Tiffany but I was always Team Debbie!" she continues.

I go on to explain that there was never an actual feud and that I've always wished people could love us and our music equally, but the tabloids love to fuel the fire of pitting women against each other and, clearly, it starts young.

"My feeling was, there are charts with a different person at the top every week of the year, so there's room for all of us!" I tell her. "Tiffany and I each had our own unique vibes back then musically, but we were even more powerful when aligned and supporting one another because we became a genre and not just individual lanes."

Malibu Mom seems to get it when I reference her daughter: "Would you want your little girl to compete with her friends or root for them?"

But I digress. I'm always taken by surprise because I never walk around thinking, *Oh, I'm going to get recognized today*. Unless I'm dolled up and scheduled to be appearing publicly, I am just a gal going about her business.

It's so surreal that people can identify me from my speaking voice while I'm in line for coffee. It still seems like just a minute ago I was trying to get my voice heard for the first time. Back then I didn't have the luxury of figuring out where my favorite places were and who I wanted to hang out with. I was simply told where to show up. Never mind if I was exhausted and had three shows to do in one night.

There was a lot of shaking hands and kissing babies, and I tried to be the dutiful artist, but my jam-packed schedule was enough to take anyone down. I always needed a moment to switch off and thought it was weird that, accompanied by Mom, I had to schmooze a Pittsburgh program director at a dinner scheduled by the label in order for him to play my record. Things like that always made me feel energetically slutty and incredibly anxious. There I was, ordering my burger and fries, looking at this man who was old enough to be one of my schoolteachers.

What can I possibly say to this guy that he'll be able to relate to? I remember thinking. *It would be weird to tell him about Gina's slumber party last weekend...*

I wasn't feeling like my happy genuine self, and my nerves were on edge. This was *not* a part of showbiz. I was exhausted, and my lifestyle started to catch up with me during the meal. Body tingling from my toes up, chest tightening, breaking into a sweat, I felt like the walls were closing in. This would be the first in a long string of anxiety attacks. If anyone out there has experienced them, you'll know what it's like: you literally think you are dying, unsure where your next breath is coming from.

It's not that the program director had done anything to make me feel bad; it's just that I didn't understand how to connect with an adult male and didn't want to spend the little downtime that I had in this way. It made me uncomfortable, resentful, and doing what I had to do by sitting at that table went against something within me. So my body rebelled and, feeling a little lightheaded, I was given smelling salts, which was probably the stupidest thing anyone could have done because it triggered more anxiety and resulted in me being rushed to the ER.

I was a live wire, feeling on edge and constantly fatigued because my overstressed nervous system was pulling from reserves of reserves of reserves. Most teenagers don't experience that before they get to college. As a showbiz gal in an adult world, I didn't want to be perceived as an ungrateful diva for complaining or refusing to do as I was told. I got points for being a trooper. This would become a recurring theme during the first few years of my career because everything was framed as urgent and of the utmost importance by the record company.

To me, a program director saying, "I'm not gonna play her record if she doesn't have dinner with me," was very much tit for tat. That was never going to be sustainable, as there might be times when the superhero cape had to come off, but it would be concerning to the Atlantic execs who were focused on delivering a product. And listen: once labels invest millions in an artist, it is simply part of the job. You have to be tough and superhuman and do as you're told. But I was in denial over the fact that I was pimping myself out.

I'm sure many of the executives back then saw me as a commodity, not a young girl, but there were some exceptions, such as the label's sweet, elegant vice president, Paul Cooper. Imagine getting a phone call in your hotel room at seventeen years old, telling you a chauffeured limousine is waiting downstairs to take you to Disneyland! My little sister and I were literally jumping for joy. The antithesis of the norm at that time, this wasn't a case of an older male wanting to accompany me for his own salacious purposes. Paul sent us on our way, a guide met us, and we had the time of our lives. His allowing me to be a kid to counteract all the business-related adult experiences was pure generosity on his part.

I have such fond memories of visiting Atlantic's LA offices where Paul and West Coast VP Tony Mandich always made me feel warm, cozy, and valued as a creative force while still seeing me very much as a kid. Tony would fling his arms out to welcome me, then adopt a different tone with Mom, emphasizing that she was his age-appropriate peer while I was still a young girl. Again, I didn't realize back then that this was something to be celebrated, given what I know now about the power dynamic between many male execs and their young female clients.

I didn't feel like I had to put on airs or jump through hoops for Paul and Tony, but unfortunately I did with some of the other department heads. They would simply craft my itinerary without regard for my physical stamina or emotional well-being, triggering the kind of fatigue and anxiety that's caused so many young performers to get hooked on uppers and downers. Individual needs were not taken into consideration back then. I am so happy that today, many young entertainers, like Selena Gomez and Shawn Mendes, are vocal about mental health and taking breaks when needed. It's a great message to put out into the world.

There was a stigma to the word *anxiety*, but recognizing early on that I needed tools and techniques to manage stress, I began doing yoga and acupuncture. "You're sticking yourself with needles?" my less evolved classmates would squeal, mocking me. My cousin Carmella accompanied me to those weekly appointments in a home office that smelled of Chinese herbs and literally held my hand as I tackled my issues in a holistic way. But the pressure was real and it came to a head on the day of my high-school graduation.

Graduating with the class was a big goal of mine, symbolizing being a normal teen even though my academic life was the total opposite of that. To my mind, stepping foot inside a classroom to be with my fellow students meant I was at least hanging on to some shred of normalcy. I'm sure private tutors and homeschooling would've made my life easier, but Mom always said she didn't want me to look at her someday and demand, "How come you didn't let me stay with my friends at school? Why didn't you protect my right to go to the prom?"

We therefore went ahead with my graduation, but it was extraordinarily stressful and unconventional, as there was the matter of the insurance policy I had to sign. This stated that I'd be held responsible if any students, faculty, or guests were injured as a result of the media's presence, but I hadn't come all this way, enduring my journey in public school, not to graduate with my class. Mama Di and I were risk-takers and she left it to me to decide, so of course I opted to sign away and go on with the show!

Thankfully, the graduation ceremony went off without a hitch and no entertainment reporters were trampled by rabid Debheads or vice versa! If only the same could be said about the after-party, where I was now a public figure at what should have been a private event. The fact that this took place at Aunt Linda's house instead of at ours was also of note—and a contributing factor to what happened that day. Because our house was near the football field, we'd have everybody driving by; they'd be either honking their horns or knocking on our front door. I wished the celebration could have been at our house, like it had been for my big sisters before me.

It's my party and I'll hyperventilate if I want to! Not the song I had in mind. So forget feeling normal, especially in light of the photographer.

"I'm having so much fun with your nice big Italian family," he said, grabbing a plate and making himself at home.

He was lovely and we were a warm and welcoming bunch, but I felt like I was on display. I was spinning. So, totally dizzy, I excused myself, disappeared into the basement, sat down on the couch, and put my head in my hands. Cue everyone hypothesizing about what was happening:

"It might be heat exhaustion," said Uncle Carl.

"Maybe it's asthma," suggested cousin Monica.

I remember in this moment closing my eyes, shaking my head, and feeling invisible when I reopened my eyes. A dissociative disorder that would worsen with time, it made the world around me a little dimmer while, not quite in my own skin, I honestly *wanted* to disappear. This was caused by a buildup of fatigue, stress, and anxiety. And it was triggered that day by the presence of the photographer who'd been invited by my publicist to our humble backyard barbecue.

Funny enough, the press coverage would lead me to career opportunities. That was the trade-off. There was a downside to not being an unfiltered teen letting my hair down at my own graduation party. Not with media around. I was once again caught between whining—I mean, who wouldn't want one of her favorite mags to be interested in covering their graduation?—and *I am a teenager, not equipped to emotionally handle all of this*. A few years into public life, a psychiatrist would tell me that the brain and body interpret extreme success as trauma. So even though I was logically able to say, "Oh my God, amazing things are happening for me and I am excited!" I often felt out of sorts and overwhelmed.

"I don't feel like I'm in my body," I'd tell my mom.

The people who seem the most "put together" are often quietly and privately dealing with their physical and psychological problems. Cracks were starting to appear in my pretty little veneer because I was constantly either recovering from something, preparing for something, or *on*. The body remembers, but there was never enough time and space to process my life. And my teenage brain, still not fully developed, wasn't wired to understand an adult world. So I just kept doing what I was doing to the best of my ability.

Performing suited me well, as I was always in a heightened state onstage. That energy met me where I was, I met it where it was, and it was a great outlet. It's just that my energy was better suited to lights, cameras, action than it was to sitting still. A sold-out crowd of screaming people felt natural, a low-key family dinner didn't. The hoop-jumping never ended cuz, while I had to find commonality with everyone, nobody, it seemed, could relate to me.

One time, a program director spun my record after interviewing me on his show. Wide-eyed and excited, I rushed to listen to it on the car radio and heard him ask, "Is she out of the building yet?" while smashing the disc and saying he'd never play it again.

Seriously?

I guess being in a chauffeured town car was supposed to ease the hurt. It didn't. My songs are my babies, and back then, some morning-show DJs had a bitter kind of edge that wasn't conducive to being gentle with little girls or sensitive toward their feelings. I know I speak about attracting tough love in the form of people in my inner circle—including my mother—being brutally honest in the name of constructive criticism, but that's a way different scenario than folks being cruel for the sake of a laugh on morning radio. Don't have me on the show just to turn around and belittle me. That kind of thing imprints as trauma, so it was very careless for people in power to do that back then. And it still is.

Many think of Howard Stern as being like that, but Howard's the nicest, classiest guy on the planet; he knows his craft, knows his audience, and is edgy in a really professional, respectful, intelligent way. You know what you're walking into; there will be a sexual aspect and a fast, sharp, witty-banter tennis match. There will also be a deep dive because Howard is naturally curious and very appreciative of artists.

One of my all-time-favorite morning-show experiences was with Scott Shannon on the Z100 Morning Zoo's Christmas special. He had a way of bringing people together that was edgy and cool but also steeped in respect. Little did I know a couple of life-altering things were going to happen on that fateful New York City winter morning. When I sat down and took the mic as part of this ensemble of talent gathered in the live studio, I was struck by fellow guest Michael Damian's black bowler hat. Michael, no stranger to female attention, being as he was the star of the soap opera *The Young and the Restless*, gave in to my cute-girl routine.

"Oh my God, let me try on your hat," I said. "Wow, it looks better on me than on you!"

"Keep it."

Mission accomplished, wink-wink!

That hat became part of my pop image, so this was a profound moment, but something bigger was about to happen: I would connect once again with Brian Bloom, whom I'd previously brushed shoulders with on the *Club MTV* staircase and who became one of my great loves. I remember that day I was feeling less pop star and more flushed teenager, a bit clammy in my oversize sweater but cozy and protected, as I was surrounded by people who weren't out to get me.

Although Brian was at that radio show with his on-again, off-again girlfriend, actress Allison Smith, he and I didn't know our moms were forming a friendship of their own in the Z100 lounge; in fact, Linda Bloom and Diane Gibson were the catalysts for me and Brian getting together.

Those early days of dating often found us at one of our family homes, listening to music together in one of our rooms . . . with, of course, the door open. Brian was a big mixtape guy, a big R&B connoisseur, and what we had was a really sweet, innocent, music-centric teen romance. He told me recently he still has one of our mixtapes: New Edition, Ralph Tresvant, Troop, Ready for the World . . . maybe unusual for a suburban Jewish boy to be making for his girlfriend who'd resuscitated the porkpie hat from the jazz era.

Although his previous relationships had been more physical, I wasn't there yet *at all*. I was a bit of a late bloomer—maybe because Mom was always around, maybe because I had enough adult responsibilities, meaning I needed to keep that part of my life simpler, although I loved a good make-out session.

Brian is incredibly good-looking, with striking blue eyes, and the two of us looked a little like Danny and Sandy from *Grease*. However, I've never been into aesthetics as its own thing. What attracted me was how much Brian didn't lean into or play up those good looks. Instead, he's always been incredibly introspective and self-aware. The fact he was all that and a professional actor, having been a regular cast member on *As the World Turns* while appearing in films like *Once Upon a Time in America*, drew me to him. It was rare to find a teenager who was familiar with the ins and outs of showbiz but who also remained as grounded as Brian did. We were two Long Island kids who'd made good. Something right out of a Billy Joel song.

Emotionally intelligent and thoughtful in his conversation, Brian was comfortable in his own skin and made me feel comfortable in mine. He didn't shy away from true connection, and given all the things going on in my life that we could discuss, neither did I. There was an innate understanding rooted in our fame connection, our music connection, and—both of us having been raised in Merrick—our Long Island connection. We were old souls who perfected the art of writing letters.

We reminisce about the secret drawer he had under his bed full of letters I'd written on hotel stationery from around the world. But we were also kids who loved to laugh and be silly. And then there was the chemistry. Yet, all that aside, the thing to know is that we each monopolized the one and only phone line in our family homes for three to four hours at a time to talk about God knows what. What a perfectly sweet love affair.

I didn't get to see him a lot because I was touring and traveling. He recently reminded me of quite possibly the only time I actually played hooky from a radio interview—once in San Diego—to continue hanging out with him poolside at the Mondrian on Sunset Boulevard for a few more days. "My voice needs rest" was the excuse I used, and, to make sure I wasn't found out, we substituted normal communication with tracing sexy messages on each other's arms.

Writing out what we wanted to say and do, we'd erupt in fits of giggles and I'd blush whenever the invisible love notes and dares became too much for me. You see, I could write and sing about things I wasn't quite ready to follow through with, and the fantasy and tease of it all was way more fun than talking about myself on the air to some middle-aged DJ who'd probably throw my record up against the wall after I left. This was a better investment at the time. Ever the professional, I loved knowing that the romantic, rebellious teenage girl was alive and well—for a moment anyway. This sweet, sexy, teenage time that one never gets back was a pull too strong to say no to.

The body remembers and the heart never forgets . . .
So young I hadn't met me yet.
But I feel you now.*

LA was convenient, as Brian was there a lot for his work. We didn't travel or stay in hotel rooms together, but he supported me at some of my concert dates and helped to keep me grounded amid the flurry of flashbulbs and audiences chanting my name.

In April '88, I was pinching myself when I won Favorite Female Singer, cohosted, and performed at the Nickelodeon Kids' Choice Awards at Universal City in LA. Brian couldn't attend this one, but

---

* "The Body Remembers" by Deborah Ann Gibson. Copyright © 2021 by Birdsong Publishing (ASCAP). Used by permission. All rights reserved.

luckily he wasn't the jealous type, because the after-party found me sitting cross-legged beside one new-to-the-scene actor named Brad Pitt. And even though Denise and I giggled over how cute he was, I was back in my hotel room using that calling card to call my boyfriend—right after we all watched the delayed telecast of me singing "Out of the Blue" and "Shake Your Love."

The following month, both of those songs were part of my set list along with "Staying Together," "Only in My Dreams," and a rendition of "Happy Birthday" at the Atlantic Records fortieth-anniversary concert at Madison Square Garden in New York. I knew I'd be performing between Led Zeppelin and the Who, and I knew my hits so far had been dance records. This live HBO special would be broadcast to millions of people, and half my school was going to be at the Garden. I was given just enough time to do a medley of the upbeat hits.

"I need to sit at the piano and perform a ballad," I told a producer on the show. "I *cannot* appear between Led Zeppelin and the Who as a dance-pop act."

My mom and I were cut from the same cloth. Fighting our nerves, we'd take a deep breath and do what we had to do. *Only I am going to make this happen*, I remember thinking. During the rehearsal, I got down on my knees while the producer was running around with his headset and said, "You need to give me another song or I'll get booed off the stage."

He saw my point and allowed me to add "Foolish Beat." It was awesome. But I was stressed. Performing live on TV has always made me incredibly nervous. With an edgy adrenaline-filled voice, I'm not the singer who can hit it out of the park at seven in the morning on the *Today Show*. Even when my diet's perfect, I'm getting enough sleep, and I've done all my warm-ups . . . my system's a little delicate. We can dig only as deep as we can dig and work only as hard as we can work. I pushed myself to the limit.

After the show, Ahmet wanted me to pose for *Rolling Stone*, but I turned to Mom and said, "You gotta get me outta here. I'm done."

The walls were closing in.

I've always had the odd ability to be both in my body and out of my body at the same time. So the professional in me was longing to be a part of that photo, immortalized in music history, whereas the little girl in me who suffered panic attacks just couldn't fake a smile and had to run to safety. It was so hard for me to deliver at that caliber on the stage and then have a mental meltdown that would cause me to literally collapse if I didn't say no to this "opportunity."

Getting in the car, I felt like I was jumping out of my skin and was disappointed in myself for not being able to mind-over-matter this ongoing state I was finding myself in. The anguish was deep and personal, and though I was emotionally intelligent for a teenager, I knew enough to know I *didn't* know how to process what was happening to me. I felt helpless but, more often than not, also had an aggressive amount of energy coursing through my body, so I couldn't meditate this all away.

That said, the missed photo op didn't negate the fact my star was rising as paparazzi swarmed Sterling Avenue on prom night, and three days after I graduated from Calhoun, the tour bus pulled up in front of the Gibson family home. I don't know if other pop artists had their team glamorously escort them onto their bus, but this was like when the ice cream man rolled up and we, in a flurry of excitement, would pick our flavors . . . except that now we were picking our bunks!

"Denise, did you grab the Scotch tape and Pictionary?"

I couldn't wait to tape prom pictures of me and Brian, developed at Fotomat, on the inside of my bunk along with pictures of friends and family and my dog Sam.

The *Out of the Blue* tour kicked off at the Centrum in Worcester, Massachusetts, on July 1, 1988, booked by my idol Billy Joel's longtime agent Dennis Arfa, and would take in twenty-three venues nationwide before ending at Pittsburgh's A. J. Palumbo Center on September 16. It was a big deal and I was at the top of my game. But I was often breathing into a paper bag because of a panic attack, which meant I also definitely was *not* looking through the tour bus window to take in this great country of ours.

Back then, I always felt like a little kid in an adult world. Unlike now, where there's this whole community of artists between the ages of fourteen and twenty-two, the only ones in the States that I crossed paths with at the time were Tiffany, the Jets, Glenn Medeiros, Shanice, Tracie Spencer, New Kids on the Block, to name a few. This, don't forget, was the pre–cell phone era, when the only way to keep in touch while you traveled was to use a calling card in a hotel. Living in a bubble, I was probably the only seventeen-year-old who knew her calling card number by heart.

While my peers were getting ready to go to college with kids their own age, I was very much in my own world, with nobody around who could relate to me or whom I could relate to. There were aspects of my life that even I couldn't comprehend. Mom constantly asked me to meet with my business manager, Bert Padell, but the thought of actually getting paid for doing my joyful, glorified hobby was embarrassing in a weird way, so, much to her dismay, I avoided money talk at all costs.

I did apply to Hofstra University to possibly take some part-time courses before ultimately deciding not to pursue a college education. The rumors about me receiving offers to study at colleges around the country, although very flattering, were untrue. Instead, I clung tight to Denise and was so happy to cross paths with contemporaries such as actors Wil Wheaton, Alyssa Milano, Holly Robinson Peete, Brian Robbins, Billy Zabka, Kimberly Russell, and good ol' Scott Grimes.

They were all at my eighteenth birthday bash, and I had Brian by my side, his little brothers Mike and Scott in tow, after I performed at LA's Greek Theatre that August. It was a paparazzi dream come true. And it felt kind of strange but really cool to be the pop star among the actors, attracting this incredible set of talented teens. I always knew who was on the list and what each of these people meant to me. It was overwhelming to think they all wanted to be at *my* event.

The party took place at my favorite '50s diner, Ed Debevic's, which I loved because the servers sang and danced on the countertops! Being there, one of the hot Hollywood places to hang out, was like being in a big movie musical, which is essentially where I always wanted to live. Even my car was from that era: a 1957 Ford Fairlane hardtop convertible, purchased off a consignment lot from Julian Lennon. Since I wasn't into alcohol and didn't do drugs of any kind, and there were no musical peer gatherings for me to go to, this kind of retro innocent soirée was the pinnacle of excitement!

In those days, I needed a security guard to leave a hotel or step off the tour bus. This meant there was none of the independence I had once known and I couldn't be as free-spirited as I would have liked, as I already had stalkers, including the one who killed Rebecca Schaeffer and was written about extensively in famed security specialist Gavin de Becker's book, as well as another who was married with children. After the latter started sending me overly amorous fan letters, my father phoned him and told him to forget about me. But instead of acting as a deterrent, this only inflamed the guy more—and so did a weekend in jail due to his written threat to blow up our home... before arriving in front of the wrong house, where he was arrested, much like the naked escapee mental patient who jumped our gate.

Welcome to the dark side of fame. Work hard, *pay* hard. There's a cost to your soul too.

The death threats against Dad and me—and eventually Denise—continued for another year, and being exposed in public settings wasn't great for my nerves. At that young age, I couldn't fathom being a target and actually losing my life. In fact, more stressful to me was picking up on the vibes of everyone around me, from family to band members and crew personnel. So I deflected with humor to keep everyone from freaking out.

"Relax, guys," I'd say with a wink and a smile. "If we do the dance steps double time, it'll be harder to take us down!"

Rolling his eyes, Buddy couldn't help but laugh. It lightened things up. As did me saying I should move up, down, and all around on the piano bench during the ballads so that anyone with a gun would be aiming for a moving target.

Mom and the promoters weren't laughing, but they also weren't canceling any shows, despite a stalker being found with a trunkful of weapons in his car at one of my concerts. Everyone knew they would never convince me to live in fear and disappoint the audiences. Steering my thoughts away from the kinds of serious circumstances that my teenage brain couldn't fully comprehend, I'd go inward and focus more intensely on my craft.

Three hours before rolling into a venue, I'd start my routine of breath work and vocal practice with scuba belts strapped to my body while holding weights . . . on a moving bus. I was living for the show that night, living to hit perfect high notes—or what I perceived as perfect. My concept was to go vocally and physically where I'd be by the end of the show in the most exaggerated way so that it all felt effortless. A great concept if you have double or triple the energy required for a normal show day—which I did. Ahhh, my electric youth!

Think of me as a hiker wearing a weighted vest so that, when the vest came off, all the hard work would be wired in and singing would feel like second nature. Very disciplined but also ritualistic and maybe a little over the top. Still, it was the only way I knew to perform at the desired level—*my* level—stemming from a common mentality that saw many of us over–work out in the '80s and '90s. A show of hands if you're guilty as charged!

Repeater, repeater, repeater . . .

These days, when I walk, run, and dance, there's a flow to it and I try to avoid the tipping point that is outside the normal range of recovery.

I was very self-motivated and thanked my lucky stars that Mom wasn't like those traditional stage mothers I'd see in audition rooms . . . like the one I witnessed telling her kid to change her outfit, give a fake name, and go back in after she wasn't asked to return for the callbacks. I *wanted* to do it, and when my nerves sometimes got the best of me, Mom would give me that gentle nudge. It was as if she and I were both walking into this fire with blinders on. We had no idea what was ahead, it was uncharted territory, but we knew we wanted the outcome of getting the role, the hit song, the tours. And we got it—*all*.

During that first rush of fame, I was like, *Oh my God, people are singing my songs around the world. People who don't speak English are singing my songs!* I was so proud and so excited to be this little girl who'd just left high school and was big in Japan. I was also awestruck by all the artists I got to meet, but I wasn't in my body half the time; I wasn't fully present. Everything was so overwhelming, I couldn't take it all in and process what was happening.

Continually anxious, I was still tormented—not least by my ongoing obsession with performing those perfect vocals. I never had stage fright, I was never paralyzed with fear; I wanted to get onto that stage, but I wanted it to be so great and I wanted it so badly, I would literally make myself sick over it, go into a kind of freeze state, and become a little short-tempered. Adrenaline was not always my friend during the preshow buildup and I was virtually unable to deal with the nerves, the anxiety, the "excitement"—as I called it to distance myself from the perceived stigmas.

I wanted to be able to do simple things like sit calmly at the dinner table. Being unable to do so during a family vacation to the Caribbean was a source of embarrassment for me, as I had to keep getting up from the table. Mom had a deep compassion for what I was going through, while everyone else around me did their best to understand, even though it could have been mistaken for prima donna behavior—which it wasn't.

I needed to be able to intentionally switch off, to quiet the noise. I just didn't know what to do with all the excess energy, overthinking, and terrifying physical symptoms, like feeling out of my body, shallow breathing, and tingling in my extremities. This problem was intensified by my conviction that I should feel nothing but happy and grateful about my privileged existence. It actually compounded things and made it worse to feel that people thought I desired any sort of negative attention. On the contrary, when not in professional mode, I just wanted to blend in and be one of the gang, like I did after singing the national anthem at the World Series.

Let me take you back to October 15, 1988, for game 1 between the Los Angeles Dodgers and Oakland Athletics, which began and ended with a Gibson. I performed the national anthem, and in the bottom of the ninth inning, injured outfielder Kirk Gibson (no relation) hit a legendary pinch-hit walk-off home run. Who knew I'd be connected to such a historic event? And who could tell that, despite looking and sounding calm and confident, I was on the verge of yet another full-scale panic attack?

Beforehand, I'd been so thrilled to be included in this monumental sports event, although not more so than my dad and Uncle Carl, who'd traveled just under three thousand miles to be at Dodger Stadium with me. Following the sound check, adrenaline coursed through my veins because this was one of the biggest career moments I'd ever had in front of a national audience. And it turned into the most petrifying one minute and twenty seconds of my life.

Singing the national anthem is nerve-racking because, unlike having the arch of a two-hour show to build into your peak performance level, you have to nail one of the most famous, rangey songs in the world right out of the gate. Yet I got through it with all my little signature DG nuances and took my seat in the stands, only to then tell Dad and my uncle: "I can't breathe. I have to get outta here." Here we go again!

I'd channeled every ounce of strength I had and there was nothing left. Unable to believe this was still happening, I wasn't going to let it put a damper on their good time.

"Guys, you flew all the way across the country to see this game," I said, pulling a brown paper bag from my gear bag. "Just put me in the car; the driver will take me to the hotel. I know what to do . . . Enjoy the game!"

No way was this happening. It was one thing for *me* to miss out on things . . . but they wouldn't hear of it. "Put you in a car?" my dad replied. "Absolutely not. We're both going to the hotel with you."

"No, no, no," I pushed back. "If you do that, I'll feel even worse."

I was spinning.

"Deborah, don't even give it a second thought. We've loved just being here."

I can hear my uncle's reassuring voice now.

Arguing with them was a waste of time, so the three of us left, and after battling the traffic and eventually arriving back at the hotel, we walked into my room and switched on the TV... and at that precise moment, Gibson hit the winning run.

Shouting with excitement as the fist-pumping limping legend rounded the bases, Dad and Uncle Carl tried so hard to disguise their disappointment over what they'd just missed out on seeing in person. Instead of being witnesses to history in La-La Land, here they were, looking out for *me*. Even now, I shake my head and absolutely cannot believe that happened.

I didn't let this latest episode diminish my enthusiasm for seeing one of my all-time favorites, Elton John, only five days later back in New York at Madison Square Garden. And thank goodness, because he invited me to share his keyboard and the stage with Billy Joel on a rendition of "Lucy in the Sky with Diamonds"—and he even complimented me on my piano chops and ability to play by ear as I spontaneously jumped in. Pinching myself and managing to sit through the whole show anxiety-free was like the universe granting me a one-off gift, but it was a problem that would continue to grow worse.

Something that always served as my refuge during times of overwhelm and disconnect and anxiety was songwriting, which would instantly take me back to center. Yet even though I'd done the impossible—writing and releasing a hit album—little did I know the powerful, life-altering creative moment that was about to come.

Chapter Six

POP-BULLSEYE GIRL

Electric youth, feel the power, you see the energy
Comin' up, coming on strong
The future only belongs to the future itself
And the future is electric youth.[*]

This phrase really turned into something, encapsulating a movement that was all about empowering young people. When I wrote "Electric Youth," I knew it was the album title. And sitting at my baby grand, I also knew the opening—"Zappin' it to you"—was quirky and kitschy, but I kept it because it was quintessentially me and painted a picture. Perched at the upstairs piano, fixated on my bird's-eye view of the front door, I'd wait for Mom to walk in, poised and ready to play that dramatic intro before she even had the chance to put down her pocketbook. She remained transfixed till the clos-

---

[*] "Electric Youth" by Deborah Gibson. Copyright © 1988 by Music Sales Corporation (ASCAP). International Copyright Secured. Used by permission. All rights reserved.

ing chord. We both knew I had something, just as I did with "Lost in Your Eyes."

Arriving home from school one day, I sat downstairs at the upright piano and that melodic, heartfelt ballad just poured out of me, a composite of my puppy-love experiences. I recall the time I gave Brian Bloom a sneak preview, and though I often felt like a giddy, awkward teenager, I became bold when communicating through music. It was a shared love language and such a sweet moment, which always ties Brian to that divinely channeled song. But every great song must come to an end.

Acknowledging the different places we were in both geographically and emotionally, we gradually phased out the romance, which left me once again with my constant . . . music.

From a songwriting standpoint, "Lost in Your Eyes" has a bit of an uncommon structure where the verses are catchy and the chorus is more like a bridge, but it's still a hook. The intro is part "Through the Eyes of Love" from *Ice Castles*, part "What I Did for Love" from *A Chorus Line*. It came so easily to this little girl who was getting inspired by life and her inner monologue.

Excited, I decided to debut it before it was properly recorded, on the *OOTB* tour. Without cell phones or digital devices, you could do that back then without fear of a recording getting leaked. Worst case was some crackly cassette being passed around at summer camps across the nation, which I didn't mind. I knew it was a hit!

At that time, I was rolling hard, and the songs were coming to me as fast as my pen could write. "No More Rhyme" spoke to my fear of complacency in a safe relationship. Nothing was wrong, but was it dynamic enough to withstand life's challenges and keep me intrigued forever? Heavy thoughts for a little girl. My entire life, I've had a fear of being bored; to me, it's a fate worse than death.

I actually wrote "Who Loves Ya Baby?" with Olivia Newton-John in mind. After it was turned down for her album *The Rumour*, I kept it for myself. I don't know if Olivia ever heard my recording, but one girl's trash is another girl's treasured track. That song ended up opening both the *Electric Youth* album *and* the concert tour.

I was never a strategist. I was a visionary, so I'd work backward from a goal. "Let the music lead the way," I would always say. You know, "What's the music telling me and how do I best serve that production-wise?"

In this case, I was collaborating with Fred Zarr. He produced "Who Loves Ya Baby?," "Electric Youth," "No More Rhyme," and "Shades of the Past"; we coproduced "We Could Be Together"; and he did some of the programming on the other tracks that I produced solo. The result was Fred and me at our best, doing some really cool work.

Released January 10, 1989, *Electric Youth* topped the *Billboard* 200 for five weeks, and the leadoff single, "Lost in Your Eyes," was #1 on the *Billboard* Hot 100 for three weeks, which prompted that mag to assert my "knack for churning out punchy, well-crafted tunes is stronger than ever ... Gibson leaves no doubt that her first-time success was not a fluke."[*]

"This eighteen-year-old New Yorker is heir to the great tradition of the Brill Building," wrote Mark Coleman in *Rolling Stone*, adding that "the best pop music always mirrors its time, and anyone who's interested in a jolt of the here and now during this era of cultural nostalgia should plug into *Electric Youth*."[**]

Despite the fact that the public embraced me, there was so much cynicism about me at the time. Still, in working on this book, I've

---

[*] Billboard, *January 28, 1989.*
[**] Rolling Stone, *April 6, 1989.*

done a deep dive that's led me to some reviews I can now celebrate and kind words I am grateful for. I was more seen than I thought I was. In "the great tradition of the Brill Building"? *Wow!* I appreciate that, Mark! Only took me thirty-five years, but now I can thank you properly.

When I recorded my first single, I had no idea if it would be heard by a hundred people, a hundred thousand, or millions. I'd hoped, but I had no idea. Now I knew I had an audience, and, having a great time, I felt zero pressure despite the classic sophomore slump. That didn't occur to me because I knew I had the material and the audience.

I was even invited to cohost and perform at the American Music Awards alongside Rod Stewart, Anita Baker, and Kenny Rogers. I will never forget the feeling of walking into rehearsal, reading the teleprompter, and being guided by Dick Clark himself. It was like I'd trained my entire young life for this. Having not been the coolest kid in high school, I didn't know how to rub elbows with Axl Rose, Olivia Newton-John, DJ Jazzy Jeff, and the Fresh Prince. But they all welcomed me with open arms.

There were bids at the time from the likes of MCA Records, who threw me a soirée in a big suite at the Mondrian Hotel in the hopes of buying out my contract. But I was loyal to my label and the boys in the back office who'd taken that first chance. Atlantic and I were doing groundbreaking things together.

My career was like a bullet train with happy passengers who were having a great time. I was living the dream, dropping by the set of crush Kirk Cameron's *Growing Pains* and the show *Family Ties* while repped by Michael J. Fox's agents, and flown on the Westwood One plane to dine backstage with George Michael. Everyone around me was making lots of money. Touring Europe on a private jet with my translator, Jacqueline (who, upon seeing a hot guy, would shout, "Have him scrubbed and sent to my tent!"), making small talk with everyone from Cher to Sammy Davis Jr. on exclusive MGM flights . . . I was on a roll.

I was chased down a London alley behind Capital Radio and pulled from a mall autograph signing when the crowd shattered the floor-to-ceiling glass trying to get to me. And it never got cooler than getting to share an office that served as a makeshift dressing room at the Palladium for one of the early, humble Jingle Ball concerts in NYC with the New Kids guys. Jon Knight jumped over a desk in a single bound to greet me when I walked in. With Denise in tow, we giggled like the schoolgirls we were. It was that moment when I was everyone's darling, but even then I didn't walk around in a star bubble. I've always enjoyed being approachable in the light of day while giving my audience the diva onstage.

No matter how big things got, I was determined to connect with my audience in the most personal way possible. So I created D.G.I.F., the Debbie Gibson International Fan Club, with handwritten notes in homespun mini-magazines that my staff of gals—including Buddy's mom Julie, Aunt Linda, Janet, Addie, Karen, and Grandma—would lovingly mail out as I sat on the Long Island office floor signing 8×10s.

With mass adulation coming at me from all directions, I was still a typical teen, curling up with my oval-shaped push-button landline phone and talking to friends who pulled me right down into my true self and my teenage existence. This included moving into a new home between finishing the album and kicking off the tour.

For security reasons, we knew we had to live behind gates. And with the money to buy a big house for the first time, I wanted to have fun spending it. I'm still that way. I live my life, and, maybe to a degree that scares my business manager, I don't save for a rainy day that might never come. I remember looking at some more modest places that would have suited Denise and me just fine. But when she, Mom, and I walked into an upscale property and were like, *Oh my God, we could possibly* live *in this house?!?* it quickly turned into *Let's do it!* Sure, we could have conserved the money—maybe it would last, maybe it wouldn't—but I am still here, I'm still on my feet, and I still believe in living life to the fullest and going for it when you can.

I had the grandest version of that experience at the time, purchasing a brand-new, ten-thousand-square-foot, six-bedroom, seven-bathroom house with Mom as my partner on the appropriately named Soundcrest Lane in Lloyd Neck, New York—close to Billy Joel's place in Cold Spring Harbor, overlooking Huntington Bay. Marble and hardwood floors, vaulted ceilings, spiral staircases, a sunken conversation pit with throw pillows, a balcony walkway from wing to wing—it would be a great party house. And I'd continue living with my folks while, despite the adult pressures, I was in that bubble where I could still be me.

I even hosted foster boys from St. Mary's Children and Family Services at Christmastime and brought budding young musicians from the home into the studio to get inspired. Unfortunately, that was stopped by the powers that be because, I was told, as a celebrity I was showing them things they could never have. Can you believe that? I know I showed them what they *could* have and provided many a blissful experience for me and for us all.

Sad to say, my parents' own marital bliss was often more like marital blitz, featuring rip-roaring arguments that they'd been getting into ever since my preteens. "I feel like I have four daughters and a son," Mom would "jokingly" say—which was a little unfair to my dad because, if you measure a man by how he creates joy and provides for his family, he did great. It's just that, through his eyes, she had evolved from a humble, non-college-educated secretary into this go-getting executive ballbuster. I don't know if they ever discussed their life goals and their vision, but Mom was always going to be a risk-taker, my dad wasn't, so she left him in the dust.

Whereas Dad was politically incorrect in an innocent, childlike way, assuming everyone shared his sense of humor, my mother was intentionally unfiltered—meaning I couldn't go out with either one of them in public because half the time I didn't know what they were going to say. One time, we took my father to Japan on one of the promo tours, and hearing the locals refer to plum wine, he couldn't resist mocking their pronunciation: "What's *prum* wine? I've never heard of it."

"Dad, you've got to knock it off," Denise and I responded, trying to clue him in on the fact that he was being culturally insensitive.

He wasn't slick. Mom might say something really sharp, but she wasn't going to accidentally insult someone's ethnicity. So they were like a comedy duo, with her elbowing him and saying, "Joe, cut it out," while he just shrugged: "What did I do?" Wide-eyed, along for the ride, he wasn't pitching in with the business and he didn't have to, but it was clear that he and my mom were growing even farther apart, which happened to many couples of that generation who married in their teens.

I know a lot of kids mourn the loss of their parents' marriage, but I had no attachment to whether or not mine remained a couple. I never fully understood why people stay together if they're unhappy, so their back-and-forth shtick was just slightly embarrassing and mildly annoying.

At least money wasn't an issue, what with *recoupable funds* being a vague grown-up business term that I wouldn't come to understand 'til much later, when it would become apparent I should have more to show for all the record sales. I always put art first over commerce, opting to not cut a minute and a half off "Electric Youth," from 4:58

to a cuter, more palatable radio length even though I knew it could chart higher than its #11 spot and ultimately earn me more money. That said, I was a creative kid living my best life. I mean, who gets to make a pencil sketch of a castle, show up on set for a music video, and see it fully built in living color? That is exactly what happened when I codirected the "Electric Youth" video with Jim Yukich for half a million dollars, which felt like Monopoly money. Atlantic fronted that budget, which, to this day, is not wasted on me.

Added to the mix was my coveted, groundbreaking Revlon endorsement and my custom-designed perfume, aptly named Electric Youth. It's easy to forget that it was highly unusual for a teen artist to have such a deal in play. Even *The New York Times* reported on it. And I was still riding high in January 1989 after meeting longtime idol Michael Jackson in LA, as he not only told me how much he was loving watching my career unfold but also invited me to be in his "Liberian Girl" video. My cameo was filmed during the "No More Rhyme" shoot with Yukich once again at the helm.

Shortly after the video's release that July, I headed to Worcester, Massachusetts, for the first date of my *Electric Youth* tour, opening at the Centrum on July 28, 1989, just as I'd done for *Out of the Blue* a year earlier. This tour would take in not only more than thirty dates across North America but also a concert at London's hundred-thousand-person-capacity Wembley Stadium and a dozen dates in Japan and Australia, where passionate fans chanting *Deb-bie! Deb-bie!* left an everlasting handprint on my heart.

At Wembley, I opened for Brit pop duo Bros. Matt and Luke opened for me on part of my US tour. I don't think American audiences really understood their music, which was rooted in classic soul with ultrasophisticated productions. So it was tough for them to break through with Sony hyper-focused on the ultra-American hooky music of my friends NKOTB. Considering their level of stardom in the UK, I was baffled that they didn't blow up in the US. I was particularly invested in their journey because I had gotten to know Matt quite well, having logged hours and hours on the phone, even sending care packages with presents back and forth.

Matt's love language was always gifts. He would send me thoughtful things from across the pond in a big box and it was like Christmas when it arrived. One of my favorites was a radar detector with his voice saying "God bless" so that, when I passed a police car, I'd hear him say it over and over in his distinct, soft, British voice. So sweet. I also recall chatting to his mum, Carol, on the phone when I called to thank him—while she was peering out the window, making sure he was okay as he graciously said hello to the five hundred or so fans gathered on his front lawn.

During a trip to London to perform at the Prince's Trust Concert, I had the *honour* of meeting Princess Diana before performing "Electric Youth," introduced by Sean Connery. It was such a surreal evening, with me telling the princess how the special gown I'd wanted to wear for my receiving-line moment had been vetoed by the producers because they wanted me ready to open the show. They had insisted I wear my video-look performance outfit—blue-jean cutoff shorts, a vest, and a bandana in my hair—but she could not have been more gracious.

"You look a heck of a lot more comfortable than I am," she leaned in and whispered.

As if that weren't enough, the evening was made even more special by a wonderful date night at a restaurant Matt persuaded to stay open with the house band playing. I wrote a song about it a few years ago called "The Band Plays On," because it was such a memorable life moment.

That sweet scene we started
I can rest my head upon
Proof that love stays like the band plays on.*

On tour, I'd often find a little bag in my dressing room containing either a belt that I'd mentioned having seen in a store or a piece of his own clothing that I had complimented.

"Here, you take it and wear it onstage."

In Houston, while we were lying on the hotel's back lawn by the pool following an October 4 concert at the Summit, Matt and I were sure we saw a UFO. Performing in front of twenty thousand fans every night, I'd always find ways to escape—and being around that lovely gentleman was never boring. We had this beautiful dynamic, but as the tour progressed, the business aspects started pulling us apart—like Mom not allowing the Goss twins to use the "ego ramps"** that I used to build excitement on song three of my set. Everything was too intertwined, and pretty soon, that little romance was gone.

Behind the onstage smiles, overloaded with responsibility, dealing with a breakup, and determined to make everyone on my crew feel special, I would often call tour masseuse/nutritionist Lisa Giannini at two or three in the morning because I couldn't sleep due to all the stress. She'd come to my room, and after we talked and did Jin Shin Jyutsu—a Japanese form of acupressure that helps calm the nervous system—I'd finally get the rest I so desperately needed. But it wasn't always enough.

When I was headlining a packed arena in Denver, the altitude got to me, and, out of breath and dizzy, I thought I'd have to cancel

---

* "The Band Plays On" by Deborah Ann Gibson. Copyright © 2025 by Birdsong Publishing (ASCAP). Used by permission. All rights reserved.
** A proscenium, catwalk, runway, or stage spur that extends into or over an audience.

Sisters on campus at Vassar, 1985.

Christmas dinner at Grandma and Grandpa's house. Ready for Santa!

I'll drag my own chair, thank you! Moving day 1972.

Placido Domingo, as warm and welcoming as he is talented. Backstage at the Metropolitan Opera before a performance of *La Bohème*.

Always right at home with class act and kindred musical spirit Fred Zarr.

Club kids! Buddy, Robert Alvarez, and me up past our bedtime in 1986.

My album release party's real star, the life-sized bear from the *Out of the Blue* cover! Club 4D in NYC, 1987.

Despite rumors to the contrary, I always loved this girl and despised women being pitted against each other! Me and Tiff on *Top of the Pops*.

NKOTB and me!

Doug Morris and Mom beaming with pride while presenting me with my double platinum *Out of the Blue* at my 18th birthday party.

With lifer Bobby Watman in his SiriusXM studio in Miami.

Moments before hats and hearts were stolen. Z100 Morning Zoo's Christmas show.

Filming at South Street Seaport in NYC turned into FANdemonium... and I loved every minute!

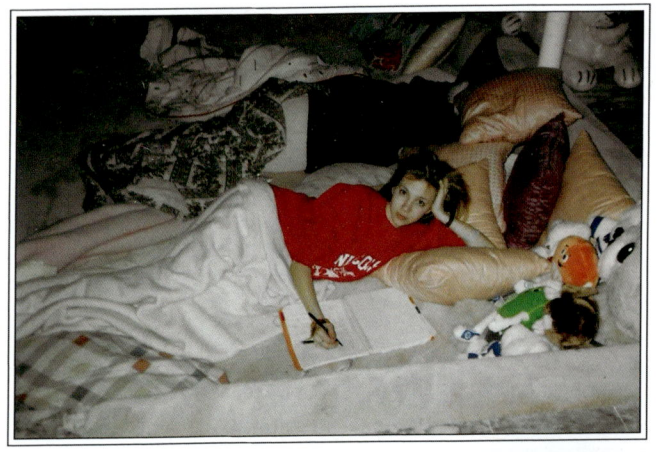

Slumber party writing inspiration in the conversation pit at the Lloyd Neck house. Iris is asleep!

Forever besties! With Iris in the Merrick backyard.

My second mom on the road Lisa Giannini, Bernie Taupin, David "Snappy" Salidor, me, Elton John, Mom, and her younger beau Mike Portnoy, backstage in New Jersey, 1989.

Where the boys are... Scott Grimes and Mackenzie Astin visited us on Stepp's opening day at Magic Mountain!

Still pinching myself! Billy and Elton at MSG... and me!

Post-club performance on Long Island with school friends, including bestie Mike Provenz!

A candid moment with the King! Michael Jackson was as present and as sweet as they come. Backstage in LA before MJ took the stage for his *Bad* tour, 1988.

With my fabulous Aunt Linda and Uncle Carl at NBT's Black & White Ball celebrating my Woman of the Year honor in Las Vegas!

Cheers to prom night with love Brian Bloom! Chrissy Gerani looks on.

"An angel with a dirty face," Éponine in *Les Miz*. A dream come true.

Chris Bruno flies in to visit me in Singapore on my Southeast Asia promo tour, 1995.

Grease press day with Craig . . . happily tired and leaning on my Danny Zuko.

Preshow in my *Beauty* dressing room but fully immersed in rehearsing for my *Chicago* audition.

The Elephant Girls backstage in Korea!

With Betty Buckley in the infamous *Gypsy* dressing room scene.

With Rutledge before The Race to Erase MS Gala in LA.

The "emotional fluffers"! Marissa, Mom, and Stepp seeing me emerge naked for my *Playboy* shoot!

Party time at the House That Pop Music Built with Lamont Dozier, Jellybean Benitez, and Taylor Dayne.

With Justin, Joey, JC, Chris, and Lance, who made sure I was treated like royalty on the PopOdyssey Tour!

Lisa, JT, me, Elizabeth, and Heather celebrating the finale of *America's Most Musical Family*!

Pop Soulmates selfie it up! Joe Mac on my 53rd birthday in Culver City, California.

Your love is "The Gift"! With Sylvia at Ray's wedding in Bay City, Texas.

Me and my boys reaching for the stars onstage on *The Body Remembers* encore tour performing our ABBA medley! Johnny C holding it down on drums and my soul sister Ariel shredding! Can you feel the joy?

Sharing the stage to duet on "White Christmas" with Daddy Joe, who has brought so much magic to my life.

Ya know... just lounging on a slab of cement in thigh-high boots! My first shoot with Nick Spanos in Las Vegas for what would become *The Body Remembers* album artwork.

How many blondes does it take to demo songs for *Skirts*? Orfeh and I share the mic and some laughs!

Jimmy Van Patten after hours at my LA *Winterlicious* meet n' greet, where he kept me and all the Debheads entertained!

Longtime friend Ron Luparello was at the *Electric Youth* tour the first go 'round, and here we are backstage at EY35 at The Town Hall!

"Love Don't Care"–but my team does! "LDC" video shoot, 2023.

The two greatest Richards who have always been there for me, Richard Weitz and Richard Jay-Alexander!

At home with The Gibson Boys around the Liberace piano. Las Vegas!

Big Al.
The Body Remembers tour 2023.
With pupstar Joey.

For more photos that didn't make the book, visit EternallyElectric.com.

It's always a festive time at meet 'n' greets like this one in Ohio in 2024!

the show. I remember lying on the couch in my dressing room, inhaling oxygen between sips of orange juice while makeup artist Donyale glammed me up just in case.

"I don't think I can do this."

The promoter was having none of it. "Get her on that stage," she growled at Mom.

"Forget it," Lisa intervened. "This isn't brain surgery, it's a show. You're not well. We're going to cancel."

"What about all those people in the audience?" I replied, feeling the walls closing in.

"That's what insurance is for," Lisa reassured me, ignoring Mom and the promoter who, she recalled, "looked like they wanted to choke me."

After about ten minutes, I started to get that burst of energy that only my musical mission can bring: "Fire up the band," I shouted to my beloved musical director Gary Corbett. "I'm going on!"

I even recall going overtime that night, adding the rarely performed "Helplessly in Love" to the set list. It was a weird tour. I sold out New York's Madison Square Garden; I sold out LA's Forum; but at Houston's Summit, they had to paper half the house to fill the empty seats. How could I feel so loved and adored one night and then feel like such a failure? I never felt that way while touring the Far East and Down Under. It was amazing. After one of the Japanese shows, I took the bullet train and can still recall the faces of crying fans pressed up against the window. I also remember the concert audiences appearing very conservative from my vantage point, all clapping in unison. So I dreamed up a fun way to bump up the excitement by running down the aisle from the back of the house. Little did I know the prim and proper fans would swarm the aisle and make it impossible for me to move more than three feet. It was a safety nightmare but made for one heck of a moment on the *Live Around the World* concert video when my six-foot-four head of security, Bill, got trampled to the ground.

That was the height of my Asian success. Soon after, having already launched Electric Youth perfume through Revlon and assorted teengirl makeup essentials through one of my sponsors, Natural Wonder Cosmetics, I even had my own clothing store in Tokyo's Harajuku neighborhood. DGNY sold designs that were based on my personal style and people lined up around the block. Again, I was thinking, *I'm halfway around the world and people know me.* It was kind of insane. And Australia was equally awesome.

The group Indecent Obsession opened for me there and had such a big reaction that, during the first show in Melbourne, I was convinced the audience was there to see them rather than me. Then I walked onstage and the wall of energy I felt from the fans was so powerful, it made me weak in the knees. As did Indecent Obsession's lead singer, David Dixon. He and I had such a fun little romance for that part of the tour and beyond, as he visited me in the States for a lovely New Year's Eve. And we also had a ton of laughs with his bandmates at a big co-ed sleepover party in my Sydney hotel room with Stepp and Buddy, as well as with my school friends Iris and Christine, who sang background vocals on the tour.

My amazing vocal coach Guen sometimes joined me on the road to prepare me for specific shows. She was that supercool older lady whom everybody adored. "Is Guen going to be at the party?" they'd all ask. She and her techniques were a big part of my life. And I mention this because, during the Australian trip, I told my great friend dancer Ray Garcia, "I'm having trouble hitting the high notes today." With weights already attached to my body, I proceeded to give him a piggyback ride around my hotel room, singing, "Wooo-ooo-oooh," as the opposition just made my voice fly. As I often say, I'm an extremist who will stop at nothing to achieve the desired result, even putting my bestie on my back. Ray and I laugh about this moment to this day. My friends have always known me to be a bit of an eccentric extremist! But it got me through a rigorous schedule, and all while having fun.

Okay, if I add more weight, will I get higher notes? Will I get more power?

"You don't have to do that," people would say.

"Unless you have a better idea, I'll show you how I sound when I *don't* do it," I'd reply.

Regular warm-ups just didn't cut it for me. As soon as the tour ended, I was supposed to start work on a dance-based movie called *Skirts* that had first appeared on my radar before the release of *Electric Youth*. Kenny Ortega was the director—he had just finished choreographing *Dirty Dancing*—and, still interested in acting, I'd been on the Sony lot for several months of auditions and screen tests, both on my own and with Marisa Tomei, Juliette Lewis, and Rosie Perez. I had only ever seen a movie set on a soundstage during a Universal Studios tour on a family vacay courtesy of TWA perks! This was a whole new world and I was loving it.

Every dancer in LA had auditioned for the film. Marisa and Juliette had initially both competed for the same role, and Marisa had ultimately been cast as my spicy Bronx cousin Monica. I was supposed to play Betty Bonatello, the good girl from Scarsdale, and I have to say that, as the newbie screen actress, I learned a lot from those two amazing gals in terms of how different their respective characters were on paper and what they brought to portraying them in the audition process. Both were phenomenal—and while in character, Rosie intimidated the heck out of me. She was so committed and present.

Reading with Billy Wirth, who'd just appeared in *The Lost Boys*, and Jamie Walters, who'd be in *Beverly Hills, 90210*, was also enlightening and fun: *Oh, so* this *is what it's like to have great movie chemistry with other actors.* Those boys affected me in ways you cannot fake and everyone in the room felt it—yet another art form that I love to this day because I love feeling so alive in the moment.

I had lived and breathed *Skirts* for close to a year, jumping through a lot of hoops and even writing music for it. But despite that project being a huge part of my life, the film never got made and I ended up performing some of those songs in my shows.

My mom sat me down and prepared me for the worst: "Deborah, *Skirts* has been put into turnaround."

What did that even mean? She went on to say that Sony had bought Columbia and they were shelving the project that had been so dear to me. Weirdly, I'd spent so much time working on it, I actually felt like I had already made the movie. But I knew in my heart that I hadn't. Here I was, my turn at bat, and the game was rained out.

"Well, Mom, what are we gonna do next?"

Programmed to not feel disappointed, I instantly flipped the script and put on my queen-of-pivoting crown. It would be one I'd wear again and again.

"Time for another album, I think. Yeah . . . let's go do that."

Now, at this point you're probably thinking, *Well, surely she's gonna be curled up in a ball on the floor or paralyzed with disappointment.* But nope! It's not that I wasn't heartbroken over having to leave my dear Betty Bonatello behind. This movie had, after all, been a huge part of my life, but my coping mechanisms were greater than my desire to wallow. Maybe it's just that I didn't have the emotional skills I needed at the time to process. I would process this and many other disappointments years, even decades, later in my desire to go on with the show.

ETERNALLY ELECTRIC

What I now refer to as "The House That Pop Music Built" was ready for us to inhabit full-time, but not with Karen and Michele, who were each doing their own grown-up things. And also not with Dad, beyond a short period of time. When he and Mom finally got divorced, as you know, Denise and I were neither shocked nor devastated. It was just sad that, having been raised an orphan, he now felt like he'd been abandoned twice by his family.

I recall stepping out of the studio when he knocked on the door during a recording session to hug him goodbye at the top of the staircase. His suitcases were packed and in the car, but he had a little case in his hand, which made him look kind of like a traveling salesman off on his next adventure. Life didn't stop. The musicians were on the clock and we kept rolling. As was often the case in showbiz and maybe in everyone's world, I didn't have the time to process. Workers keep working, parents keep parenting, recording artists keep recording... so there was no fanfare. Dad just left. But I knew he didn't want to. Nothing was wrong, in his opinion, though often in relationships one person is content while the other feels something is lacking and wants more.

Goodbye
How do you say goodbye?
Do I just look you in the eye,
Shake your hand, wish you well
After all this time...
*I never wanted for goodbye.**

---

* "Goodbye" by Deborah Gibson, Carole Bayer Sager, and Narada Michael Walden. Copyright © 1992 by Music Sales Corporation (ASCAP), Carole Bayer Sager Music (BMI), and Gratitude Sky Music (ASCAP). International Copyright Secured. Used by permission. All rights reserved.

Maybe that's why, in my adult life, I still manage to find lost boys and advocate for abandoned animals.

Although this was a hard moment, ultimately I knew our mother needed a different situation. And, truthfully, our father did too, even if he didn't know it yet. Mom needed an equal partner and Dad needed a nurturer. Soon after, he got together with Florica, the stable, low-key, simple-life lady who became his second wife and is still with him to this day. They are a fantastic team, settled into life in St. Augustine, Florida, with their fur-baby family and daily routine.

Meanwhile, my daily routine was really suiting me. I mean, who gets to roll out of bed and into their own state-of-the-art recording studio? At a certain point, Mom was like, "Why are we renting the Hit Factory? We can build your dream studio right here."

We had some great times there, recording a lot of the *Anything Is Possible* album, despite having to pay the musicians' cartage fees to transport their equipment and listening to them bitch about traveling all the way to Lloyd Neck. Vocalists Fonzi, Robin, BJ, Michelle, and I had so many laughs in that vocal booth and often kept the tape rolling so I could include our banter on the records. Even famed trumpeter Chris Botti, who was then unknown, dropped in for a session.

"You're a little behind," I quipped, referring to his timing.

Without missing a beat, he stood, glanced at his tush, and hit back: "Why, thank you!"

We're friends to this day and have a laugh about that moment whenever we chat.

Adding to the party atmosphere, Freddie Jackson—who sang a featured vocal on "Mood Swings"—cruised around the neighborhood with me on a pair of little Zuma scooters that I'd bought. Naturally, we were photographed, and, just as predictably, the tabloids asserted we were dating. That wasn't happening, but the camaraderie between everyone was amazing and nobody wanted to leave, especially when it was late and there was snow on the long, dark, winding road to our house. They eventually stopped bitching about how far they had to travel and packed their jammies... just in case!

During the summer months, we often barbecued; a resident fox would come up on the deck, seeking out food, and we would all run into the house—especially the rock 'n' roll tough guys, screaming like little girls! I smile recalling my cousin Lisa taking a bubble bath under the skylight in the guest powder room with her glass of wine on the side of the tub. I love that my crazy career provided all these moments for my loved ones! To this day, I sometimes go a bit beyond my means, but it's for this very reason: to be able to give people moments and memories. Which is why, if I'm running to catch up a bit, so be it.

When no guests were around, I could be found painting a manifestation mural on my bedroom wall while eating dinner by myself because I couldn't sit still with my family at the table; if I did, they might think I wanted attention when the brown paper bag came out. Believe me, I didn't need it *at all*. The anxiety wasn't as bad when I was in the music, out of my own way. But when evening came and everything was quiet, I'd be alone with my thoughts and it would be hard for me to stay still. I was relentlessly continuing on my holistic journey with acupuncture and yoga, but it was clear I needed something more than what was in my current antianxiety toolbox.

See, when you're having a panic attack, you're struggling with every thought and you feel like the walls are closing in. Breaking down every motion and sensation in my body every second is torture. Which is why I will never forget the day I was put on Xanax and could actually go to a movie theater for the first time in years. Crying with joy that I was able to sit through the entire film without jumping out of my skin, I was like, *Oh my God, I have my life back.*

I'd eventually find the balance, but it's always a work in progress. Medicines like Xanax and Prozac were a first step to helping dig me out of the hole to find more sustainable organic solutions. Ultimately, nothing can take the place of a break, which was the last thing I wanted. This was the first time I'd have to learn that lesson. Later, I would be forced to learn it again.

Between the end of touring and the start of recording my third album, Chris Cuevas, a Mississippi musician who Mom managed, moved into our new home and became my next serious boyfriend. He was a sweetheart of a guy with a distinct singing voice and natural musical ability. I understood him, but it was hard for other people to wrap their heads around why he wore sunglasses indoors. I felt like this was to avoid looking anyone in the eye, lest they'd see how anxious he was . . . I felt like he understood me at a time when I really needed that point of connection. Different coping mechanisms for the same underlying issue.

Nineteen going on twenty, living life in my own way but under a roof with my mom, I had a two-bedroom suite in one wing of our house, she had the grand diva suite in the other, and Chris was in the basement. Nigar Okyar, our amazing, comedic housekeeper who had been brought in to help with Denise and all our family needs, was policing everyone because all she saw was a young guy in the house.

"Chris like snake," she'd constantly say in her thick Turkish accent, making a snakish motion with her hand, all five foot nothing of her. It was hysterical.

He wasn't a snake, but because he was super-talented, we hooked him up with Fred Zarr, who helped produce songs that would eventually also get Chris a deal at my home, Atlantic Records. It was fun to kind of piggyback artists like Chris and an Aussie gal named Jo Beth Taylor, who was managed by Diane and coproduced by me, Jellybean

Benitez, and Ric Wake, of Taylor Dayne fame, who lived down the street. Both of those artists were worthy and had the chops, so if Mom and me breaking new ground made their journey a little bit easier... why not? It made me happy to contribute in that way. We had a bit of a stable going and I also wrote and produced for Columbia artist Ana, Japanese artist Remy, and Hollywood Records group The Party. I would later even cowrite a song for Jennifer Love Hewitt!

Not that our desire to nurture new talent was without its share of drama. Politics led to heartbreak when one of the up-and-coming artists Mom and I were working with was propositioned by a very prominent music man/label exec who was married with children. Because the artist I'm referring to is male, he was ultimately dropped from this major label and we ate the two hundred fifty thousand dollars we'd put into making the album.

"Stand Your Ground" was the final collaborative song released by me and Fred, and it was for an album on which I experimented with different styles of music that reflected my transition into becoming a young woman. So *Anything Is Possible* was an East and West Coast affair, with sessions also taking place at the Hit Factory in NYC, Z in Brooklyn, and Sunset, Tyrell, and Inner Sanctum in LA.

While Jellybean produced "One Step Ahead," Motown legend Lamont Dozier cowrote that song and three other tracks with me, all of which *he* produced. A big Holland-Dozier-Holland fan, I'd been performing a medley of their hits in the *Electric Youth* show. Working with Lamont was amazing to me. He was really nice, we got along great, and "Anything Is Possible" almost didn't sound like either one of us, as it was organically born of our collaboration. That was exciting. As was the lovely, legendary Paul Buckmaster delivering the album's exquisite string arrangements, taking me under his wing and delighting in my interest in the finer nuances of the orchestral world.

Divided into a ballad side called "Mood Swings" and a dance side called "NRG Up," the record was released on November 20, 1990—and, unlike my previous albums, failed to sell millions of copies or make the top 10 on the *Billboard* 200. While that magazine praised my "more adult image and vocal style," as well as my "true gift for crafting memorable pop songs,"* the *Los Angeles Times* described my latest effort as "a redundant, over-produced, 72-minute sprawl."** I wasn't fazed. Sure, I was disappointed when the leadoff single, "Anything Is Possible," was *thisssclose* to cracking the top 20, but I thought an eight-album deal meant I was allowed to experiment and evolve naturally. Sadly, no such grace was given.

Some people get it, some people don't. That was my attitude. I loved the album. Sure, it was a bit eclectic with its various styles, but who is just one thing? While it confused much of the public and the label folks—who signed off on it—my diehards understood and embraced it. To this day, I find that "One Step Ahead" and "Reverse Psychology" radiate a cool vibe, while the gorgeous waltz "One Hand, One Heart" remains a big fan favorite.

I also loved the video that we shot for the title track, with all the vignettes, the war scene, the cameo by Lamont, and the dancing in the streets on a highly stylized set. We auditioned a lot of dancers and picked eight to join me for what I decided would be a more heavily choreographed tour, with Buddy beautifully doing the honors of coming up with the routines.

Among the dancers was one of my lifelong besties, Ray, who I spoke of earlier from the piggyback vocal practice and who I met and cast that same day. Also on the soundstage that afternoon was my

---

*Billboard, *November 17, 1990.*
***Mike Boehm,* Los Angeles Times, *December 9, 1990.*

effervescent Aussie kindred spirit, Kylie Minogue. I recall us meeting for the first time right there, where we filmed the "Anything Is Possible" video. "You stole all the great dancers in LA for your video and I couldn't get any for mine!" she joked.

Kylie was lovely, and the album brought me many gifts. However, everyone at the label went into panic mode, wondering what was up with their "pop-bullseye girl."

The fact that they'd accepted the record upon delivery meant there were no surprises, so maybe they had just assumed I could do no wrong. Not even psychic Ann Cervone, whom I'd frequent because she was always spot-on with her predictions, saw this downfall coming. Regardless, this was a moment where not having an A&R person backfired, because by the time of my album's release, the American music scene itself was also transitioning—from hooky pop to Seattle grunge. Which was why, even when the "Electric Youth" video was on the air, there was a backlash from people writing to MTV, saying they hated it.

It was a new decade, things were swinging another way, and the Atlantic execs weren't very forgiving. Instead of being my teammates who were in it for the long haul, they were more *What have you done for me lately?* and I felt betrayed.

Chapter Seven

SHOCK YOUR MAMA

On October 26, 1990, I was one of the headliners at the Carousel of Hope Ball, which, staged every couple of years at the Beverly Hilton Hotel in Beverly Hills, benefits the Children's Diabetes Foundation and Barbara Davis Center for Diabetes. As I sang and danced my heart out, my inner monologue marveled at the luminaries in the audience: *There's President Ford . . . There's Luther Vandross . . . There's Michael Jackson.* And seeing the Reagans was so lovely after having been a part of Nancy's "Just Say No" campaign.

After my performance, I ran into Uncle Vic, aka Vic Damone. For a guy who never envisioned me in this landscape, he was really warm and welcoming. *Sweet!*

"Debbie!" he said, reaching out his arms . . . and possibly an olive branch.

Nobody in my immediate family ever calls me Debbie, so that felt kinda weird. Nonetheless, he gave my mom and me a hug and introduced us both to his wife, Diahann Carroll, then extended an invitation: "How about you girls joining us for dinner tomorrow night?"

We instantly said yes. Naturally, we were going to make this happen, though Mom and I could always read each other's energy and I felt like, in that moment, we were both cats with our fur standing on end.

Is this the same Vic who discouraged me only six short years ago?

The idea of sitting still at any dinner table still terrified me and harkened back to the dinner with that program director. A bit fish-out-of-water in this adult setting but ever the dutiful daughter, niece, and professional, I flipped the script and suddenly got excited. Diahann was such a badass trailblazer; this would be fun! But the usual thing happened: I crashed from the heightened energy of the star-studded event.

By the next evening, I was hyperventilating, spinning in circles, and couldn't gather myself to go to this dinner. Disappointed, I told my mother, and, not in the least bit surprised, she was very nurturing. She truly understood that if I could, I would.

"You know what, Vic's *my* cousin, he's my age, and he really just wants to have dinner with *me*. Don't worry about it. I'll explain your situation and I'm sure they'll understand."

When Mom showed up at the dinner, Vic immediately asked where I was. Then, when she explained I was in my hotel room suffering from a panic attack, Diahann asked for my room number in the name of calling and checking on me. Instead she called . . . to ream me out.

"Debbie, it's Diahann."

Upon hearing her voice at the other end of the phone, I naively expected her to say something compassionate; surely, as a showbiz veteran, she, too, had her rough moments.

"Who do you think you are, standing us up for dinner?"

Crying hysterically, I was like, "Oh my God, don't yell at me," while she went into a rant that pushed me over the edge. No mention of my anxiety, no empathy, just letting me have it. Mom tried to explain it away, but I didn't understand that kind of attitude and I still don't. There was no good reason for Diahann to be so mean.

Years later, she apparently had a "Change of Heart"* when I ran into her at an Upper West Side nail salon. (I know, you can't make this stuff up.) She apologized immediately, citing a certain place she was at in her life at the time. She became incredibly girlie, sharing with me that she was getting a mani-pedi in anticipation of a date night with her man. I'm someone who needs very little in order to move on and create a new dynamic, so just this acknowledgment satisfied me. Who doesn't love a good "Come to Jesus" moment?!?

I got it. I was in a certain place back then too, under all sorts of stress, including the planning of my international *One Step Ahead* tour. The rehearsals were in a big warehouse for what we thought would be a large-scale production to promote the *Anything Is Possible* album, which we expected to skyrocket. When it didn't, the tour was scaled down, but that didn't bother me as much as it did other people so long as I could keep performing.

It wasn't like the *Skirts* scenario, where the whole thing was being called off; surely, if I was able to handle that disappointment, I could handle *this*. I always felt like I was the leader and the energy trickled down from me, so if I kept my head held high and everyone's spirits up, we could all focus on the task at hand: putting a great show together regardless of the venue size.

You have to remember, I had come from performing on a teeny,

---

* *"Change of Heart,"* written and recorded by Diahann Carroll in 1960.

odd-shaped stage at Something Different for pie and ice cream, and I never lost sight of that. This was still the big leagues. Maybe the label and promoters got dramatic about it and saw it as a strike against me as a commodity, but despite the hit I took in ticket and album sales, I wasn't going to let the business bottom line dampen my creative spirit.

In fact, I got *so* creative that I put "On My Own" from *Les Misérables* into the show as my encore and Mom called Richard Jay-Alexander to say, "You must come see Deb perform as Éponine. Her fans go crazy. And you want them in your theater."

I was so nervous knowing that Richard was in the audience, but I used that as fuel to hit it out of the park that night and he immediately got it.

The tour itself was a blast. The meds, therapy, and yoga were kicking in and I was able to enjoy myself more, which was thrilling. Nobody focused on the downsizing. The audiences were passionate, and the Asian leg saw me being treated like pop royalty with grand suites and butlers and the fans singing every word at the top of their lungs. After the tour ended, I had barely unpacked my bags when Richard called us into his Manhattan office for an official sing-through of the entire *Les Miz* score accompanied by musical director Robert Billig to hear if I could nail all the highs and lows. Which I did. And though there were some places where maybe I fell short, he knew I would put in the work and that I was willing to be directed.

"Okay, we're going to do this," he said when I finished.

"Wait, what? You're telling me right here and now that I've got the part?"

I was so used to auditions being "you leave, you wait, they deliberate." But Richard had already made up his mind.

"Yeah, I want to make this happen."

I literally walked out of that building on cloud nine.

"Oh my God, Mom . . . I'm going to be on *Broadway*!"

I had exactly eight rehearsals over the course of two weeks and was locked in the garage with a piano while preparing in isolation at home with those freaking weights. When I started my run, my answering machine's outgoing message said, "Hi, this is Deborah. I'm not talking for the next three months because I am on Broadway. So you can write me a letter."

This was before email. Not speaking, just practicing my singing, I was super-dedicated to an extreme, doing all my own prep work ahead of time.

January is typically a slow month in the theater and it became a thing to cast a big name. However, little did I know back then that when longtime Éponine Natalie Toro was asked to take a leave of absence to put *me* into the show, the cast would become really protective, and rightfully so. *Who is this pop princess taking a job from our beloved Natalie?* was the vibe. I had no idea what I was walking into. But that energy immediately shifted as soon as they realized how serious I was about doing justice to Éponine.

They were all disarmed when they realized I came to serve the piece, to be one of the gang, and that I was prepared and had ultimate respect for this art form. I assured Natalie at the big farewell party she threw herself that Éponine was being put in the most caring hands. As Tito Puente provided the soundtrack, I looked around the dance floor at the wonderful folks who would become my new theater family. I'd just have to prove myself every night onstage to show audiences my casting wasn't some publicity stunt. And I did just that: newspapers were reporting that *Les Miz* had unleashed its secret weapon, and the rest was Broadway history.

Natalie later shared with me that this shakeup ended up being a gift in disguise because she was able to venture out to LA, procure a fantastic agent, and explore new opportunities, which led to her having a diverse and successful career. This moment in time beautifully bonded us and we are connected today.

Éponine and Cosette shared a dressing room that was about eight feet long, and my side of the counter was considerably messier than that of Cosette, the prim, proper, lovely soprano Melissa Anne Davis. I lived in a suite at a nearby Marriott because it was two hours—and way longer in traffic—between the theater and home. As Richard was the first person to take this kind of chance on me, I did *Les Miz* for scale plus perks like the suite and driver instead of a star salary.

I would have done anything for the opportunity to take on the role of Victor Hugo's impoverished "angel with a dirty face" street urchin who was once a spoiled, pampered child. Now Richard, who took pride in "teaching wood how to walk," took delight in his creation by running up and down the aisles of the Imperial Theatre, shouting, "See? I made fucking Éponine out of Debbie Gibson!"

A few months earlier, sitting at the table in the Atlantic Records conference room, I'd watched squiggle marks appear above the heads of the label when I told them I was going to appear in *Les Misérables* on Broadway. "But you guys have Bette Midler. What don't you get?" I reminded them, prompting one to reply, "Yeah, but *you're* young," inferring my passionate turn for musical theater was the most uncool career move I could possibly make, a detour instead of part of my own lane that I was carving, full of new adventures born of versatility.

"Well, I have an eight-record deal and being cool isn't exactly my calling card," I'd pointed out, ever the realist. "So we could do a Broadway album too."

Cue a collective "*What?*" from the suits, who were more comfortable with the urban-pop trajectory. So imagine how elated I felt when, on my opening night in January 1992, they all showed up, dressed to the nines. The Broadway scene was foreign to them and they probably felt out of place, which was why I really appreciated their support as well as their evident pride. I just never understood the disconnect between theater and pop or the perception that a young pop artist must stay in only one lane.

When a cynical reviewer turned convert wrote, "I came to pan her, but couldn't," I thought, *Mission accomplished!* because that's exactly what I'd been aiming for. Following all the work I'd done with Guen to figure out how to produce certain notes and bring a sustainable street edge to my singing, I could feel the reciprocal energy from the audience that let me know my voice and emotions were reaching everyone.

There's a big difference between holding a microphone an inch away from your face during a pop concert and having a tiny mic tucked under your wig on your forehead for a stage show where you have to be in pristine vocal shape, projecting to an audience that's seated and calm. You can't change a note and you can't riff. As Éponine, I had rich low-register vocal moments and the line "I'm gonna scream, I'm gonna warn them here" had me doing a blend in my high register, in addition to a big, belty C to sustain in "On My Own." I'm a B-flat girl, so that was hard, but I got there. And maybe the best advice anyone's ever given me in terms of performance was when Richard came into my dressing room on opening night and said, "I can already tell you're thinking about the big note in act two. That note doesn't exist right now. Just do what's in front of you and don't think ahead."

That tip would come in handy throughout my career journey. Trusting I had what was required for the beginning of the show, I could find my way to the climax; hearing it ring out and reverberate when I sang "That I have never knoooooown" was thrilling, as was my death scene. The guys would always try to tickle me when they were carrying me offstage and nobody wants to see a laughing corpse; the cast had great camaraderie and I loved that. So although I was a star name, I quickly became one of the gang, inviting everyone over to my little suite at the Marriott for Chinese food between performances.

Among the things I liked best about *Les Miz* was that Fantine, Marius, and Éponine are disguised within the ensemble until they emerge as principals. This allowed us to burn off our nerves and warm up our voices as peasants *and* as "Lovely Ladies"—and then have half an hour to get ready for our big moment.

"Look for me," I'd tell my friends. "I'm on the right, wearing the bonnet."

Buddy still can't get over seeing me as a prostitute!

I don't know if this was done to help us or to have extra bodies in the ensemble, but I had a blast as a singing prostitute. And I also loved hearing the glorious music, even when I was backstage.

I wasn't carrying the whole show, and there was an understudy should I fall sick. But theater was intense in a different way—more so than concert work because of the mental focus—which is why I soon felt anxious and exhausted while putting a ton of pressure on myself to be as great as possible. The yogi breath work I did before each performance began making me dizzy because I was running on fumes, doing eight shows a week sandwiched between morning press interviews and signing autographs outside the stage door. So I gracefully bowed out when I was asked to do the same in London's West End following my three-month stint on Broadway.

It pained me to do this because who wouldn't want to star as Éponine in the West End? But it was a turning-point moment where I knew I couldn't get a leg up on the exhaustion and anxiety without rest. What I needed couldn't be found in a pill.

"I need a break," I told Mom, finally surrendering to what I'd long known I had to do. "If I don't want to burn out for good, I can't sing another note."

The Xanax wasn't working. Nothing was working anymore. So, without any pressure from her to accept the London-related offer, I took that break, which lasted maybe a few months. In my fast-paced world, that was an eternity—and I think the signal I sent the universe and myself was what let me off the hook: *I am acknowledging that I am exhausted*. I had to get off the merry-go-round. My closeness to the *Les Miz* cast was really within the context of the show; I didn't know how to have a social life *and* be in a show. So I needed a moment to breathe, live, and not just be hitting certain notes every night.

To this point, I bought my first-ever apartment, on East 79th Street, and moved in. During this time, Denise was apartment-sitting for my Baldwin Pianos artist rep Myron Martin, who'd acquired Liberace's mirrored six-foot, three-inch Jonathan Livingston Seagull grand piano upon his passing. It was love at first sight, and before long Mom was persuading Myron to part with it, even though he had no desire to sell at the time.

I recently ran into Myron, who now runs the Smith Center in Las Vegas, and we had a laugh over how convincing Mom was while he shared her text with me:

"Myron, you are straight. You're moving to Las Vegas to run the Liberace foundation and museum. If you move there owning his mirror-covered piano, you'll never get a date with a girl. They'll all assume you aren't straight. So, you should sell the piano to Deborah. She'll take good care of it and you'll get plenty of dates with pretty Vegas girls!!"

"Needless to say," Myron added, "I sold you the piano . . ."

I was refreshed and ready to hit the high notes once again when I got the prestigious offer to record "Sleigh Ride" for *A Very Special*

Christmas 2. So many icons had been a part of the first album—and producer Jimmy Iovine, vocalist Darlene Love, and so many fabulous artists would be a part of this very special recording session. It was done live in Los Angeles with the whole band playing at once and with me singing live to capture the most exciting version possible.

I'd long been a fan of the Special Olympics, which these albums benefit, having volunteered locally at their camp on Long Island in my early teens and now having been introduced to gymnast Casey Mangan. She defied all the odds to live a quality life despite her parents being told when she was a baby that she should be institutionalized because she had Down syndrome. We connected immediately, and recently I was delighted to see she's joined my modern-day fan club, the Diamond Debheads! The record would go on to raise tons of awareness and money for this beloved charity each and every holiday season.

One memory that makes me giggle to this day is being at the Denver Stadium for the big opening ceremony and Warren Beatty flirting shamelessly with Diane. I tried to get a word in, and looking me dead in the eye, he said, "I'm not talking to you, Debbie . . . I am talking to your *mother*." He then went on to marry Annette Bening, who also had that cropped auburn hair. Coincidence? Mom had many hot suitors in her day. Smokey Robinson would call the house looking for her, prompting my cousin Monica, hand over mouthpiece, to scream, "Aunt Diane! Smokey Robinson's on the phone!," which I never quite got over!

I started recording *Body, Mind, Soul* in June of '92. The original songs submitted to and rejected by Atlantic included the vibey, syncopated "Different Time," which I did with Fred Zarr; "Keeper of Dreams," which was in the Wilson Phillips vein; and "Feels So Right," a straightforward piece of Whitney Houston–type vocal pop, which I thought was authentically the right lane for me. Yet when Doug Morris and Ahmet Ertegun heard these and the eight other tracks, they said no to all but six of them and I was shocked.

They loved what I had done with Elliot Wolff of Paula Abdul fame and with the Narada Michael Walden/Carole Bayer Sager collaboration "Goodbye," as well as with the self-penned "How Can This Be" and "Tear Down These Walls" produced by Phil Ramone, my idol Billy Joel's producer, though they turned down two of his other tracks as well.

I never had an A&R person on the front lines for me. I had the CEO, founder, and president of Atlantic Records picking my music from day one, though I usually was the one essentially handing in my album without anybody weighing in. In the beginning, I would walk into Ahmet's office with individual cassettes in a brown paper lunch bag and dump it on his desk, proclaiming, "Here's my album!" The dance department guys were now a thing of the past, just working the remixes.

Doug was encouraging me to go in an edgier, more urban direction, suggesting I start wearing little black dresses and heels.

Comfy in my youthful vibe, I generally opted to perform in high-top sneakers.

While he and Ahmet hit me with every cliché in the book, I was like, *Right, cuz when you think* urban*, you think* Debbie Gibson.

Sure, I have soul, but my soul doesn't come out in the form of riffing, as that wouldn't be rooted in anything real. As a music fan, I can always sniff out an imposter—and the last thing I wanted to be was *that*. So when they brought up the idea of me collaborating with Prince, I knew they'd really lost the plot. He had already worked with Sheena Easton, Martika, and Carmen Electra, and if I were in my thirties and knew who I was musically and as a woman, I would have given my right arm to do the same. But, in my early twenties, I didn't want to be just another of the girls in his stable where he's the genius producer creating this *thing* that's really his and I'm simply a featured vocalist.

This just didn't feel aligned with where I was in my journey. I thought it would confuse my audience, which was tracking my evolution in real time and growing up with me. That was important stuff. Besides, didn't I prove myself by solely writing all my hits and producing my number ones? Now we were going to scramble to change things up because one album missed the mark? Atlantic's loss of faith in me because the previous album had underperformed was, to say the least, disappointing.

Never mind my success on Broadway or the fact that *Anything Is Possible* had been certified gold for selling over half a million copies. We were still in the metals, right? Convinced I had recorded a really amazing, melodic pop album, I questioned why Doug and Ahmet wanted me to reinvent the wheel, but they were hell-bent on doing that and kept using the word *urban*. So next they suggested that I work with Carl Sturken and Evan Rogers, the New York–based songwriters and producers who'd crafted Donny Osmond's big hit "Soldier of Love" and, more recently, "P.A.S.S.I.O.N." as part of the R&B group Rhythm Syndicate.

I didn't understand why everybody was into the formula of "plugging that artist into this will definitely work." But what were my options? What this suggestion had going for it was that I was a fan. And I did love the Sturken and Rogers sound. So, being that I'm adaptable as a composer and creator, I ended up thinking, *All right, let's try to do stuff my way, their way, my way, their way.* The question was, how malleable should I be when it was my name and photo on the album cover? Remember, I was the little girl standing in the hall, unable to sleep because I'd told a lie. Honesty has always been my calling card, and looking fans in the eye and trying to pass off someone else's idea of who I should be as my own was never gonna fly.

The songs I cowrote with Carl and Evan were more to the urban side because, as a huge Babyface fan, I could channel that sensibility. "Love or Money" and "Do You Have It in Your Heart?" were fun to work on, but whereas I can now own a sultry ballad like "Losin' Myself," who had I actually lost myself over at twenty-one? I enjoyed using my low register on that track, while for the video I'd get into tip-top shape because, if I was going there . . . I was going there *all in*. By this time, I'd decided I was playing a version of myself. In the name of stretching, I had learned to justify the things that weren't 100 percent me. But I would come to learn it's a fine line.

I ended up going into a period where I lived in a hotel in the city and went into a health-and-fitness zone, working with a fitness guru named Radu whose trainers would run me through Central Park to warm me up for the man himself. My sole vocation was getting in shape, so we'd do all kinds of drills, and I'd also lift weights. Every other minute of the day, I pretty much rested and recovered—and it was transformative, helping me with my singing and making me feel really good. It was also preparing me more for diva status visually, as the baby fat was melting away and I was sculpting my body, fulfilling a longtime desire to do a sort of Gypsy Rose Lee burlesque routine in a music video.

Debbie Gibson becomes a stripper! News at 11:00.

The tabloid TV shows would run with that and I learned an invaluable lesson in terms of what the public would and wouldn't accept from me. Whereas other artists could transform themselves, the public hadn't given me that permission yet. Still, Doug and Ahmet appeared oblivious. Upon listening to some of the new songs I'd written with the boys, they encouraged me to push the envelope even further: "You need to go write the kind of song that would shock your mama. We want you to stretch."

So Carl, Evan, and I wrote "Shock Your Mama" and, I think, executed it beautifully.

Though I'm all good news in my Sunday shoes
I'm gonna wear you out on Saturday night.*

When Mom and I played Doug and Ahmet the new song—the one for which I'd taken their songwriting advice—they listened and, though pleased, were in cahoots to stretch me even further. Ribbing each other playfully, they were like the old curmudgeons on the balcony in *The Muppet Show*.

"Hey, Doug, you know what she needs to do?"

"Oh my God, Ahmet, I know exactly where you're going on this: those dirty limericks we were singing last week."

Putting their arms around each other, they began swaying from side to side.

I wish all the girls were like diamonds and rubies
'Cos I'd be a jeweler and polish their . . .

They stopped short of singing *boobies*, but it was implied to illustrate their suggestion of something naughty and a bit taboo if sung by me before the "Shock your mama, shock your mama, baby" chorus.

---

* "Shock Your Mama" by Deborah Gibson, Evan Roger, and Carl Sturken. Copyright © 1992 by Music Sales Corporation (ASCAP), Bayjun Beat Music (BMI), and Could Be the Music (BMI). International Copyright Secured. Used by permission. All rights reserved.

ETERNALLY ELECTRIC

This would inspire Carl, Evan, and me to come up with the part where Evan raps:

If anyone thinks we're movin' too fast
Tell the whole world they can kiss my . . . [scream].

I love that song with its mischievous tongue-in-cheek edginess. And I always had a kitschy side, which is why the video we shot in Paris features me wearing a long rip-away skirt with a high slit over a miniskirt. No stylist could find that outfit, but when Mom went on a mission, she usually came through. So Diane Gibson added *stylist* to her résumé when she combed the unfamiliar streets of the French capital and found it the day before the shoot, enabling me to look prim and proper in one context and then sexy in another with a leg poking through the slit.

That's how we made it work, although I can't imagine male execs in the #MeToo era getting away with the kind of suggestion that Doug and Ahmet made to me back then. Seeing them giggle like teen boys over the sexual innuendo was amusing and endearing and disturbing, all at the same time. Mom and I played along, wanting to please them. But we're also talking about my natural evolution as a young woman, being subjected to the age-old power struggle between the male record-company exec attitude of "Hey, babe, it's rock 'n' roll, so sex it up," and me trying to avoid being pushed into my sexuality before my time. It was an easier sell to just sex me up. I think girls transitioning into womanhood makes men lose their minds, especially when the young girl is a business commodity. They needed to protect their investment . . . but not me. I even had a man posing as a journalist turn a supposed interview into an obscene phone call.

Watching two of the most powerful men in the music business giggling because they almost sang *boobies* made me wonder: *Where have*

I landed? How did it get away from me arriving home and writing "Lost in Your Eyes" with nobody around, no interference, and no instruction to create a dirty rap to sell a record, pursuing a style and direction that's not at all connected to me and my audience?

I would come to learn, if you feel like you need to take a shower after a meeting... you're in the wrong meeting!

There was a lot of back-and-forth about tweaking the material, and it really started sucking the joy out of the art. Mom and I would sit on the couch, Doug and Ahmet would have their own chairs, and we were basically performing surgery rather than making music, which often left us girls in tears. I am transported back to the time in the second-floor ladies room at 75 Rockefeller Plaza, where, side by side, Mom and I stood washing our hands, deflated, knowing that soon enough we'd be washing our hands of this historic partnership with these legendary music men. There was just no meeting of the minds anymore—and no magic within this foursome.

Today, many of my fans love the *Body, Mind, Soul* album, but at the time of its January 1993 release, people were wondering, *What's she doing?* Everyone had to navigate and adjust their mindset to try to understand what was going on, including me, feeling like I'd been backed into a corner to make this kind of music that I had figured out how to justify in the press knowing full well it was born of strategy, not pure inspiration. I am always best when thinking with my heart instead of being strategic.

When the album didn't deliver in terms of sales or chart positions, the Atlantic guys were the first ones to run scared and drop the ball, taking zero responsibility for the fact that this was primarily their vision, not mine. Nonetheless, it was another bullseye missed, making it two in a row that had fallen short of the stratospheric impact of my first two albums. Not good odds in the fickle world of pop music.

There was, evidently, more interest in me within the more stable world of the theater. The theater world prides itself on performers with the chops to deliver and it isn't trend-based, though modern times have seen their share of "stunt casting." I was never about that, and by this point, certain producers were well aware of how seriously I took my craft.

One role on my ingenue wish list was Sandy in *Grease*. I vividly remember going to the sixty-nine-cent Gables movie theater in Merrick to see it with Karen and Michele, and it was life-altering. I instantly related to Olivia Newton-John's sexy innocence, even as a little girl, and that ignited a lifelong dream. Little did I know this dream would come true on the other side of the pond during a trip to promote *Body, Mind, Soul*—an unexpected side benefit of this album. I was about to be the token American in the British revival of one of the greatest American musicals of all time.

As luck would have it, I was in the right place at the right time to play Sandy onstage with the film score intact because Robert Stigwood, who'd coproduced the movie with Alan Carr, was now producing his own stage revival of *Grease* in London's West End alongside Paul Nicholas and David Ian.

After seeing me being interviewed on BBC TV, Robert called Mom and invited me to audition. Singing "Hopelessly Devoted" onstage at the Dominion Theatre, I felt like I'd been born to play Sandy. *This is perfect.* Robert knew it, the director, David Gilmore, knew it, and so did I—even though, in true theater fashion, they put me through my paces again the next day.

The callback took place at a rehearsal studio, where I danced for the show's choreographer, Arlene Phillips, and acted out scenes. Having not done this in a long time, I wasn't the best actress in the world when it came to delivering lines. In *Les Miz*, the dialogue was all sung, and that added a layer of comfort, but everyone still had to be very accommodating and patient with me when it came to finding my way with the spoken word, particularly Arlene. I knew she was working behind the scenes, championing my getting the role. We are kindred spirits.

"Go home, pack your bags, and come back in six weeks," Robert told me.

I had no problem leaving behind a boyfriend who'd eventually cheat on me anyway.

Hired to do a nine-month run, I was psyched. There were three months of rehearsals before opening in *Grease* and I had a great time in London, living away from home . . . without my mom. This was now *my* life. I'll never forget the first day of rehearsal; I instantly felt at home, like I was with my tribe. Everyone was open and loving and insanely talented and supportive of one another. After that rehearsal, I experienced a first: sitting in a restaurant and eating by myself. I even signed up for a philosophy course!

It was strange at first, but I exhaled and took it all in, knowing this was the start of a new time where I'd embrace the enjoyment of my own company. As the cast got tighter, I'd hang out with the gang after rehearsals and entertain the relatives and friends who took the opportunity to make the trip across the pond on the regular.

Soon I was like, *If I have to do one more tour of the Tower of London . . . enough beheadings!*

Mom had met a younger man, Mike, during the *Electric Youth* tour, a videographer she'd started dating not long after divorcing Dad . . . before having a facelift. Some people in our orbit were judgmental about her choices. I didn't have a problem with any of it. Having made some real money for the first time in her life after finding her way without a college education, she was in a power moment—being herself, looking her best. So what if she wanted to be sexy for her young guy and buy him a car with what she had earned? I celebrated it.

In a world where no one appeared to blink an eye at older men with younger women, I was like, *Go, Diane!* But I do have to say that what she went through with the facelift was brutal. Denise was scared when Diane arrived home scarred, bruised, and bandaged. She had lost a lot of blood during that day's procedures and it was very hard on her body. Things were not as refined back then, but this cautionary tale is still relevant today. And this desire for alterations would later become life-altering for Mom.

Okay, our showbiz family has now taken things too far.

I could hear Denise's inner monologue when she saw Mom looking like a mummy. That visual is scary for a young girl.

I myself had to question how much I'd be willing to traumatize my body for an aesthetic. Just like doing anything to have a hit record: Are you transforming and stretching yourself, or selling your soul and sacrificing your identity? I don't judge anyone for doing whatever makes them happy. I, too, live somewhere between making the most of what I have and living up to some fantastical aspirational vision I've created for myself. I was taking notes at the time to make my best decisions in all areas of my life and discovering a lot of those boundaries during that period:

How am I going to sleep best at night? I must do things that are authentic.

The theater was providing that for me. It simplified my life. Sure, eight shows a week is a lot, but it requires a singular focus as part of a community. Putting on the costumes, singing, and dancing to the *Grease* music every night with my peers was pretty much guaranteed to bring me joy. Which was more than I could say at that point about my relationship with Atlantic.

There were no more meetings with Doug and Ahmet. Starring in *Grease* in the West End opposite the wonderful Craig McLachlan, I was in another happy place. I made so many close friends like Drew, Liz, Anna-Jane, and Daniel—whom I dated briefly and who is now married to a man. When my ankle got injured and I had to take ten days off from the show to heal, I'd go see movies on crutches with his very straight brother Jamie, and I think Daniel himself questioned if that's who I was meant to be dating.

It was like my college experience. Everyone was always going for a curry between shows and having sleepovers. And I even invited the US cast of Disney on Ice's *Beauty and the Beast* to my flat for a Halloween party, where I became great friends with skater Patrick Hancock, who later went on to run my music camp programs with me.

Craig, meanwhile, was such a divine gift for me: a true star, leader, and confidant. He had so much charisma and was always in the moment, onstage and off. It was hard to keep my straitlaced Sandy face during performances—and offstage he was a kick. He came up to my dressing room to meet my grandparents wearing nothing but a dance belt and his electric guitar. They were charmed as he said, "Hello, Grandpawww, hello, Grandmawww," in his Aussie accent. We've stayed in touch and remain friends to this day.

Meanwhile, back home, my mom was dealing with the day-to-day of my record-deal reality.

"We can keep going with this deal," she said on a business call with me, "but it's just going to be the same problems over and over."

Although I had about ten million dollars in advance money still coming to me per my contract, no price tag was worth going back down the same dead-end road. So there was no big farewell. Breaking the contract was totally mutual. Nobody was feeling it anymore. I'm just sad that, having tried to contact Doug over the years to reconnect, clear some air, and form a new adult relationship, he's never taken my calls.

Ahmet was really invested in me whether I was on the label or not. Later, when I was no longer on the label, Mr. Ertegun would invite me to his office, listen to my music, and give me some beautiful opinions because he loved music and believed in my writing. He was so elegant and so kind. That was the Ahmet I knew. Never hitting on me or doing anything salacious, he was always grandfatherly—to *me*, at least, though I'm aware of the allegations and hope the women coming forth find resolution. Though there have been constant murmurings about many record execs, I wasn't targeted. Mom was often around, and I truly feel that it's thanks to her I don't have any #MeToo stories. Nobody likes an overprotective mother, but it wasn't about that for her. She always said, "It's not a popularity contest." And though in a way it was, it first and foremost was about my safety and my sanity, especially in this realm.

Having cut my ties to the label, doing *Grease* in London was a big chapter for me, especially when Brian Koppelman, the A&R chief at SBK and EMI—also my music publisher—called to say, "I know you've left Atlantic. What are you writing these days?"

"I'm doing a lot more singer-songwriter-type ballads with a kind of modern-day Carole King vibe," I replied, piquing Brian's interest.

"I'd love to fly over to London and have you sit at a piano to play me your new songs," he said.

Now *I* was interested. Nobody at Atlantic had asked me to do that for the last album. Everyone there was working from the outside in, not from the songwriting on out. So Brian jumped on a plane and came to my flat. I could see and feel his enthusiasm as soon as I started playing him some of my latest compositions.

"I want to help you make your singer-songwriter masterpiece," he told me. "You need to produce this album by yourself and I want to make that happen."

I could not believe what I was hearing. This was so life-affirming after all I had been through artistically. What a beautiful relief to know I could just make my music again.

Chapter Eight

BOBBIES IN THE LOBBY

The entire time I was in London starring in *Grease*, the Dominion Theatre was sold out. Rave reviews, mania at the stage door, Craig and I handling most of the press responsibilities.

I'd taken on the role after being told the producers weren't allotting a full-on star salary for Sandy, as they'd been looking to cast an unknown. The pay was still decent, so I could afford to do it, but it was a fraction of what Craig was making. When they offered to renew my contract at the end of the run with no increase in salary, I was, to say the least, surprised. *Seriously?*

I guess *Grease* was *not* the word for *me* anymore. Nevertheless, having once vowed to never do a theater run for more than nine months because I felt I wouldn't be able to keep it fresh that long, I left on a high note with my dignity intact. Although I was bummed, I returned to London sooner than I thought for a grand adventure both onstage and off.

I was invited to headline *The Music of Andrew Lloyd Webber* at St. Paul's Cathedral in front of the royal family. During rehearsals with a symphony orchestra, I met *Starlight Express* star Greg Ellis and there was an instant connection, with a flirty vibe happening all day. So we did the concert, which was a thrill and it all went fantastically well, but that was weirdly the inconsequential part of this story. After the show was when the fun *really* began, with a big cast and press party at Planet Hollywood.

Everything was at Planet Hollywood; we'd had the opening-night party for *Grease* there too. Mom came back with me to the UK for the show and we had a suite with a living room between each of our two bedrooms at the Waldorf. We hadn't lived together for quite some time, but old habits die hard, so I indulged her. And although it was unlike Mom to let me fly solo out on the town, she felt tired at the party and left me there to hang out with my West End friends, as well as with my new pal Greg. She knew I was in good hands.

When the party was kind of winding down, he and I were like, *We don't want this night to end.* So we took a cab back to the Waldorf, which was oh-so-posh, and were then like, "What do we wanna do? Where do we wanna go next?"

There was a café in the hotel and, although it was closed, we snuck inside, as the door was unlocked. It was dimly lit and there we were, sitting at a table, talking, laughing, and making out. We were young and having fun and feeling like we were getting away with something sneaky! It was now probably three in the morning, and Mom and I were getting picked up at about six a.m. for our flight, so in my mind I had three whole hours to pack. I was gonna take every minute of this time to enjoy myself with this cute guy.

Suddenly, two London bobbies walked in, complete with truncheons, walkie-talkies, and those distinctive high custodian helmets.

"Excuse me, miss, are you Deborah?"

Oh my God. My mother...

I just knew.

When we exited the coffee shop, there were all these bobbies flooding the hotel lobby. Mom had been calling and waking up people all over London: Arlene Phillips, actor Darren Day's manager Peter Powell... everyone in the West End received a call that night. In a big Italian family, people are either presumed dead on the road or an axe murderer is involved. It's always a drama of epic proportions. But, because I'd dated Darren at the end of my run in *Grease*, Diane thought maybe I had ended up over at his flat.

"My daughter's missing! Maybe she's with Darren." Peter was so tired, he literally ran out in a button-down shirt and teeny athletic shorts before showing up at Darren's door. Darren didn't know where I was. So the two of them looked for me all over the West End before making their way to the hotel.

"Why didn't you tell them I was here?" I asked the guy at the front desk. "I've been right here all this time. You *saw* me go into the café!"

"Well, Miss Gibson, I wanted to protect your *prih-vicy*."

That is upper crust for "privacy."

"That's nice of you, but you allowed half of Scotland Yard to look for me?!?"

Despite me shaking my head, this was as amusing as it was stressful and surreal.

Greg and I were escorted upstairs by the bobbies. When Mom opened the door, I saw Darren and Peter. Grabbing me by the scruff of my neck, she said, "Deborah, get in here! And *you*," she added, poking Greg's chest with her finger and giving him *that look* that only an irate mom can give. "Call your girlfriend. She's looking for you!"

He apparently had a live-in girlfriend who I knew nothing about 'til Mom detectived Greg's apartment number and called.

Darren looked like he got a kick out of this moment in particular.

I was always so responsible, no one was used to me doing anything remotely scandalous. However, Mom was out of touch with what my life was right now.

"Didn't you know we were getting picked up at six?" she asked.

"Yes, I was timing it. I haven't missed a flight yet."

"But you'd normally call me."

"I wasn't gonna wake you up at one in the morning. You said you were coming back and going to sleep."

I was twenty-four years old—I wasn't used to being micromanaged.

Greg had me paged at Heathrow Airport because we hadn't exchanged numbers; how else were we going to keep in touch in this pre–cell phone era sans social media? I know it's a recurring theme throughout this book and my life, but . . . I am indeed still friends with both Darren and Greg today and share laughs about this story all the time. I must call my friend Ken Jeong to make the movie version of this real-life escapade with me!

With all things London-caper-comedy behind me, I was excited to dive into the album that SBK had recently signed me to record. I had written most of the songs in London, but after a country music–writing trip to Nashville, I added the new original treasures "Dancing in My Mind" and "You Don't Have to See." One song that didn't make the cut was "I Never Took to a Taken Man," a message that would become important to me . . . though not without its failed attempts!

Despite Brian putting together a powerhouse band—including original session guitarists Ira Siegel and John Leventhal, keyboard player Steve Rosen, bassist T-Bone Wolk, OG percussionist Bashiri

Johnson, and drummer Russ Kunkel—it would prove to be a challenging process.

The vocals were a huge priority on this record, so during the *Think with Your Heart* sessions I resumed my vocal weights routine to be able to sustain properly, as well as to get the desired level of storytelling to penetrate the listener's soul. Playing back that record now, I'm proud of the reliability and strength of my high notes as well as of my songwriting, which came from my soul and from being signed to a label where nobody told me what to do. This was *my* voice.

It was October 1994 and I was a guest at the White House for a weekend hosted by the National Italian American Foundation alongside such luminaries as Nicolas Cage and Isabella Rossellini. I had been grappling with making a regime change on the creative side of this album and once I pulled the trigger, it made me ill. So ill, in fact, that, following my White House stint, I not only landed at Heathrow Airport, I also landed in the hospital.

Excited but weary, I'd arrived at AIR Studios for the recording of the sixty-six-piece London Session Orchestra with Tony Visconti—and mustered up just enough strength to record the title track, "Think with Your Heart," live at the piano with all the musicians. Even in my weakened state, I found that to be a breathtaking experience, as was the creative fulfillment of recording a song called "A Million Pieces" for which I hand-wrote the arrangement, even though it didn't make the album. However, ready to enjoy watching the strings for the remaining songs being cut live, I ended up being hospitalized for fatigue, dehydration, and an undiagnosed virus—which usually translates to something stressful in life causing an all-out system meltdown.

Because I was the sole producer of the album and strings were still being added to the tracks, a messenger kept running back and forth between the studio and my hospital room with cassettes of the recordings and Tony's charts so I could send back comments in real time for them to make the changes. Oh, what I would have done for FaceTime to have been invented back then!

I'm quite sure, looking back, that emotional stress was what wore me down. And this would become a recurring theme. In fight-or-flight mode much of the time, I'm a strong woman, but one who's always needed to be surrounded by soft, nurturing energy. That can be an outwardly confusing dichotomy. Which is why, when someone's presence starts to take me down, I start questioning whether the interaction is worth it.

I replaced my recording engineer with renowned mix engineer Niko Bolas to put the finishing touches on the album. Niko had a great spirit and energy about him that shifted me out of the bad place I was in. His main goal was to facilitate my vision and empower me, so the mixing process with him was awesome. As was another project he invited me to be a part of.

"Have you heard of the hardcore LA punk band Circle Jerks, Deb?"

"No."

"Do you know what a circle jerk is?" Why did everyone smirk when they asked me this question?

"No." Ahhhh . . . I'd find out.

"They're such big fans of yours," Niko continued. "I'm producing their new album and they'd love to have you sing a guest vocal on one of the tracks.'"

"Oh, *absolutely*!"

I ended up screaming a little and having a lot of fun on "I Wanna Destroy You." Then, when the *Oddities, Abnormalities, and Curiosities* album was released, the guys asked me to perform the song onstage with them at the iconic East Village punk venue CBGB.

"Here's the set list," singer Keith Morris told me when the night arrived. "The way this place is set up, it's best if you wait until we start playing the song before 'I Wanna Destroy You,' then go outside, walk along the back alley, and come in through that back door to get onto the stage."

Aware that MTV was filming the event, I had opted for my version of a grungy, punky look: baseball cap, braided hair, yellow Circle Jerks T-shirt, blue jeans. What I hadn't bargained for was my very own *Spinal Tap* moment. Waiting in the back alley, I heard the "I Wanna Destroy You" intro and the fans screaming—which was why nobody could hear *me* banging on the metal door, yelling to be let in. It was a minute that felt like five before someone finally heard me. And it was so punk rock. I shared a mic with Keith, and, not exactly an expert at stage diving, I launched myself headfirst into the crowd. A total let-my-hair-down night; I enjoyed the heck out of it.

That was great because it was one of the last moments of pure joy I'd have before hearing some not-so-great news about my *Think with Your Heart* album and a regime change at SBK, which took place immediately before the record's July 4, 1995, release. This resulted in the album's transition from a big deal for the label to an irritant for the more rock-oriented guy who'd taken over as president. Forget me promoting it in theaters or arenas; the budget was slashed and I was relegated to doing a two-week acoustic tour of some retail chains, many of them Borders Books & Music stores.

This was not exactly what I'd had in mind for what I considered my best songwriting to date. I'd walked away from millions of dollars and started over, only to have a regime change get in the way of me doing things properly?!? Of course, my mom pushed back. And if Diane Gibson can't get it done, it ain't gonna change.

Fan favorite "Didn't Have the Heart."
This pic is from my self-funded music video.

    I felt there was zero support, and yet again, I had to make the most of things while thinking, *Why am I being forced to be the Queen of Pivoting again?* Aware that these were still high-class problems and that nobody appreciated a whiny girl singer, I was like, *Chin up, tits out, cheerio!* After all, I was now an honorary Brit. And I was determined to blow the lid off every record store I played.

    My diehard Debheads showed up in full force, and they'll confirm it was a stand-up moment within our community because they loved the intimacy, while the music spoke for itself. No matter that I was singing at the top of my range under fluorescent lighting while shoppers were busy perusing the shelves for self-help books or the latest Stephen King novel. I would connect with my audience by doing exactly what I would have done if this were Madison Square Garden, because what was the alternative? You look as desperate as you feel, and in a flip-the-script moment, I decided to make this one of the quirkiest yet most meaningful stops on the DG Express!

The only other people with me on that tour were my sound guy and Heather Moore, whom Mom had invited aboard immediately after Heather quit her job as manager of the country-music dance club Denim & Diamonds. The two of them had done business when Bryan Austin, a country singer managed by Diane, was booked to play the venue. And they had become friendly when my mother went there for line-dancing classes while I was in London.

"She's one of us," Mom told me.

I knew that meant *You should meet her.*

So I did. Heather was spinning many plates—and did so with the hottest jeans, cutest cowboy hat, and best poker face I've ever seen. It rivaled Diane Gibson's, which is saying a lot. When Heather mentioned she would be flying to London to visit family, we invited her to drop in on the orchestral session at AIR Studios, where she watched me do my thing—and instantly got it.

After returning to New York and my little apartment on the Upper East Side, I began visiting Denim & Diamonds myself. Mom had been doing her best to turn me on to country music and I liked the idea of learning how to line dance from the hot DJ and dance teacher DA. Think Johnny Castle in a cowboy hat. Here I was allowed to blend in with people who just wanted to be part of a traditional, old-school music-and-dance community.

Located on Lexington Avenue between 47th and 48th, this outlet had nothing to do with who I was professionally and didn't play the kind of music I was making. Which was why I'd often throw on a cowboy hat and walk barefoot all the way from East 79th—yup, my barefoot thing—to enter a world that allowed me to lose myself on the dance floor. Mastering the Boot Scootin' Boogie and the Tush Push at Denim & Diamonds was so much fun, while watching Heather in action as the skinny-Minnie, cigarette-smoking, take-charge gal who ran the show left me in no doubt as to why she and Mom hit it off.

When badass women get together, they recognize kindred spirits. And in Heather, a boss babe overseeing sixty employees, Diane saw a twenty-five-year-old version of herself, someone who could free her up to do whatever she needed to do by replacing her on the road; someone she could trust to handle me with the desired care to achieve our joint objectives. So she told her, "If you ever decide to leave this place, we'd like you to come with us."

"What does that mean?" I remember Heather asking tongue-in-cheek with wide-eyed enthusiasm. "Where are we going?"

I don't mind not knowin' what I'm headed for.*

Little did she know . . . on the adventure of a lifetime!

Her dad's recent pancreatic-cancer diagnosis had been testing her emotionally. And a lifestyle that, as she describes it, consisted of her "counting thousands of dollars until six a.m. and then unwinding at a bar until eight" was no longer sustainable. So she eventually quit the club and became my day-to-day management person as well as Mom's

---

* *"Lost in Your Eyes" by Deborah Gibson. Copyright © 1987 by Music Sales Corporation (ASCAP). International Copyright Secured. Used by permission. All rights reserved.*

right-hand woman. Diane was relieved; she'd finally found someone who, she felt, could pinch-hit for her.

That August, following a show at the House of Blues in West Hollywood, Heather accompanied me on a thirty-day tour of Singapore, South Korea, Malaysia, the Philippines, Thailand, and Japan. And in Singapore we were joined by my boyfriend, actor Chris Bruno, who had just been cast against type in *All My Children*, playing Michael Delaney, the first gay character on daytime TV. We'd been introduced by our mutual friend Jim Davidson; our first hello, which was not intended to be a matchmaking setup, was at Disneyland and found us hitting it off with instant chemistry.

Chris was outgoing *and* easygoing as well as artistic, athletic, and handsome. I was at a point in my life where I was ready to embrace my down-home tomboy side, and Chris appreciated my playfulness and sense of freedom, traits that we shared. We also had a shared love of the phone and fax machine whenever our careers separated us. His four-day stay in Singapore—during which he saw me perform on a barge out on the water in Boat Quay while the audience watched from the shore—was a breath of fresh air at the start of a challenging trip for two American gals whose sense of humor was certainly tested in the Far East.

Beforehand, the label had called to ask me for a list of my special skills and favorite things because the TV shows in the different territories wanted a unique angle for me. "I love baking, tap dancing, juggling," I replied, "and I also love foreign languages."

Cut to me wearing a chef's hat and making mooncakes (akin to Twinkies) in a factory at midnight, speaking Chinese off cue cards and singing in Mandarin with the TV host. I learned it by ear and drilled that song so much on the plane, I could play it on the piano for you right now. I also tap-danced to "Tea for Two," sharing the stage with these larger ladies who, wearing kids' clothes and pigtails, were called the Elephant Girls. As two strong women touring Asia by ourselves, Heather and I were taken aback by this but chalked it up to how things were done on the other side of the world. There was a chauvinistic attitude in South Korea at that time; nobody at the Seoul record label would help us with our bags when we arrived for a performance. Fortunately, pop star twins Gunnar and Matthew Nelson were there to swoop in and lend a hand.

Up in my room, I called to ask for a massage, unaware that, in South Korea, all of the registered masseurs are blind because they have a really strong sense of touch. When they sent someone, I opened the door, said, "Come in," turned, and it slammed shut behind me. Then I looked around—the woman was nowhere to be seen. *What's she doing?*

Knocking on the door again was what she was doing. After reopening it, I realized she was blind and led her in by the hand. But she didn't speak English, so we had a hysterical time while I tried to communicate what I needed.

In Kuala Lumpur, I wasn't allowed to show my arms on television. And in the Philippines, there was absolutely no security when I signed autographs at a shopping mall, sitting behind a table while about five thousand people lined up between red ropes. It was like the store managers had just thrown us to the wolves. Heather stood at the front of the line to make sure there wasn't a stampede, but it was quite a learning experience.

Not long after I returned home, I was offered the role of Rizzo in *Grease* on Broadway. However, I decided I'd prefer to do the national tour, which would enable me to also promote my new album via press and radio stations around the country while on the road from November 1995 through March of '96.

Craving another theater moment, I again wanted to be one of the gang without the focus only on me. A nineteen-year-old unknown named Sutton Foster—who would become Broadway royalty—played Sandy, and I recall her doing a thirty-second warm-up before hitting the craziest notes onstage I'd ever heard. I knew that girl was gonna be a star. Meanwhile, my Kenickie, Steve Geyer, and Marissa Jaret Winokur, who played Jan, would become two of my best friends.

I ended up living on a couch at Marissa's North Hollywood apartment after our *Grease* run ended. It would be the second time I did that, the first being a few years earlier when I took Richard Weitz and his then girlfriend Lori Glass Berk up on their kind offer to stay in the guest room for what turned into months as I auditioned for projects as one of Richard's clients. I even doubled-down on their dare to move my piano into their living room because they loved a good singalong.

Lori and I cry with laughter to this day when we look back on that evening she arrived home from work to find my family photos atop the upright! I can't tell you how many times I belted out showtunes in that humble apartment off Santa Monica Boulevard. I've always loved a good slumber-party vibe and looked for nurturing in a friendly nest wherever I could get it.

Marissa and I like to joke we were the *Two Broke Girls* sitcom long before it existed, and shenanigans ensued when, following an audition, I walked in one day carrying a new pet goldfish. Yup. We eventually signed a deal with Norman Lear and had a blast singing and dancing in TV executives' offices all over town to pitch our show, which never hit the airwaves. And then there was Adrian Zmed, our Danny Zuko, and Sally Struthers as Miss Lynch . . . two of the most fun-loving and warmhearted people you'll ever meet. Playing Rizzo was a blast, but staying healthy on the road challenged me. Trying to retain body heat at night for my always-faltering immune system, I wore a wool hat and scarf in bed. When Marissa heard Chris was going to visit me on the road and asked if I was going to buy some sexy lingerie, I just said, "Nah, he's used to me sleeping all bundled up in a onesie." Not such easy access!

Chris recently told me my dedication to doing *Grease* was maybe a bit intense and more akin to me playing, let's say, the lead in an opera. He knew then what it would take me decades to learn: that I'd have to cultivate a trusting relationship with my instrument, knowing it would show up without so much fanfare and rigid ritualistic practices. He's right. I'd go into such a zone about my performing, I didn't know how to simultaneously entertain a boyfriend and do my best work. Still, *Grease* was a ball and I loved traveling around the country to promote my music as well as the show.

No sooner had I finished that tour than I embarked on a thirty-city tour of *Funny Girl*. I'd auditioned for the late Jule Styne's wife, Margaret, to replace the original first pick, the brilliant Carolee Carmello, in the role of Fanny Brice. They wanted a recognizable name to play the lead character and I was their best option, preapproved by Jule, endorsed by Margaret. But I was also forced down the creative team's throats and needed new vocal input.

Sammy Dallas Bayes, the director, was a little like, *Where's my diva Carolee?* So I cold-called famed voice teacher Joan Lader.

"I've got the lead in *Funny Girl*," I told her. "I know I hit it out of the park at the audition, but I also know I'm doing this eight times a week. So even though you're probably overbooked, can you help by seeing me *twice* a week?"

There was momentary silence on the other end of the phone as I let this big request hang in the air. But Joan did just that and changed my life.

I worked my *arse* off applying her unique techniques, and I'd also do things like hang from a bar to open my ribs, run up and down stairs, do backbends, and strike a full plow pose in the wings before a scene with my knees literally massaging my head. I found a whole new voice. Sammy got the poppier version of Fanny Brice, and when Mike Provenz—the same high school friend who'd been blown away by the caliber of "Only in My Dreams"—came to see the show, he was blown away all over again:

"Holy crap, I had no idea you could sing like that!"

Neither did I. It was a tour de force and I was at the top of my game.

I prepared three months for the first day of *Funny Girl* rehearsals, enlisting the help of a dialect coach to sound as authentic as possible while channeling my own Fanny Brice to perfect the segue between the singing and the speaking. I also read books about her and went to the library to watch archival footage during that pre-internet era. I did my homework. So it was a crying shame that, when the promoters asked the director, "What's the minimum amount of rehearsal time you need to put up this show?" he answered, "Three weeks."

Sammy, his eye on the budget, wished he was able to say, *Three months*. This revival was supposed to end up on Broadway. No way would that happen in three weeks.

I was doing previews with blue bloomers under a Victoria's Secret robe because my costumes weren't ready. Still, I loved our fabulous musical director, Sheila Walker; she and I had great musical communication and I was very proud of the work I did in that show. My visceral, accessible Fanny Brice lived inside me. Although I'm not Jewish, I *am* from Brooklyn and Long Island, so I leaned into my street-savvy brassiness and did my best to represent these soulful folks and the culture I had grown up around. Unfortunately, I had zero onstage chemistry with my leading man, the lovely and talented Robert Westenberg, who had been nominated for a Tony for *Into the Woods*. I think that was part of the problem. But once again, I had a fabulous experience with the cast.

Starting its run in Pittsburgh on November 1, 1996, the show had mixed reviews, and the November 12 to 24 booking in Denver was canceled. That would have been okay had the California dates not required rescheduling on top of a two-week break, creating a seven-week gap between performances.

"In this business, you're allowed six weeks off, but after seven you either have to post a closing notice or keep the cast on salary," producer Greg Young explained in a *Playbill* article.* "That's a lot of money and the show wasn't out long enough to make it worth the payroll. So we posted a closing notice, but we're definitely going back out in January."

That never happened. When the show closed, everybody freaked out: "Where's my next job coming from?"

The cancellation hit us all like a bolt of lightning, but in true Queen of Pivoting fashion, I threw everyone a party, and after we hugged the last person goodbye, Mom and I turned to each other and said, "Okay, what's next?"

Truth be known, I was relieved not to have to hit those high notes anymore. There were other ladies better suited for that job.

My immediate focus was on reviving my music career. I wanted to return to my pop roots on my own terms, in my own way. That meant forming my own label, Espiritu Records, and spending a ton of my own money on recording and then promoting an album that, reflecting my reinvigorated authenticity, would be titled simply *Deborah*.

I'd worked really hard for my gut-renovated West 81st Street duplex, which for a spell found me living the life with a seventy-five-year-old live-in French butler named Guy. But, ever the gambler, I was

---

* David Lefkowitz, "Debbie Gibson *Funny Girl* Tour Cancels 1996 Engagements," *Playbill*, November 26, 1996.

about to literally hock the ranch and give up my elaborate lifestyle to do my music my way. Calling Mom, I asked her how much money I had to play with.

"About a mil," she replied.

I knew enough to know it would take more than that to record this album and properly promote it. So I nonchalantly said, "Well, then, I'll have to sell my apartment to give this next album the best shot."

You must remember, these were pre-streaming days, pre–social media. This was an indie record requiring a major-label budget to even be in the game. And I wanted to be in the game. Remember that song from *A Chorus Line*? I felt *nothing*. I wasn't nervous and I didn't doubt my decision for one second, although my sister Karen and Aunt Linda were very vocal about telling Mom not to allow me to invest all my own money into my music career. We didn't listen. I was restless sitting at home staring at that glorious exposed-brick wall, wondering what could be if I went for it. So I had to. And I did . . . as Deborah.

Ever since I could first speak and articulate my disdain for nicknames, I've always preferred to be called Deborah. So after years of building the brand name *Debbie Gibson*—which was akin to "the Hamburglar" from my quirky perspective—I decided to go deep within and back to my roots. The *Deborah* album was that moment, although we bridged the gap by still crediting my artist and songwriter contributions to *Debbie Gibson*.

Much was made about the name change, which wasn't really a change at all, just a return to who I always felt I was at my core. I wasn't trying to sound pretentious or more grown-up; like my short haircut in the '90s, when I didn't confer with any of the powers that be, it was a simple thing that just made sense to me. I never overthought the public response, so the fuss surprised me. Still, in hindsight, I get it! If Billy Joel suddenly became William Joel, it would have felt like a whole new person with a brand-new identity and would have taken some getting used to.

As time went on, I evolved. Just like those of us who once couldn't bear to look at our high-school yearbooks but can now go to theme parties of that era, I not only got past the Debbie thing, I embraced it. And I also love it these days when new friends who know me as Debbie want to call me that. Ringing in my ears right now is Vegas friend Dayna Roselli—introduced to me by Matt Goss—saying, "Debbie, let's grab dinner on the Strip tonight!" That feels cool and sexy and relevant to who I am today. But I still stand by the decision I made to swing things all the way back to Deborah to now embrace the new version of Debbie.

"You were indie before indie was cool," Heather says these days about the *Deborah* project and my move from the Upper West Side.

I reimmersed myself in dance pop and melodic ballads.

"Now that she's proved her ability to compose serious ballads and work a Broadway stage, Gibson has decided to have a little fun again," *Billboard*'s Larry Flick remarked about "Only Words." "She hits the dance floor with exhausting energy, romping through this fast-paced anthem with an infectious grin and a sing-along chorus. This may be characteristic of Gibson's past club glories, but it sure isn't indicative of superstar remixer Junior Vasquez's past efforts. He momentarily eschews the tribal darkness of his previous recordings in favor of a sunny sound that is awash in delightful, pastel-like keyboards. Perfect for the tambourine-shaking tea-dance set."[*]

"Only Words" made the top 40 of the US dance charts but failed to register anywhere else, foreshadowing the fate of the *Deborah* album. This, remember, still predated the era when I could record it at home

---

[*] Billboard, *March 29, 1997.*

and promote it online. Having spent a fortune on the studio sessions, I had to do the same to get it into stores all around the country. So Heather hit the phones, procured orders on consignment at seventy or so record stores, then went a step further, getting a commitment for front-window displays in Tower Records. These included the Manhattan outlet on 66th and Broadway, where it stayed in the window for over six months.

"I just asked," Heather loves to tell people who wonder about the mystical way in which she achieved this feat. "It's amazing what happens when you do that!"

The traction our efforts created resulted in a distribution deal with Nile Rodgers. But the financial return on my huge personal investment was hugely disappointing.

"We sold all thirty records that we had in there today!" Heather was excited when she called with that news following one of my Tower Records promo appearances. So was Chris, who'd been there with me.

"That's *awesome*."

"Yeah, that's awesome," I exclaimed.

Here I was, getting excited about much smaller numbers than I once had. Major label versus independent was quite an adjustment. Millions then, thirty now. At the same time, it was all relative—and super-gratifying to see our grassroots efforts paying off. We were having fun.

It's great to look forward and have big dreams. And it's also wise to be grateful for where you are right now rather than live in a constant state of disappointment. I've always tried to remain realistic. Glass half full . . . at least I *have* a glass.

While I was firing on all cylinders doing my Southeast Asia press tour, Chris was trying to balance his career with focusing on the fact that his mother had stage-four breast cancer. We'd been flying all over the world to see each other, sometimes at short notice and with only a few hours to share. That spontaneity was exciting. But it was taking its toll, and our lives were going in different directions.

"You were the most driven woman I had ever met in my life," he recently told me. "I remember telling your mom, 'She does more before nine a.m. than the US Marines!' I never saw anyone put so much into their career or show your level of determination. While you're tough when you need to be, we had a very sweet, kind, caring relationship where neither of us did anything to hurt the other. We had a lot of fun and that's why we're still friends today."

He's right. Whenever I need some Bruno time to lift me up, I still give him a call.

Deborah was released in June 1997 and it wasn't long before the theater once more came a-callin'. Mom was asked by associate producer Tony McLean if I'd be interested in playing Belle on a national tour of Disney's *Beauty and the Beast* and her reaction matched mine: "Not another tour."

"What about Broadway?" she asked.

Disney was the star of Disney, so this was new by its Broadway standards. I was hired to succeed the incredible, very kind Kerry Butler as Belle, and that September, following two weeks of rehearsals, my nine-month run began.

Belle was a spunky, gutsy girl who wanted more than just her provincial life. Audiences picked up on the energy and I was in my element. But while I was now earning considerably more than I had in *Grease*, the star treatment didn't extend to the dressing room I was given, which was tiny and right off the side of the stage. And this is where Mom, who'd already helped shake things up in terms of my casting, broke down another door.

"We need a bigger dressing room to entertain VIP guests," she stated on my behalf.

Very often, my mom and I fought for the bare minimum. I never asked for anything gratuitous, but it was kind of like, *If you're hiring me to do all the things I do and bring all the things I will bring, you need to find me a bigger, better dressing room—not because I need to run laps inside it, but because you're going to want me to entertain as your star. Let's do this right.*

Meanwhile, stage management didn't think I was doing it right—and I was given a note that said, "Deb, you're getting a little too rock 'n' roll with your body language on 'Be Our Guest.'"

Dancing with silverware lit me up. What can I say? The pop girl was getting picked on. "Belle *is* rock 'n' roll," I fired back. "That's the whole point of doing this show in a new time."

This was a battle I would always fight. Bring someone to the table for a specific and unique quality, then try to keep them neatly in a box? I was pretty good at walking that line, so I straight-toned it up and kept my movements crisp as well as a bit smaller.

Eventually realizing how well a pop personality fared in a Broadway show, the producers would start taking more chances—such as casting Toni Braxton as the female lead once my run was over in June of '98. That did my heart good. I didn't always win the battles, but the next girl had that much more freedom. Not only did they let Toni carpet the floors and paint the walls of the dressing room that Mom had gone to bat for, they also let her change the keys to suit her voice.

The top Disney brass thanked Richard Jay-Alexander, who took the chance on me and set the stage, not only for putting pop vocalists into Broadway roles but also in the color-blind casting of Ricky Martin, Shanice, Lea Salonga, and Melba Moore—and Disney followed suit. Little girls of every ethnic background should see themselves represented as Disney princesses and ingenues. Together, we were all breaking ground.

Oh, the Great White Way, with front-row seats at the Tonys, getting dragged around the stage by my dear friend Marc Kudisch (whom I'd met through Chris Bruno) as Gaston, and then by Chris Monteleone, also a supportive friend to this day! The pop-culture tides were turning, with an invite to perform at the Macy's Thanksgiving Day Parade. Sharing a trailer with five cute up-and-coming boybanders called The Backstreet Boys, one of whom—Howie D—I'd go on to briefly date, was a fun surprise! I'd pop over to my mom's Midtown apartment she shared with David Reichman, her soon-to-be husband—who, not too long after, would become her ex-husband—for a home-cooked meal. It was a very cool time, one that allowed me to figure out how to have some semblance of a life—with the new guy who was now a part of it.

I first met entertainment reporter Todd Newton when he interviewed me on the red carpet at the press opening of *The Lion King*. We had instant chemistry—and he had all-American good looks in addition to being affable, charming, witty, and direct in a way that was refreshing, not aggressive. This led to a really fantastic relationship, one of my faves ever.

Once, when I had some time off following eight shows in five days, Todd was flying back to LA and I escorted him to the airport and through TSA during an era when that didn't require a ticket.

"Surprise! I'm coming with you!"

That's how crazy-spontaneous I am. I had bought a ticket to hop on the plane with him and Todd loved it.

He'd come to visit as often as he could and we had a blast traipsing around the city together. When we were apart, I also enjoyed our routine of phoning each other every night after the show. Oh, how I long for the days before text messaging, when people spoke in real time. There were also love notes via fax. He was a great gift giver, and one of my favorites was an antique music stand that I still have in my Liberace piano room . . . despite Todd suddenly falling off the radar, breaking our beautiful rhythm when seemingly everything was in a really fantastic place for both of us.

There we were, talking marriage, naming the kids, and then one night he just disappeared. He hosted a radio show, and afterward he normally called me, but not on this night . . . or any of the days to come. He went MIA and I couldn't get hold of him. It was so strange.

I remember feeling like I had missed something. I'd been blindsided. The '90s version of "ghosted." I contacted a buddy of Todd's to make sure nothing bad had happened. That's how out of character the silence was. It was that moment where I felt like the murmurings behind the scenes could have seen me labeled a "crazy girl." This thing where a woman is heavily courted and made to feel safe in a consistent relationship, and then, suddenly, the guy changes direction without explanation, driving her to question things. This still happens to me today. And although I'm often guilty of ignoring red flags, this is a continuing narrative that unfortunately never seems to go out of style.

Confiding in my Beast Chuck Wagner in the library scene of *Beauty and the Beast* while our backs were to the audience, I felt utterly despondent. He suggested I was being a bit dramatic, but I literally didn't know how I would go on without answers or closure—and, feeling completely wrung out and heartbroken, I lost a ton of weight from the crying during this stressful time. I'd visualize putting my issues in the prop basket in the wings before going on to perform. But as I've learned, it's hard to mind-over-matter matters of the heart.

Alas, I didn't go on for act 2 of a performance the week it ended because I was so physically weak and unsteady. Stage management felt I'd go toppling down the castle stairs.

Eventually Todd would face me, though he couldn't articulate why he needed to walk away when I asked for some sort of closure. He has since opened up about not really being in the place I was in at that time. This would be a recurring theme. I'm told I am "too real-deal." I can say this: What you see is what you get and I'm definitely full-on when I'm into someone.

Todd and I have talked about revisiting the relationship a couple of times, but for some reason it doesn't feel right these days.

You know people move on
You don't love them back, one day they're gone
Not the story that you want to hear
*But love don't go, Yeah, well, maybe next year.**

It's a tricky thing to reset and regain the hopefulness I once had if someone walks away. Once I imprint a memory of rejection and break that sweet flow, I might never be able to come back.

I'm glad to say Todd and I are now great friends, but his disappearing during the run of *Beauty and the Beast* really did a number on me. When I invest, I invest.

After many sleepless nights trying to figure out what went wrong, I started to move on and find inner peace again, which was a good thing. I'd soon need all the sleep and stamina I could get, as I would be rolling right into another great adventure, this time with one of Broadway's most infamous leading ladies.

Here she is, boys! Here she is, world!

---

* "Strings" by Deborah Ann Gibson. Copyright © 2021 by Birdsong Publishing (ASCAP). Used by permission. All rights reserved.

Chapter Nine

SING OUT, LOUISE!

My good friends know I am super particular when it comes to venturing out in the evenings. When not touring, I tend to keep farmer's hours—early to bed, early to rise—but this last-minute invite from my friend Jason Feinberg to go to Nobu with his brother and sister-in-law was just perfect to get me out of the RV and dressed up to join "young hip America."

There we were, kibitzing over the fact that when Stewie sang "Lost in Your Eyes" for his *American Idol* audition on *Family Guy*, I was suddenly pop culture royalty in *Jason's* eyes! The laughter was escalating when suddenly...

"Hey, look, there's Kris Jenner."

He spotted her instantly from his days of interviewing her on E!

I immediately recalled how kind Kris was to me when, in 2006, she and the pre-fame Kardashian girls were in a dressing room down the hall from mine while pre-Caitlyn Bruce competed against me and

Kurt Browning on Fox's *Skating with Celebrities*. Kris had the utmost respect for my mom, even referring to her a time or two as "the original momager" in the media. So I promptly went over to her table and we had a lovely chat.

The momager energy is one that immediately resonates with me. It's a frequency I know. There's a toughness and a quality about a momager that is at once strong, vulnerable, and, in a way, longing to let down the hard exterior when in the presence of someone who doesn't demand it. This was that moment, and we had a tender chat about the loss of my mom as well as the circumstances surrounding it. This instantly brought Mama to life—and reminded me of another famous mother, Mama Rose.

Toward the end of my run in *Beauty and the Beast*, I heard about a new production of *Gypsy* at the Paper Mill Playhouse in Millburn, New Jersey, where high-caliber actors work for scale and the productions are Broadway-quality. You may recall my playing both Baby June and Baby Louise at different times in my childhood, and I was even considered for the Bette Midler TV version in my twenties. But I was about to have the time of my life playing one of the greatest characters in theater history, opposite one of the greatest stars in theater history, Betty Buckley. Before I go there, let me set the stage . . .

Known as a burlesque queen, Louise—aka Gypsy Rose Lee—started out as a very awkward tomboy, famously playing the back end of a cow to the precocious, baton-twirling, high-kicking, crinoline-wearing, banana-curled Baby June. I had therefore auditioned with the tomboy vibe, wearing jeans and a flannel shirt. Always looking to feed my performance even in an audition setting, I never felt funny about doing whatever I had to do. So I brought along a huge bag of stuffed animals to sing "Little Lamb," before taking out the braids, shaking out my hair, throwing on heels, and removing the young Louise getup to reveal the bustier bodysuit that had been custom-made for my "Losin' Myself" video's striptease scene.

My mentality has always been to make sure I can look back and say, *I gave it everything I had.* That makes it easier to deal with disappointment and move on. It also makes auditioning more fun and I get to keep that expansive experience, which, as you know by now, I'm a fan of in every aspect of my life. Now my time had come and the creative team behind the Paper Mill Playhouse version of *Gypsy* decided to check me out.

On May 10, 1998, after hearing the legit side of my voice while seeing me play the spunky down-home Belle in *Beauty and the Beast*, they also attended the midnight performance of the Broadway Bares charity event, benefiting the Broadway Cares/Equity Fights AIDS organization. Well, my burlesque-style striptease coupled with what they'd heard as Belle sealed the deal: Without auditioning, I was cast in the title role of *Gypsy* . . . starring Betty Buckley as Mama Rose.

Signing on to do that show was a real moment in my career. Known as a pop star, I'd still been trying to prove myself in the legit theater despite my history in the business. Now, cast in this prestigious production, I felt validated. The rehearsals began that August, and while I had already been working hard with voice teacher Joan to refine my "Little Lamb," the big, belty "Let Me Entertain You" was more innate to who I am—and always fun for me because my pop edge and grit could come through.

Betty, already celebrated for her Grizabella in the original Broadway production of *Cats* as well as for her Norma Desmond in *Sunset Boulevard*, was poised, professional, and incredibly intense. At the same time, here I was, this carefree, well-prepared twenty-eight-year-old, driving to and from New Jersey in her little red Mercedes convertible and dating a sharp, hot New York TV executive named Mark, loving how everything was in a nice flow.

Rehearsals of the earlier scenes didn't demand much of me as an actress, and in regional theater there isn't a lot of time to get a show on its feet. So, by the time we got to the mother-daughter relationship, which is the centerpiece of the story, there was a lot of pressure to deliver and expectations were high.

One day in rehearsal, Betty said, "I don't think you understand what this is like for me, Deb. I feel like the quarterback of this team!"

The director, Mark Waldrop, called a break.

"*I* don't know what it's *like*?" I asked him. "Having headlined at Madison Square Garden, I know *exactly* what it's like."

I was offended and hurt. But I found out what was behind Betty's intensity soon enough. During the break, she and I ended up in the ladies' room. Looking me straight in the eye and softening, she said, "Just put yourself in my hands. Trust me."

I haven't been acting nearly as long as this woman has, I remember thinking.

Little did I know that Betty was trying to help me reveal what was at the heart of me being perfect to play the part of Louise. Which was that *I had that mother.* Betty was trying to jump-start the process of my truest connection to the role and I—though I didn't know it at the time—was resisting.

"Make no mistake, Deb, Diane Gibson is a stage mother," she would say.

She, too, had had a critical mother living vicariously through her and she recognized this as a way to draw a parallel to help me tap into my connection to our characters' very complex dynamic. In hindsight, it's amazing that Betty took the time and care to help mold me. It is a gift I have taken with me.

Recalling how fiercely I'd defend my mother, Betty recently shed some light on her comment and how she immediately sensed I was very restrained in rehearsals because I was afraid of hurting Mom. This protectiveness was keeping me from letting it rip in the big dressing-room scene where Mama Rose disregards the sign that says "The Mother of Miss Gypsy Rose Lee is not allowed backstage at this theater." I hadn't yet gotten to the place in my life where Diane and I parted ways in business. But, with Betty's guidance, I accessed those emotions that helped me come into my own as an actress.

No matter how much acting I had done, in certain people's eyes I'd always be the pop star who'd come into the theater world. So in her way, Betty was saying, *Let go, be vulnerable, and I will help you grow and evolve if you let me.*

So I did. I can see now that Betty was lovingly pushing me into my own truth by design so we could create the authentic mother-daughter duo who'd bring truth to our version of *Gypsy*. Betty can read people with a depth of awareness and is an actual acting teacher with a masterful knowledge of psychology. I feel like this is part of an ongoing theme in my life, to attract tough love in a desire to elevate, and this would be a turning point for me as an actress. Betty will forever be credited as an important mentor.

After asking Betty and me to stay late, the director had us do an exercise around a line of dialogue in the big dressing-room scene where Mama Rose tells Louise, "You know what you are to them? A circus freak! This year's novelty act!"

Mark had us play verbal tennis with the phrase *circus freak*, getting out all our angst in this beautiful way to bond and grow. It translated to what people saw onstage. Ever the pop-music people-pleaser, I experienced a newfound freedom. For her part, Betty was out for the good of the character and the show. I was excited to learn how to get deeper into my work.

A couple of days later, I bought everyone who'd been in that room—Betty, Mark, the assistant director Patrick, and myself—baseball hats with CIRCUS FREAK on them. It was monumental.

I've now been there myself, because it *is* different in your twenties than in your fifties when the stakes are high. The longer you're in the business, the higher the expectations; when you're Betty Buckley playing Mama Rose and theater is your life, it doesn't get any more important than that.

Fans were flying in from all over the world for our critically acclaimed production. Every time she performed "Everything's Coming Up Roses," maneuvering me around the stage in my pre-burlesque tomboy getup with braids and newsboy cap, I witnessed the great Betty Buckley in action up close and as personal as it gets. We even got unprecedented standing ovations in the middle of the show—several of them a night.

I had never seen anybody cry and sing at the same time. I didn't know that was humanly possible. A lot of people have a perception about how they would play Mama Rose: Keep on the suit of armor while the emotion is bubbling underneath. Well, Betty was wiping away actual tears with the palm of her hand while belting at the top of her range. And she was so visceral, it was awe-inspiring. This was real emotion and I'd forever hold it as the high bar for all acting—especially in the theater, where the line between feeling and projecting is thin and separates the good from the spectacular.

Women have to be tough in this business, but Betty has a wonderful soft side. We share a love of advocating for animals . . . and of our voice teacher Joan, whom I remember telling before a lesson, "I have to cry, but I can't cry because I have to sing tonight."

"You can't sing if you *don't* cry," she replied. "You have to release all that emotion, Deb."

Betty showed me that firsthand, but I had yet to integrate it into my life and work.

I came from the teen-pop school of never letting people see me being emotional. There to sing "Shake Your Love" and make people happy, I was supposed to be poised and put on my own little suit of armor because everyone was happier when they thought I was fine. Now, however, there were people in my life saying, "No, you're supposed to break away from that."

I was starting to learn that vulnerability was a superpower.

One of the fascinations I've had with doing regional theater is that we're allowed to experiment more. Doing *Gypsy* without being cast on Broadway or in the movie, I was permitted to play Louise outside of the rigid parameters, and the result was that Betty and I were pretty rock 'n' roll in terms of our visceral interpretations. That was life-altering for me.

The vaudeville days in *Gypsy* transported me back to being in the trenches with Mom, doing the club dates, doing the Orpheum Circuit in East LA. Rose's toughness also reminded me of her. When Rose turns and says, "You know, I could have been bigger than *all* of you," that could have been my mother; had Diane been able to sing and dance, she probably would have been bigger than me because she had such a presence. Isn't it amazing how art sometimes really does imitate life? I'd love to play Mama Rose someday. And I would definitely seek out a production that allows me the freedom to come from the inside out and put a new spin on it. Maybe Betty can direct it!

I gleefully returned to the Paper Mill Playhouse to lead the cast as the Narrator in *Joseph and the Amazing Technicolor Dreamcoat*. That was the kickoff to a national tour that lasted nine months and took us into the new millennium. It was so fitting to belt out the show's theme of turning visions into reality, shades of "Only in My Dreams."

Strange as it seems, there's been a run of crazy dreams...

Joseph's brothers were played by seven of Alan Osmond's eight sons; David, the eighth son, was doing Mormon missionary work in Spain, and as his brothers weren't supposed to phone him there and distract him from his mission, I'd use my calling card to circumvent the rules and help my adopted brothers. That's how I got to know all eight boys, bonding with the ones on the tour and the one who wasn't.

Patrick Cassidy played Joseph, and after we got past some tension at the urging of his mom, Shirley Jones, we became great friends. His Joseph was beloved by audiences and his fellow castmates. So... there were Osmonds, a Cassidy, and a Gibson in the same cast, providing teen-idol lineage down the years. And we had a lot of fun. It was a hard show to sing, but, in great vocal shape following *Beauty* and *Gypsy*, I was able to let my hair down a little on that tour. Which was good, since I intended to keep doing touring theater and check off all the remaining ingenue roles I wanted to play now that I was in my thirties.

Theater, theater, theater—I couldn't get enough, playing all these roles I had dreamt of as a little girl and getting compensated nicely, which was a great thing, considering I'd be ready to do my pop-music thing again and fund it all myself. Doing touring theater, while good for the soul and my bottom line, didn't translate to anything in terms of the pop-culture landscape, and it wasn't elevating me in any way career-wise.

Even though I was doing cool things like duetting with acclaimed vocalist Peabo Bryson, I needed to create my own music again. So during the summer of 2000, I recorded my seventh studio album, *M.Y.O.B.*, with a title track written by Billy and Bobby, the Alessi Brothers. Recording a new song by outside songwriters was something I had never done, but I loved this funky, playful, true original.

I cowrote "My Secret" and "Wishing You Were Here" with my gay friend/former boyfriend (all us pop divas have at least one!) Jerry Sharell; "Down That Road" and "What Part of No" were collabs with Gary Haase. I also wrote "What You Want" with Rudy Haeusermann and "The One" with Chynna Phillips, my Upper West Side neighbor, with her hubby, Billy Baldwin, popping in and out to make sure we were hydrated and to hear our progress. Sweet times. There was even a tribal techno dance remake of "Knock Three Times" that found me duetting with the legend himself, Tony Orlando.

Though Tony was happily married to Francine, I think it's safe to say Mom had a big crush on him. The two of them had such a great friendship. I was always asking him, "Can't you be my stepdad?" He is an awesome guy. And although the album, released on my own Golden Egg Records label, again failed to chart, it garnered positive reviews, including that by AllMusic's Peter Fawthrop. Telling listeners to brace themselves for a thirty-year-old '80s teen idol who was now following the trends of her 2000s successors, he pointed out that "if anyone other than Gibson were singing this material, exactly as she sings it here, it would make the Top Ten. You get the feeling that no big label or producer wants to lay their hands on jump-starting an old career when there are so many new faces (and lesser talents) to scout."

As you can see, this was an ongoing theme: A select few people would get it while I'd essentially exhaust myself doing my best work in a vacuum. I was always having to prove myself. Although I didn't mind that part, I felt like I was banging my head against a brick wall trying to change people's perceptions. And that was not how I wanted to spend my time and energy.

Thankfully, the theater was still calling my name. In October 2000, I signed on to play the lead opposite Eartha Kitt's Fairy Godmother in a national tour of Rodgers & Hammerstein's *Cinderella*. Directed in a really inspired, avant-garde way by Gabriel Barr, it was an amazing four-month experience. Eartha was seventy-three at the time and still kicking her leg over her head; she'd wake up early every morning to put in a couple of hours at the gym. The ensemble boys were just trying to keep up with her. And I remember that fabulous way she spoke, rolling her *r*'s when she'd say, "The earrrly birrrd gets the worrrm."

"I'm not putting the Catwoman *purrrr* in the show," she initially insisted. However, after she tried it once and it got a laugh, she used it *everrrywhere*.

"As if life isn't sweet enough in fairty-tale fantasyland," I used to joke.

I mean, there's nothing better than dancing with a spatula and a whisk to take the seriousness out of life, right? Now, in *Cinderella*, I may have topped that fantastical experience with these beautiful puppet mice crawling on my shoulders while I sang. That was great, as was waltzing nightly with my dashing Prince and friend Paolo Montalban. January 2001 was the end of my run, but I was psyched to be asked to rejoin the tour that July for three weeks after Jamie-Lynn Sigler left the company due to health reasons.

On August 16, four days after my final *Cinderella* performance, I capitalized on an opportunity to indulge my pop side by appearing as a special guest for twelve days of stadium shows on *NSYNC's Pop-Odyssey tour. Always a singer-songwriter at heart, I wanted to play my own piano. So when the boys' management declared I was a "track act"—"We're not traveling with her grand piano for one song; that's ridiculous"—Lance Bass went to bat for me: "You give her whatever the fuck she wants." He and I have been friends ever since.

Joey Fatone could be seen peering out from behind the side stage speaker to watch my set. He, too, is a forever friend and it was a really sweet time; I even saw my longtime Debhead turned head of merch design Jourdyn meet her now-wife Daisy while they were both part of my street team. I love that my career experiences are sprinkled with these memories that are as important as—or more important than—what happened onstage. Real lives are what I care about, and music indeed makes people come together.

Around this time, Heather left the fold because, feeling like she'd learned all she could from a management perspective, her relationship with Diane was getting a bit strained. She also wanted to try different things, such as getting married and having a family. That was a loss for our team. There was a lot of change and loss at that time, including the loss of my grandmother.

She had gone into the hospital shortly after seeing me in *Beauty and the Beast* and had never returned home. Instead, she ended up in the same assisted-living facility where Grandpa had been since being diagnosed with Alzheimer's at the age of sixty-five. My sisters and I had always been close to Mom's parents, especially because we never knew Dad's. They lived ten minutes from our home, so we'd see them all the time and we were with them for all the holidays; we spent Christmas Eves and many a New Year's Eve at their house.

During the last afternoon of 2001, we got the call that Grandma was about to pass. My sweet friend Jonathan Kanterman—who would soon become my boyfriend—especially showed such a caring side in this moment. Just before midnight, he drove me to the family gathering at the assisted-living facility on Long Island, where we played Andrea Bocelli's music because Josephine loved him so much. Sisters, cousins, Mom, my aunt and uncle . . . everyone who could make it to her bedside did.

It was moments like this one that made me realize we were a tight-knit group even though we were all adults off and running in different directions. We had such a strong family foundation from childhood; the gang would get together to come see my shows and we'd try to find each other for the holidays. Dad often got the short end of the stick, as our family was so much about Mom's side, but in these later years we've been sure to spend quality time with him as well. These cozy times are woven into the fabric of who I am. I always could and still can let down my guard and be just Deborah around my relatives.

I was holding my grandmother's hand when she took her last breath during the early hours of New Year's Day. She was seventy-six. The women in our family have always been powerful manifesters, and this was the ultimate example: Grandma scripting her exit to take place immediately after New Year's Eve, her favorite holiday, when she loved getting everyone together.

Soon after, I also lost my first instrumental voice teacher and friend, Guen, to pneumonia. Grandpa lived until June 2004, but without a doubt, this was the beginning of the end of an era—which was why I was so happy to have a little time to travel for pleasure in the early 2000s between stints in musicals.

One such trip was to visit and cowrite songs with my old friend Jerry Sharell. We had so many laughs that autumn in 2001, and we didn't want the party to end. Whenever we got together, Jerry would sing out Ahmet's favorite line—"Get the pen!"—when inspired to write a song . . . but as Cher. His Cher impersonations were the best, bar none, complete with a "Whoaaaaa" and a hair flick after every sentence. My other favorite Jer impersonation was of his younger self asking his mother, "What didn't you know?" in reference to his *Yentl* poster on the wall/coming-out moment. So we went to bed in fits of laughter the night before I was to head back to NYC, where I was living in Gramercy Park.

I was waiting for my car service to arrive the next morning when my mother called. "Deborah," she said in her usual hushed, dramatic tone. Little did I know, this time it was warranted. "The country is under attack. Turn on the TV."

It was wild to think I would have been heading to the airport to take a flight from the West Coast to the East Coast on this very day. The tragedy was incomprehensible and it's still hard to process as a New Yorker—and just as a human being. Those images are ingrained in all of us forever.

I couldn't go back right away, as they were using the streets surrounding my apartment building as a morgue. New York was part of the fabric of my very being, its people the stitches that held me together and added the pops of color. I don't know who I'd be today without bento boxes and gossip sessions with Orfeh; Bruce Wayne coming to do my glam for an event and bringing me a coffee from the cart on the corner at five a.m.; A. J. Hammer meeting me at Columbus Bakery; and texting Kudisch to meet me on his break from rehearsal for a walk around Central Park.

If 9/11 taught us anything, it's that life is fragile and unpredictable. So now more than ever, I was grateful to be surrounded by people who brought deep meaning to my life.

It was at the North Shore Music Theatre in Beverly, Massachusetts, in late October 2002, that I met one of my best friends, dancer-choreographer Eddie Bennett, while starring as the merry murderess Velma Kelly in the Kander and Ebb musical *Chicago*. He was eating outdoors with the cast on a lunch break and someone who wasn't familiar with my music said, "What does she sing again?" and Eddie climbed onto the picnic table to perform a mini-concert of all the songs from *Electric Youth*, as well as some from *Out of the Blue*. By the time he walked indoors, I had already caught wind that he had done this unbelievable homage to my songs.

"What's your favorite song of mine?" I asked him.

"'We Could Be Together.'"

That was also a favorite of mine. So I pulled Eddie into a little backstage rehearsal room that had a piano. It was a fall day, and the blazing colors of yellow, orange, and red leaves were streaming through the window—a very vivid East Coast scene. I sang and played "We Could Be Together" as he leaned up against the piano, echoing those precious moments when, as a kid, I'd perform my music for the family in the living room of our Long Island home. Eddie still talks about this particular moment when the universe introduced us and appeared to be telling him, *She's gonna be more than just a work buddy, she's gonna be a lifelong friend.*

The universe was so right.

While starring in *Beauty and the Beast*, I had auditioned for *Chicago* on Broadway. Again, pop-culture names had never been hired for that show, but in this case, the Weisslers, who were producing, knew me from our *Grease* days. So they put me through a three-month training process with their dance captain Lillie Kae Stevens—I was working with her three to five hours a day and doing *Beauty* at night—which implied they were grooming me to take over the role of Velma.

I was in that flow where I had boundless energy. If I was focused on something, I didn't run out of steam, *period*. All the yoga classes and weight training and even gymnastics lessons here and there helped me in this very physical undertaking. I prepared hard, doing cartwheels in high heels, and learned all the nuances of Bob Fosse's original choreography, after which I was put through a two-day, two-part audition so

ETERNALLY ELECTRIC

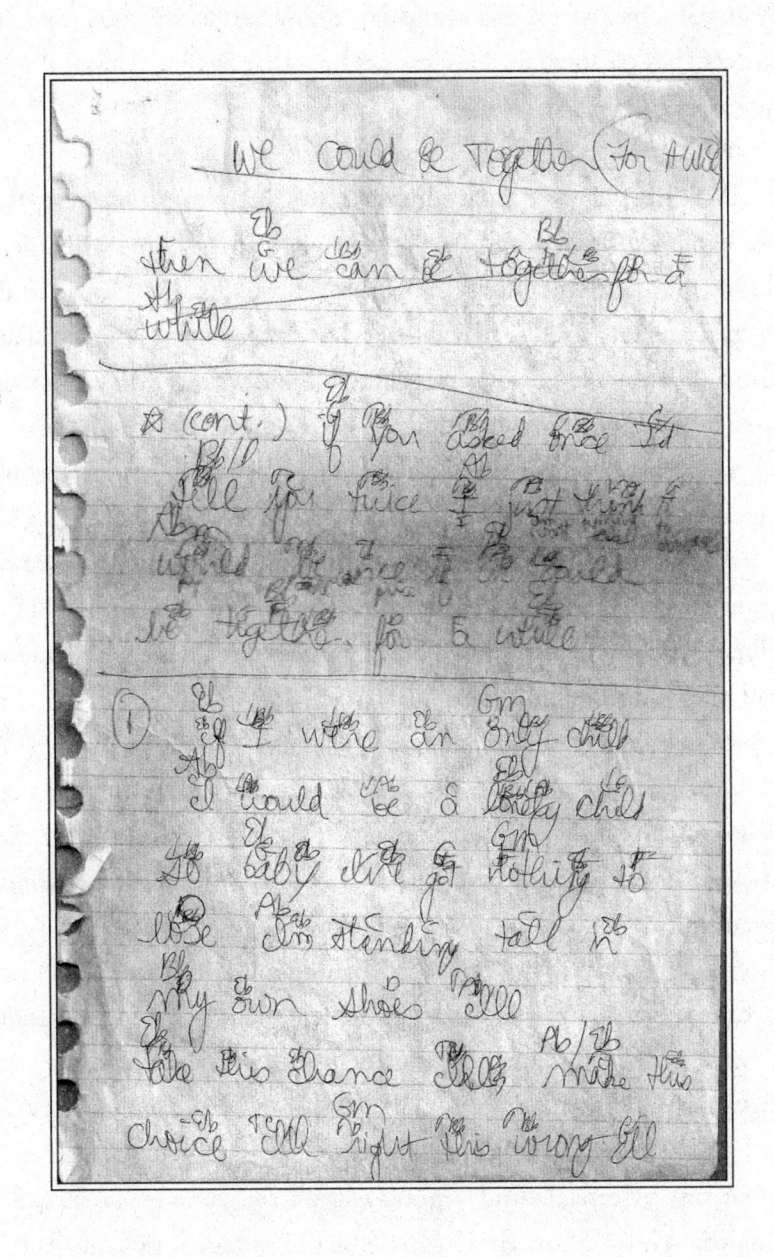

the creative team could see me sing, dance, act, and take direction from Walter Bobbie. At the end of the day, all my hard work and attention to detail boiled down to "I just can't believe that Debbie Gibson would murder somebody."

Huh?!?

At least, that was the feedback passed along to me through the grapevine. At one point, in character, I was so overcome with angst during the audition, in the scene where Velma talks about Roxie stealing her publicity and her trial and her shoes, I aggressively threw a chair across the room. I know when I suck and I know when I do something special, and in the moment, it might have been the thought of the stolen shoes that got me. I kid. But seriously, I was, at the very least, quite capable and directable.

The bottom line was that they didn't want me and no amount of hoop-jumping was gonna change their minds. You thought the "Hot Honey Rag" was a popular number? I was about to do my most famous and finely honed dance... You guessed it: *The Pivot!*

Once again, on with the show!

I searched for a theater that might welcome me and my spin on Velma and found a home in the perfect production for a short run just outside of Boston. It was so much fun doing theater in the round. There's nowhere to hide; you're visible at all times—and that's what is thrilling about it. Oh my God, I'm laughing thinking about one of my favorite memories: Mom sitting in the front row, filming everything with my little 8 mm camera, then denying it was her when people said they saw what she was doing.

"Who, me?" She didn't break a sweat. She had a great poker face.

It was hysterical. And *Chicago* was an awesome experience. So after that North Shore theater run ended, I spent a lot of time auditioning for other shows—including reading opposite the brilliant Philip Seymour Hoffman, and Kander and Ebb's *And the World Goes 'Round*. Not because I was dying to do a musical revue; I just needed to be seen by the powers that be at the Roundabout Theatre Company so my number would eventually come up to play Sally Bowles in their exquisite Broadway revival of *Cabaret*. As I felt they had no way of knowing that my energy was grounded and gritty, it was up to me to show them.

I worked backward from my goal, but I'm conditioned for things not to pan out. So imagine my surprise when, sitting at lunch with Culture Club owner and dear, amazing, New York-to-the-core friend Bobby Watman, my phone rang. It was Mom.

"The Roundabout Theatre Company wants to know if you'll go see *Cabaret* tonight at Studio 54 and then decide if you want to play Sally. If you do, they're handing you a script; you'd start rehearsals tomorrow and open in two weeks. They've tried to use an unknown as Sally and it's not working. As the Emcee, Neil Patrick Harris is fabulous and sells tickets, but everyone's asking, 'Who's Sally?'"

Oh my God!

They wanted a pop-culture name but also one who could legitimately play the role.

My strategy worked, and that night, I did indeed go to see *Cabaret* and picked up the script. The three months of prep and two days of auditioning for *Chicago* versus being entrusted with this coveted role—unproven and in only two weeks—was reassuring. I guess some things are meant to be. I was their go-to girl and I wouldn't let them down. Physically, mentally, and vocally ready, I started rehearsals the following day while drilling the choreography at night in my apartment and doing daily yoga to stay open, limber, and focused. Could I pull this off in two weeks? I was nervous, but I thought, *I am nothing if not bold.* Just like Sally Bowles herself.

That's what I did, and the results validated one of my favorite quotes: "Luck is what happens when preparation meets opportunity."* The creative team put me into the seamless machinery they had going and taught me the choreography, dialect, and music. Though the show's director, Rob Marshall, worked with me for only a day, he imparted genius advice and encouragement about trusting my own instincts and following them to the ends of the earth. I'd carry that with me through my life and career.

There were a lot of layers to this role and I had to ask the team putting me into the show how to convincingly look like I was doing cocaine as Sally, as I had never been exposed to it in real life. I know this may sound kind of shocking for someone who went to music industry parties so young, but I always purposely gave off a certain air that let people know I wasn't there to go down that road.

Working with Neil Patrick Harris after getting to know him a bit through my dear friends Ray Garcia and Sylvia MacCalla when he and I visited the national tour of *Rent* was a really sweet experience. NPH and I duetted on "Little Fall of Rain" back then, around an upright piano in Ray and Syl's Gainsborough Street apartment in Boston, and I got to witness his desire to do Broadway in such a unique way. So, now sharing the stage and watching his meticulous attention to detail and beautiful abandon in the role of the Emcee warmed my heart.

During the run of the show, NPH hosted the best game nights with fellow actor Brandon Wardell, which became a Broadway community tradition. When Neil's man, David Burtka, came on the scene

---

* *Attributed to the Roman philosopher Lucius Annaeus Seneca.*

during this run, I was super happy for him and have loved watching them build their family over the years.

Jonathan was super supportive of me and he was often at the performances. He and I did casual NYC things, like grabbing wonton soup for lunch and seeing a movie on my day off. I could always be my full self with him in my life and I loved hanging out with his friends at Shabbat dinners and learning about Jewish culture. A far cry from my days of accidentally bringing two dozen Dunkin' Donuts to Mike Provenz's family's seder in the '80s.

Ahmet Ertegun graced me with his presence in the audience and floored me postshow by saying, "Darling, you've become so many things." Quite a wonderful compliment from this legend who no longer had a vested interest in me. He encouraged me once again, saying, "Come up to the office and play me what you've been composing. If you'd like, I'll give you my feedback."

I remember playing him a song called "In Blue" from *M.Y.O.B.* that I had submitted to Anita Baker.

I guess he likes me in blue
*Those tears they make him feel like a man.**

"That is a magical lyric," Ahmet told me. "You're such a competent, capable composer, you will always come up with a good song. But a magical line is what makes that song a hit, what makes it extraspecial."

He was trying to say, *Keep going for the magic, girl. Don't ever sell yourself short.*

---

* "In Blue" by Deborah Ann Gibson. Copyright © 2001 by Possibilities Publishing Inc. Used by permission. All rights reserved.

It was time to make magic by realizing another lifelong dream: making a Broadway record.

Colored Lights: The Broadway Album found me performing music from *Gypsy, Les Miz, Shall We Dance, Funny Girl,* and *Flower Drum Song,* to name a few. Even my original song "Sex" from the musical version of *Skirts* that I was developing with the original screenwriters, Hillary and Katie, made the cut. Featuring stellar orchestrations by Ron Abel, Steve Orich, and Lanny Meyers, the album introduced me as a theatrical artist to all who hadn't seen me in that setting—and it would be my last US release for eighteen years. And *Cabaret* would be my last Broadway show in over two decades... and counting.

After my four-month run in *Cabaret,* I began my stint on *American Juniors,* a spinoff of the hugely popular talent show *American Idol,* with fellow judge Gladys Knight and host Ryan Seacrest, who, contrary to tabloid fodder, I did *not* date at the time. Filmed in LA, the show focused on creating a vocal act composed of the five best contestants, featuring a then unknown Lucy Hale. But there was no follow-through with the group postshow, so that was the end of that. Still not ready to hang up my black shoes with the rhinestone buckles, I commuted back and forth to Oklahoma City to play Velma one more time!

I had split from Jonathan upon leaving New York. After seriously contemplating converting to Judaism to fit into his world, I realized the relationship lacked the passion it needed to endure and there was nothing keeping me there anymore, despite the fact that the tabloids had us heading to the altar. We were never actually engaged.

ETERNALLY ELECTRIC

Can it stay so good forever in time?
I've always felt the rhythm
*What happens when there's no more rhyme?**

My relationship with Jonathan and NYC had run its course. Now was the time for me to explore what LA and this new chapter had in store. One thing I knew for sure: It was time to break free of everyone and everything. And break free I did!

Can you feel the genuine love?
Ahmet and me sharing a moment.

---

* *"No More Rhyme" by Deborah Gibson. Copyright © 1989 by Music Sales Corporation (ASCAP). International Copyright Secured. Used by permission. All rights reserved.*

Chapter Ten

MS. NAKED VOCALIST

I landed in a retro West Hollywood townhome from the 1920s that was so old, it didn't even have a dishwasher. That suited me just fine because, along with being the Queen of Pivoting, I was the Queen of Takeout!

I recall puttering around in my PJs one morning with my dogs Rosie and Daisy when Mom called to say hello and go over business stuff. On this particular call, she quipped, "Okay, ready to talk showbiz? As in, are you ready to show your biz?"

I instantly knew what she was asking. You see, *Playboy* called us like clockwork about every two years or so, asking if I would like to do a cover and a celebrity pictorial, and up to that point, I had declined. When the calls started, soon after my eighteenth birthday, I wasn't yet comfortable in my own skin. Then it became a matter of not trying too hard to be like, *Oh, look at me, I'm all grown up and a woman now because I'm doing a naked shoot.* But by the time I reached age thirty-four, I had done my fair share of musicals where I was baring both my soul and my body to a degree—not in the same way I would in *Playboy*, but pretty close.

At this point in my life, I was super comfortable in my skin and ready to experience this iconic moment. So, I was flattered by the call and also had a kind of wink-and-a-smile attitude about it. Once my sisters reassured me my nieces and nephews wouldn't be scarred for life by Aunt Deborah's naked photos, it excited me more than it scared me. But as with everything I take on—or, in this case, take *off*—I knew I wanted to look and feel my best, so I sought out one of the most popular trainers in Los Angeles, Gunnar Peterson.

Unlike during my Radu days, I didn't diet to any extreme degree and I didn't train to the point of exhaustion. I thought, *If I'm toned but a little soft and have that glow that comes with the endorphin high of working out and taking care of myself, mission accomplished.* I even continued dyeing my own hair, something I often do now—an accessible bottle-blonde girl next door with an aspirational wardrobe.

Wait, a wardrobe for a nude photo shoot? Yup! Just like the cartwheels and the lounge chair and producing "Foolish Beat," I was insistent on doing it *my way*. Although I went into a zone of extreme focus, as I always do for all professional endeavors, I knew I needed some specific energy and support to make me feel my most at home on the set. So I rang up Marissa, Ray, and Stepp, and they jumped at the chance to be my "emotional fluffers."

Blasting music, we made a party of it. And of course, Mom was there as both manager and mother. Though unorthodox to have one's mother at a *Playboy* shoot, we had such a deep professional understanding of each other that she knew, once I committed to

ETERNALLY ELECTRIC

doing something, it was her job to support me 100 percent. My inner circle also made sure my body angles were flattering, my cheeks—*all* of them—were flushed and perky, and my facial expressions were authentic and strong. All in all, I had an absolute blast, and it shows.

I knew it was going to be a fulfilling artistic adventure with famed photographer Guido Argentini, whom I hand-picked, and OG hair guru Victor Vidal, who loved seeing me all the way from teen stardom to this very womanly moment.

"This is the highest clothing budget we've ever had for a naked photo shoot!" I was told.

I always thought a little peekaboo was sexier than being blatant about it.

After Hef and his people decided I didn't show enough, they exploited a loophole in the contract. I'd been led to believe that I would definitely be the cover girl; I hadn't waited sixteen years to do something this provocative, only to be relegated to the inner pages. But alas, the March 2005 issue had me on the inside of a *pullout* cover to fulfill their legal obligation. They felt readers would have been disappointed if I was on the cover but wasn't doing the most explicit kind of pictorial.

Hugh Hefner later admitted he regretted that move, as featuring me prominently would have boosted sales. Celebrities known for other things showing anything at all was worth the price of the magazine, and those parameters were loosened. Once again, guinea pig/pioneer. Still, I'm so proud of that theatrical, elegant, classy, sexy photo shoot that I did on *my* terms.

I wrote, recorded, and released a song called "Naked"—beautifully aligned with this photo shoot but about baring one's soul in a relationship.

I'm wild and free
*I am nothing but me.**

Although I loved the *Playboy* experience on its own, little did I know it was about to bring me a new best friend and creative collaborator as an even higher purpose.

When I first went to the Mansion for Hef's movie nights, I was surprised by how much it felt like being at a down-home family dinner; I was one of thirty or so invited guests for a low-key, sweats-and-jeans kind of evening. After the buffet dinner, Disney casting director Bill Shepard would call out, "Hey, Debbie! Play something from *Evita*," and I'd happily oblige by playing and singing "Don't Cry for Me, Argentina" in the old-school Hollywood piano room, which was a far cry from bikini-clad girls in the grotto. It would then turn into a bit of a DG singalong, with me taking requests.

"That was fantastic," Jimmy Van Patten said, exuberantly applauding after I played "Lost in Your Eyes." "Now play one of *your* songs!"

His brother Nels didn't know which way to look. "You dummy," he said, giving him a shove. "That was her biggest hit!"

Back in 2000, Jimmy had starred in *The Flunky*, a movie he cowrote with his brother Vincent, who also directed it.

"I'm turning it into a musical, but I don't write music," Jimmy shared. "I have lyrics and a script, which I'm handing to Thora Birch. I'd like to know what she thinks about possibly playing a role."

"You know I'm a composer," I reminded him.

"I do," Jimmy replied with a pensive grin. "Before coming here, I went to print a copy of the script in the apartment of my psychic

---

* "Naked" by Deborah Ann Gibson. Copyright © 2005 by Possibilities Publishing. Used by permission. All rights reserved.

neighbor. She told me to make a second copy because there's going to be someone else I'll want to give it to."

"Um, hello, I think that would be me!"

See what I mean about a higher purpose? I wouldn't have been handed that script without having posed for *Playboy*. Strange but true.

When I read the script later that night—about a guy, Jackie Baker, who is broke and doesn't work, yet enjoys the high life by hanging out with Hollywood stars as their flunky—it resonated. Jimmy's style of writing is genius, both modern and classic at the same time. By the next morning, I'd written five songs, which I then played to him on some rinky-dink upright piano in the guesthouse back at the Mansion, and over the course of the next year, I ended up cowriting the songs to the entire musical.

The Flunky was a passion project. After producing and reading it at my acting teacher Howard Fine's theater—and later a workshop of it at the Electric Lodge theater in Venice Beach, California, choreographed impeccably by Eddie Bennett—Jimmy and I were professionally off and running in different directions. So, it got put on the shelf, much to the dismay of Dick Van Patten and Diane Gibson, *The Flunky*'s biggest fans. Jimmy and I will pick it back up someday.

In May 2004, I appeared as sassy New Yorker Marta in *Company* at UCLA's Freud Playhouse as part of a star-studded cast. Then, that August, I went back to play Meg in *Brigadoon* with curly hair, a bustier, a Scottish accent, and a newfound fan in Jerry Stiller, who waited by the stage door to tell me how much he'd enjoyed my performance. I randomly ran into his son Ben the very next day at Coffee Bean on Sunset and he reiterated the fact that his dad loved the show and was happy to meet me. A totally surreal moment. Only in LA!

Another La-La-Land moment happened when, leaving LAX airport, I heard a familiar voice call out "Deb" from over my shoulder. It was none other than Brian Bloom. We hadn't seen each other for years and picked up right where we'd left off; friendship turned to dating, and the funniest thing was when, standing in my living room, it hit me: "Wait . . . there are no parents here!"

We had such a sweet chapter of rekindled romance that found us going to the movies, making dinner . . . and, of course, doing the things you do when there are no parents in the house. I don't think I was in the place he was in at that time. Brian was way more present and evolved on the relationship front; I was still in some kind of transition that didn't find me rising to the level of what this relationship deserved. So we parted ways yet again, and soon after, Brian started a new relationship with Marni, who he is still with to this day! He and I have remained friends ever since. Brian is that person who does a deep dive into people and things that are important to him. And he continues to show up for *me*.

I was performing at gay-pride events and on gay cruises, which was a great source of joy. I knew this community was loyal, standing by on land and at sea to celebrate me. It gave me occasions to rise to for such a worthy and grateful audience. I remember getting the call from Atlantis cruises to turn around a performance, complete with band charts, that I didn't have put together at the time. Cut to then-assistant Cade Bittner and me literally cutting and pasting horn parts, the bass line, everything needed for the show *on* the ship in record time. We recently had a giggle over how crazy-resourceful we were! Thank you, Tony Robbins.

But it wasn't all rainbows on the gay high seas. Or in the golden prison of my mind. You have to remember, I was still in this transitory phase. Once again, my efforts in the love department didn't work out and I was straddling the line between cruise ship showgirl, regional theater star, and "former teen music sensation." Often vocally struggling, I needed steroids to help me through shows about twice a year.

I recall one all-out meltdown in a dayroom in a hotel in Argentina after touring the Museo Evita with Eddie between the ship docking and my flight taking off. Eddie went on his way and I was alone on my layover. Calling Mom and sobbing uncontrollably, I barely got the words out: "I just don't know who I am or where my life is going."

My mood swing wasn't helped by being weaned off the medication, which caused euphoric highs and extreme lows. That was always my experience anyway. But the gift was that it brought to the surface all the things I was often masking to keep the freight train rolling.

But the catch-22 was that my creative spirit needed to keep going, as did my bank account. Who has time to stop working to deal with their emotions? It's not a reality for most people, even though the perception is that showbiz folks are exempt.

To that end, I appeared at the Fresno Grand Opera in *South Pacific*, auditioned for TV, did some independent films, and hit the road with my assistant Cade, in the Midwest in the dead of winter, for the O'Neill Brothers' *Someone You Love* tour, playing everything from a high school auditorium to a high-caliber concert hall. Mentally trippy and not the most glamorous era!

Some of the high points of this time were getting to skate opposite four-time world champion and Canadian national champion figure skater Kurt Browning for Fox's *Skating with Celebrities*, becoming an honorary part of the skating community with performances in *Broadway on Ice*, and duetting with Jordan Knight of NKOTB on the song "Say Goodbye," which went to #24 on *Billboard*'s adult contemporary chart. Performing it live on *Good Morning America* was a big thrill, but even Jordan's silky falsetto couldn't save me from floundering a little bit under all the pressure. Back on the psych meds I went.

During this time, mentoring was a major calling for me. One day in September 2007, I woke up with the idea of starting a summer camp, and this came to fruition the following year when I launched Debbie Gibson's Electric Youth, a children's summer arts camp at Howard Fine's LA theater, attended by over 120 talented singers, actors, and dancers from around the world.

Remember my friend Patrick, the ice skater I met in London? He became my right-hand man, producing this thing with me. Talk about rewarding. And exhausting. A fave memory was finding Howard curled up on his dog's bed during a break because he'd taken on a kids' master class and couldn't believe the level of engagement they demanded. I introduced all those young artists to songwriting and they'd stay after hours, surrounding me and my keyboard, much to the delight and dismay of their parents, who'd wait till all hours in their cars for their children to come out of the building. I even had Mom educate the parents on protecting their children's publishing.

My friend Wil Wheaton and I recently had a chat about how gross it is that this business often tries to steal from and exploit the work of naive up-and-coming artists. So, I didn't take the advice of many an advisor who suggested I insist the young performers sign away all of their rights upon walking through the door. Instead, I would sign on to help administer and place their songs while they kept the bigger piece of the pie. The passion these young creatives exuded turned into programs at my house to write and demo music in more personalized offshoots of the big camp.

Jeff Timmons, my friend from 98 Degrees, came aboard to lend his producing talents along with longtime musical collaborator Rudy Haeusermann, and we had several rooms going at once. My neighbor, award-winning songwriter Diane Warren, would bop in with her years of expertise and her effervescent personality to generously support the young talent at living-room jam sessions around my piano that had once belonged to Liberace. Quite possibly my most prized possession, it added magic to the music and this experience.

I loved helping the kids find their creative vibe and I wanted to turn that into a reality show. So, Chris Cowan, a big documentary guy who has partnered with Tom Hanks, filmed all this camp-related footage for a show that he intended to produce and sell, only for everything to fall apart after my business team haggled with Chris over percentages.

So what if I'd only get a third of the income? Imagine having 30 percent of *The Voice* right now. My motto: "100 percent of nothing is nothing." Besides, this was my baby and continuing it on a bigger scale would have been fun. But I hadn't yet learned to flex my business muscles, a skill I would eventually develop.

After that, I was like: *Now what?* I was still in this mindset that I had to be doing things as "the girl who was always working," which ultimately kept me running in place. As my mother's sole source of income, which felt like a tremendous responsibility, I was torn between being the dutiful daughter and the empowered career woman. I purposely wasn't in a marriage and I had no dependents except for my pets. But I still carried that burden of responsibility for Mama.

Even though I wanted to live a simpler lifestyle at this point, I was encouraged by my business management rep and Mom to let go of my rental pad, go for broke, and put down roots in LA. At this time, we were expecting more back-end money to roll in from *Playboy*, but because of the cover debacle, our expectations were greater than the reality. So, spending money I didn't have, I put a down payment on a rustic, two-bedroom, ivy-covered house on Forest Knoll Drive, off Sunset Plaza Drive, and now I had a mortgage. I'm not a big fan of mortgages: Don't pay the note and see who owns your home.

I had bought my two New York apartments outright, but this time around, my financial advisors encouraged me to take a loan, and, impressionable during a confusing period, I was swayed. Given how stubborn I can be, that was kinda strange, but financial investments weren't my forte. In other areas of my life, I am very clear about what I want and what I'm doing, but this was a period of emotional chaos. The musical landscape continued to change, and although I was trying to transition out of the theater, I still wanted to have a foot in it.

It's important to note that, during this time, I was having bouts of physical pain. Cracks were beginning to show in the armor, presumably from stress and from having no consistency in my life. It was hard to be my own center, my own inspiration, my own everything. I felt like I was working really hard to conjure up the stamina to keep going, probably because I didn't *know* where I was going. With no particular goal or direction, I was an expert at grinning and bearing it. I felt like I was treading water a lot of the time, trying to find my way. Back in 2005, I'd met and briefly dated Lorenzo Lamas, who was lovely and took me for super-fun motorcycle rides around LA. He introduced me to his agent, David Shapira. David then became *my* agent, as well as fast friends with my mom. Both David and Diane thought we really should be pitching a Vegas show and I was onboard with that. I had a pop-Broadway hybrid production ready to go and, with Mom, flew to Vegas for meetings with Don Marrandino, who was running Harrah's at that time.

Though I had done a lot of Broadway, nobody was sure how much the public still knew about me and how people might connect, so Don had me show up at an outdoor bar/live-music venue that was connected to Harrah's and said, "Come on, surprise everyone by doing a couple of songs with the band. I just wanna see how the crowd reacts."

Never shy, I jumped onstage and did my thing, and the people were excited. Don loved what he saw, but he *still* wasn't convinced my show would resonate with the sexy Vegas crowds:

"Okay, let's do your one-woman show in Atlantic City."

Oh, boy... I am *always* auditioning!

The East Coast casino crowd was just as important to me as the West Coast casino crowd and I was just flat-out excited to do this run with David Andrews Rogers of the Oklahoma City production of *Chicago*.

Pop Goes Broadway enjoyed a sold-out, monthlong run at Harrah's The Concert Venue in Atlantic City in the summer of 2008. This marked Eddie's first time as a co-choreographer with Buddy, and it was pure magic. I'd weave in and out of hit Broadway show tunes, fun covers, and my pop hits. With six dancers and a horn section, this variety spectacular could hold up anywhere, anytime, from cruise ships... to Broadway.

Describing it as "the best show Atlantic City has seen in quite some time... it's totally entertaining," Phil Roura of the *New York Daily News* went on to say, "she has mastered her craft to the point where she just doesn't perform a song—she embraces it and delivers it with her own special stamp of approval."

The audiences were a blend of my diehards, a lot of older people who I guess were mainly there for the gambling, and my relatives and friends.

"I remember being piled into your dressing room with your big Italian family... cousins, aunts, and uncles, all eating pizza after the show," David Shapira recently told me. "You're so *normal*."

I joked with him that I spent a lot of money on therapy to stay "normal"!

It was fun having everyone get together. Jimmy flew in, as did my new boyfriend Rutledge Taylor, aka Dr. Rutledge, who showed up at the end of the run to wine and dine me, take me shopping, and—despite being new to my world—give me his unfiltered thoughts on my performance. No stranger to tough love, at first I rolled with it. He saw that I was *performing* and was a master craftswoman but felt I could also be more present and go deeper. That was ultimately where I would land, but I wasn't quite there yet.

I remember feeling a bit like I was on a high and proud of the run I had just done, so when he said that, my bubble was burst. But there was something strangely familiar in this dynamic, having had my biggest constructively critical coach by my side my entire life. Her name? Diane. But let me take you back to how I met Rutledge . . .

My therapist Dr. Laurents had recommended that I pay Rutledge a visit to see if he could do something about my ongoing physical pain and various health issues. Dr. L was then in his sixties and I assumed Rutledge was one of his cronies . . .

Wrong.

When I knocked on the front door of Rutledge's home office in Studio City, it was opened by a young, very handsome, Southern rock 'n' roll doctor—and we definitely had an instant chemistry.

"You can't send a girl to see a doctor who looks like *thaaat* and not warn her!" I playfully yelled down the phone to Dr. L from my car after the visit.

"You know I can't date a patient," Rutledge told me after our first few medical appointments.

It was that obvious?

"Okay, then you're officially fired as my doctor!" I replied.

I meant it—I would find another doctor. A potential love interest is a rarity, and I'm a girl who knows what she wants.

Game on. I liked how Rutledge shared my sensibilities: a solo show who was unconventional, had never married, didn't have kids, worked on his own schedule, and was a lovable, charming, ambitious, out-of-the-box, don't-care-what-anyone-thinks-or-says type of guy. A self-proclaimed "lone ranger," he was a total original.

We had a shared health philosophy, as he always went back to the basics and worked from the inside out, viewing medications and invasive procedures as a last resort.

Feeling physically flimsy, I'd been in keep-it-going mode far too long. Rutledge remained my doctor for about six months, during which time we did rounds of tests and he prescribed supplements, cleanses, and hormonal treatments. I also became intrigued by his lifestyle-change program *Better Than Lipo* and would become a vocal advocate of quieting the noise while trimming the fat in order to get healthier on all levels.

It was an interesting time to be looking inward to figure out why I was in pain. I knew the prescribed meds were making me feel wacky and ultimately weren't my path. And a misread MRI by a top back surgeon in Beverly Hills had me thrown into an emergency ovarian-cyst surgery. That same high-level spinal doctor told me I needed surgery or I'd never walk my dogs up my hill again. Though Dr. L referred me to an applied kinesiologist named Rich Clayton, who turned my back issues around in just one week, the issues with my bank balance and my relationship with my mother would take considerably longer to resolve.

"I got you that red grand piano for this club!"

"Mom, we don't need to mic a piano in a club. We can use a keyboard."

"You don't appreciate anything I do for you!"

Everyone in my world will tell you I don't swear—or curse, as we Long Islanders say. But when Mom would call while I was at Rutledge's house, I'd excuse myself because I knew things would get heated every time. I'd need to be well into the middle of the street to unleash the

F-bomb before taking a few moments to cool off. Ahhh, mothers and daughters—nobody could push my buttons better. And nobody was working harder while plowing up a storm at this point, which was challenging and depressing for both of us. I so wanted Diane to be calm and capable for me within this modern landscape, but she was operating from a place of fear and desperation, a place from where no great art can flow.

She was so stuck in the antiquated ways, and there was always a fight—probably because she was scared about living off a percentage of the little I was earning and didn't quite know how to turn things around. She'd fallen out with promoters, fallen out with agents; Diane spoke her mind, and there were those who didn't appreciate it. So I'd receive calls from people saying, "Deb, your mom's emails are so long and so emotional . . . we simply cannot do business in this manner."

People always felt comfortable coming to me directly, but what was I supposed to do with this information? I was stuck in the middle and this was way beyond my area of expertise and life skill set. It's hard for a momager to avoid getting emotional when things are spiraling down and she's tired of her daughter—now just another name on agencies' lists—being lost in the mix. Besides, careers have peaks and valleys, and I was *definitely* in a valley.

In Diane's defense, she had been there to witness me headlining in stadiums and at Madison Square Garden, and the agents hadn't, so once again, she was banging those fists on the table. She kept trying to go to bat for me, but nothing was panning out—unless I wanted to do some really demeaning projects.

To make matters worse, remember when I said, "Don't pay the note and see who owns your home"? Well, guess what . . .

I had gotten so far behind with my bills, and my living situation was so up in the air, I even had to rehome my cat, Gleason. I'll never forget the day when Lance Bass's assistant delivered five thousand dollars cash in a brown paper bag, a loan from a true friend who knew I needed some support and has since never made me feel *less than*.

That was a humbling moment, one of those times where you feel so vulnerable, the earth could swallow you up whole. The way Lance didn't flinch and sent help immediately—I was so grateful to know such kindness in the midst of such a surreal and painful chapter in my life.

Other friends and family members helped me out financially at the time and never held that over me. The great writer/director/producer Andy Fickman, who championed me through an audition process for *Reefer Madness*, sent me a gift and insisted on not being paid back. *Incredible*. Mike Provenz was also someone I could turn to. He knew he'd never have to chase me for the money and that it would come back to him. But more importantly, he wanted to see me happy, healthy, and thriving.

I feel like, weirdly, everyone should have to go through this once in their lifetime. It's horrendous at first, but ultimately it builds character.

I stayed part-time with Rutledge and, when I wasn't traveling to perform, part-time with friends: Ray, his longtime roommate Sylvia—who has since become a best friend and songwriting partner—and her husband, Doug Moore. That was an adjustment, as I'd never even had a roommate. Now I love having roomies whenever possible, but at that time I felt like I had failed. And it coincided with Mom and me hitting the wall in our working relationship.

All the while, the energy put out in trying to keep up the facade, the pop-music persona, was draining me. I constantly felt on edge and sick to my stomach. I am not lazy, I love to work, but take the wrong kind of work in the short term, and your long-term career is over. That's how it goes and many performers experience this moment of juggling. It's the resilience that determines who lands on top.

David Shapira was shaking the trees in the acting world and got me a role in a kitschy shark movie that was supposed to be a little "under the radar" guilty-pleasure flick to cut my teeth on—shark pun intended! All I knew is that I would be playing a scientist who gets to pilot a submarine for not very much money but seemingly would be having a lot of fun! And *Mega Shark vs. Giant Octopus* didn't disappoint. The trailer would go on to amass over half a million hits in one day. So much for flying under the radar! Who wouldn't want to see the Golden Gate Bridge getting taken down by a giant sea creature? I was once again the guinea pig/pioneer, at the forefront of the shark movie trend thanks to The Asylum and the Syfy channel.

Back on dry land, I was now thirty-nine and my sixty-three-year-old mother wasn't transitioning smoothly into the new entertainment landscape. It was an emotional can of worms and I ultimately decided that the only way for me to step out of that was for her to step back as my manager.

"My worst nightmare has come true," Diane admitted during an interview that appeared in a pitch reel for a reality show called *The Comeback*. "She has become her own person."

Wait . . . hadn't that been her dream? She'd always said, "Should I get hit by a bus . . ." regarding her wanting me to be more in control of my own life, but when the time came, she couldn't handle it. Although most parents and children go through this when the child goes off to college, it was our norm.

It was hard for Mom to let go because, for the past twenty-two years, my career had pretty much been her entire life. She felt betrayed, but she also didn't want to stand in my way. I tried one last project that would organically keep her in the mix. The idea for the reality show, *The Comeback*, was brought to me by Shapira, and Greg Johnston at

Endemol was a dream producer. But I felt really off-kilter with the cameras around; it wasn't good for my mental health.

"We're going to film you going through your stuff in storage, getting rid of things, and burning what you no longer want to hang on to in a big bonfire."

My whole childhood was in storage, and I couldn't afford the thousands of dollars that was costing me every month. Panic, crisis, walls closing in . . . I wasn't thinking clearly, which was why my original black hat went up in smoke along with equipment from my first small home studio. How does that even happen? Metals and wood and, and, and . . .

I thought I was thoroughly sorting through my boxes, but there were hundreds of them in four huge units, and after a while, in the midst of dust, chaos, and heightened emotions, I presumed I knew what was buried deep inside each. Often, however, I miscalculated and didn't find out until it was too late. At a certain point, I was spinning too much to even care. I was in survival mode and wasn't in any condition to be doing anything this profound. I am extremely sentimental about my possessions, so how out of sorts did I have to be to allow that to happen?

One of my favorite high school friends, Ron Luparello, who has been there for me through thick and thin, was there that day. So were Buddy and Diane—although she was there to be Mom on-camera and play out that dynamic. So, ultimately, she was "on" and not grounded in her usual role of looking out for me.

These were people who'd always protect me with their lives, but that reality-show dynamic throws everyone off their center. I take full responsibility and fault nobody but myself for being so careless. I also forgive myself for being where I was; at least no people were harmed. These were only things and the lessons I learned that day were some of the biggest of *my* life.

Lights, cameras, action puts everybody in an altered state. That's what these shows are designed to do, but that was temporary and did *not* represent who I am. It instead showed me that I 1,000 percent *didn't* want to do a reality show focused on my life because I'd likely lose my mind.

The camera also captured me in the office of Warner Bros. Records exec—and friend from my teenage years, who is now sadly gone—Tommy Page, singing along to a song called "Cougar" that I had written and recorded with Rudy.

I'm hotter now that I'm older
A little wiser, a whole lot bolder.[*]

Telegraphing the audience to not count me out, I was so literal in my views of ageism, whereas now I simply live it, which is why I don't feel the need to proclaim anything. I am just *being*. Though I looked the part, with a svelte physique and smiling through the pain and confusion, this was *not* my shining moment.

After all that hoop-jumping and despite all the drama surrounding me in the middle of my "final chance at a comeback" pitch reel, the network execs viewed me as a cat who always landed on her feet. They would have wanted us to sensationalize the show even more had it gone to series and that wasn't something I was willing to sign on for.

In the summer of 2010, I played Mother Nature in *Cirque Dreams: Jungle Fantasy* at Foxwoods Resort Casino in Atlantic City. My fellow performers included a Russian family who juggled in bumblebee

---

[*] "Cougar" by Deborah Ann Gibson and Rudy Haeusermann. Copyright © 2010 by Possibilities Publishing and The Haasen Publishing Inc. Used by permission. All rights reserved.

outfits and a Korean contortion sister act. Neil Goldberg, the show's creator, threw me this big fortieth-birthday party where a multicultural receiving line of cast and crew presented me with gifts, cards, and flowers.

Who are *these people?*

A unique way to celebrate such a milestone!

Although Rutledge visited a time or two, it was really hard introducing him to this world of relentless back-to-back shows. It's easier for me to just stay in my solo zone. And he didn't love that I wasn't around to do the date nights and keep building our relationship in person.

Nothing was certain. I felt unstable and my career lacked direction and focus. Not that the randomness didn't bring its share of laughs. Like the time Bob Merrick, helping Mom and me at events, thought a private gig for the Seventh-day Adventists was actually for *seventy dentists* . . . I even got a pre-show teeth cleaning! Sometimes we have to be pushed to the brink before we make a change. Although I wasn't there yet, I knew I didn't want to just perform for the sake of performing. And I also knew I didn't want to half-ass a relationship. But I had no idea how to strike that balance between career and love.

Internally conflicted all the time, I hadn't realized I'd allowed myself to be brainwashed into thinking I had to be the girl who was always working, no matter where. When people told me, "You're busy, that's good," I was starting to rethink that theory, and I'd reply, "*Good* busy is good." It isn't good to be busy just for the sake of it.

That was the lesson. Instead of ending up in the wrong places, be patient, step back, and go through some leaner times. Forget the saying "Practice makes perfect." No—*perfect* practice makes perfect. And at some point, you must dare to change your old ways of doing things and step into the void that leads to that new reality. I had now learned I could lose it all, from a house to money to my health . . . and survive.

Making a living gig to gig, month to month, I still had this desire to do things a little outside my comfort zone, such as musicals that challenged my vocal and acting chops. It felt good to stretch and I was staying active in my craft. I wanted to act on camera more, I wanted to do something gritty, but I was also interested in doing a rom-com—and a surprising offer came out of the blue (pun intended) to do a one-album deal with Sony Music in Japan.

Gavin MacKillop, whom I lovingly call "the Grumpy Scotsman," had worked on my camps with me. Coproducing *Ms. Vocalist* with him was a quick project; it was fun, and the music was really good.

American girl covers Japanese #1 hits in a gender-bending moment of translations!

Singing for Japanese audiences to *enjoy* got me back in front of them after a long history, from headlining the Budokan to collaborating with Tatsuro Yamashita on "Eyes of a Child" and beyond. So I was so happy to be on a tour of *Billboard* Live venues with my #1 *Billboard* hit, a cover of the Yutaka Ozaki classic "I Love You." It all made perfect, purposeful sense to me. I have always vowed I will live in Japan someday. That's how much I love the people and the culture.

Still, this covers-album moment wasn't going to help me with my identity Stateside. My random theater and TV projects, the reality pitch, and the five-song demo containing an array of musical genres, from pop rock to jazz—nobody could pinpoint who I was. And that was a problem. I didn't have the luxury of spending too much time in yet another transition. The public and the entertainment community needed to be directed and I needed to pick a lane—*fast*. Ms. Naked Vocalist was *not* my ultimate identity!

Chapter Eleven

STUCK

"I need another Heather."

"Then why don't you *call* Heather?"

I missed my former assistant manager. And Rutledge was tired of hearing about it but seemingly had the solution.

"Well," I said, "Heather did run screaming from us."

"Nah," he replied, "Heather ran screaming from your *mom*."

Point taken.

Divorcing Mom was the biggest transition of my life, and although my boyfriend's communication was sometimes triggering in its directness, he was hitting me with straightforward facts at a time when I badly needed that. At the height of my success, bigwigs like Michael and Terry Lippman and Roger Davies were wanting in on the management front. But I knew that although I needed someone fearless and powerful, I also needed someone who was in touch with my very specific needs. That would be Heather. She could do what the big boys did, but with a sensitivity and nuance that spoke to me.

Flailing as I searched to find projects that ignited my creative spirit, I returned to a genre that brought a campy smile to my face. *Mega Python vs. Gatoroid* was a low-budget sci-fi monster-disaster movie released in January 2011 that starred me as animal activist Dr. Nikki Riley opposite my old pop-teen "rival" Tiffany, who played a park ranger. We had run into each other a lot during the late '80s, and despite the fact that the teen magazines pitted us against each other, there had always been a camaraderie because of our seemingly parallel careers at that time. In truth, however, they were quite different.

Tiffany would always joke about me being the wholesome theatrical one and her being the edgier rocker, which was funny since I was the one who'd played clubs at night while she'd played malls during the day. And now here we were, two boss babes three decades later, giggling together under a table while stunt doubles took over for us during the big *Mega Python vs. Gatoroid* food-fight scene.

"What on *earth* are we doing?"

"Folks have been waiting years for us to collaborate and this is how we decide to do it?"

The film was so kitschy, tongue-in-cheek, over the top, and *fun*, it weirdly made sense—not least because we each got to contribute an original song: Tiffany's "Serpentine" and my "Snake Charmer." This, in turn, led to the idea of us doing a summer 2011 concert tour. Although we've always had great love for each other and respect each other's differences, musically we have quite different tastes.

At that time, Tiffany was more pop rock rooted in country and Americana, and I was more dance pop and classic ballads. The ballads were a place where we intersected. We'd previously resisted recording or touring together because we were on our own paths, but now we realized there was something very powerful about women teaming up and supporting each other.

Making sure this was the right move both personally and professionally, I bounced it off Dr. L during a session.

"What do you think of Tiffany's *character*?" he asked.

"Oh, she's a woman of *great* character."

"Well, that's maybe the most important thing to consider."

The inevitable health crash, foreshadowed by the pain and nervous-system episodes that had brought me to Rutledge and Rich Clayton, was now upon me. It showed in my voice and I felt deeply fatigued, though I decided to take Dr. L's advice: "Let good enough be good enough."

Since my early forties, I've really had to drop the perfectionist thing: "Oh, I used to hit this note and sound like that . . ."

So, picking myself up, I went ahead with the tour, and although there was no instant meeting of the minds about what songs Tiffany and I would perform together, we eventually got there. We duetted on numbers like "Mickey" and "Sisters Are Doin' It for Themselves," and we also each performed our own sets and had a blast throughout the six *Journey Through the '80s* shows, later partnering up again for big arena concerts in Manila and Singapore.

Hey, girl, I'm in Vegas, Tiffany texted me just a few weeks ago. *Are you here? Let's have lunch and go shopping!*

I love Tiffany because she's a girl's girl—and because, even though she's known for that voice, she *always* wants to go shopping.

Some gigs provide me with enough money to do that. *Celebrity Apprentice* wasn't among them, but when I was invited to join the cast for its fifth season, I flipped the script inside my head. *Maybe I can raise more money for my charity than ever before to help children and families . . .*

The charitable aspect was always my anchor and my purpose for being there. Without it, no way. I'm aware people are curious to know about the man running the boardroom—and I realize we all know this conversation is a slippery slope. But this is a candid look at my life and I'm here to give you the facts. Mr. Trump, as he was known at the time, was a New York social-scene staple, and, with Marla in tow, he came to my 1992 opening night of *Les Misérables* and to an independent album-release party of mine where there were very few press outlets and, funnily enough, a lot of gay people.

In the fall of 2011, I put on the tight dresses and braved the war room to film season five of *Celebrity Apprentice*. That wasn't my favorite career move at the time, but my options were limited and everyone on my team was hell-bent on keeping me out there and relevant. As far as reality TV shows go, this was a biggie and, as far as Trump is concerned, in front of the cameras, what you saw was what you got.

This is the moment you might be expecting me to launch into my political views; I've made a very conscious effort to be a safe haven that people can escape to for joy, entertainment, and ways to shift things for the better. We are constantly bombarded by the divisions politics creates. This is not my area of expertise and I choose to focus my energy on walking my walk, humanitarian efforts, and all things that unify.

As I write this with deadlines fast approaching, the state of the world is ever changing, so it's hard to keep up with it all in real time. However, as you might have gathered by now, I'm not someone who stands for discrimination, basic human rights being stripped away, or anything but unity and respect for people, for animals, for culture, for tradition, for all the things that contribute to the very fabric of what I wrote about way back when in "I Come from America."

Meanwhile, back at *The Apprentice* . . . Ever the diplomat and the professional, I pulled my focus together and, despite people trying to throw me under the bus left and right . . . I won my task, which meant fifty thousand dollars going to my charity! As the founder of a female-run business, I was thrown by the catty backstabbing women. But there I was in that pressure cooker, determined to come out with something to show for it. With my winnings, I was able to help build a new Children's International Center in India. I knew at that moment I was done. I wanted out. I didn't care about winning the whole thing, nor was I shrewd enough to do so. I was ready to move on and the idea of getting "fired" amused me.

Until someone can fire me from being Debbie Gibson, what did I just get fired from?

> *You might like to think you're strong*
> *You can't break me, you can only free me.**

One of the side benefits of appearing on *Celebrity Apprentice* was getting to know my awesome Vegas neighbor Penn Jillette and Twisted Sister's lead singer-songwriter Dee Snider, who has become a great friend. Not only that, but I got to sit in the guest seat opposite Jay Leno for the first time ever. Hilarity ensued when we did a bit about tweeting and twatting in relation to the network having to censor my skirt flipping up during my jousting debut.

Meeting up with Heather after filming, I confided in her about my plans to part ways with Mom and told her I was looking for a new manager to help me refocus on my music career.

---

* *"Free Me" by Deborah Gibson, Evan Rogers, and Carl Sturken. Copyright © 1992 by Music Sales Corporation (ASCAP), Bayjun Beat Music (BMI), and Could Be the Music (BMI). International Copyright Secured. Used by permission. All rights reserved.*

"Look, I know you better than most people do," she said. Little did Diane know back in the Denim & Diamonds days that she was casting her own replacement.

This was a very haphazard time for me. I was still trying to find my footing, still trying to make ends meet, still not feeling great. The day after completing the *Apprentice* shoot, I ran into a former colleague at the checkout counter in CVS on Columbus Circle who expressed dismay at me doing the show. That was a gut punch, coming from a friend. I don't feel the need to name names because that isn't the point of this story. The point is, take a beat to find out what people are going through. I could've used a hug in that moment, not judgment.

I wished this person well on their long-running TV show, yearning for something as deliciously artistic and mainstream to be a part of. But instead there I was, making appearances as a *personality* that weren't congruent with who I was at my core: doing things like allowing a staged house to be passed off as my own, looking for real estate far above my means. This was the era of reality TV, and this was what was happening in the entertainment business. At least that's what I told myself. I was keeping up with the Joneses, but I was a Gibson! I needed to be higher frequency and authentically me.

When I realized I was selling a fantasy to people that wasn't 100 percent true, I had to reassess and trust that more meaningful things where I got to utilize my talents would appear. And they did.

The movie *Mega Shark vs. Mecha Shark* saw me reprise my role from *Mega Shark vs. Giant Octopus*. It was meant to be fun and easy, but I experienced memory loss hours before I was to shoot my lengthiest monologues, which were full of scientific jargon. That was scary. Let me explain . . .

I had gotten Botox treatments twice in my thirties and they were fine, but suddenly I was sensitive to the chemical. Unbeknownst to me, my body was dealing with an illness and its overloaded detox mechanisms weren't functioning properly. I was always told that the Botox stayed local, but I was feeling like I'd been poisoned. I realize medical literature doesn't support the theory of memory loss in conjunction with this treatment. But I'm here to tell you that, as a sensitive patient, I've had all sorts of symptoms triggered by toxins put into my body or by anything physically jarring, like getting poked with a needle.

In a panic, I called Heather from my car.

"I'm on my way to the set and I can't remember any of my lines."

She reassured me, saying to trust that the work I'd put in would come through and the lines would appear right when I needed them, which they did. So I'd traded having no forehead lines for being scared and possibly not knowing *my* lines. Worth it? In the moment, no . . . though I sometimes miss my smooth forehead! At a time when I was making compromises on the home front, I had to forgo the aesthetics, as well as some of the *luxuries* I'd become used to on the home front.

It's always an adjustment to move into a partner's space, because they are used to their routine *within* that space. So Rutledge and I found a home to rent in Vegas after we'd been back and forth a lot between Sin City and Studio City. I had a separate guest room for naps and meditation as well as a custom-made dressing room that he put a lot of thought and effort into, building shelves for my hat collection and racks for costumes.

Gals reading this might be able to relate when I say that, in a romantic relationship, there should always be an air of mystery. I loved going off into my little dressing room and transforming for a date night. And Rutledge was very big on experiences. If a restaurant didn't have white tablecloths, he'd insist on somebody finding one to put on our table. This often created a moment of tension and discomfort for me, as the servers didn't always want to comply.

"Remember, you can make a Popsicle stand into a five-star restaurant with a white tablecloth," he'd say.

He wasn't wrong.

Rutledge initiated my brief foray into red wine. He could man a tractor and could also spiff up for a black-tie affair and be totally charming. Let me take you back to the event where he turned to me and said, "Oh my God, there's Clint Eastwood."

When we introduced ourselves, Clint asked, "What do you do?" And without missing a beat, Rutledge joked, "I'm a *gynodontist*."

Clint looked puzzled for a moment. Then, glancing at me, he said, "Yeah, she does have really nice teeth."

We laughed and laughed and laughed about that one for years!

A typical Friday night would find us barbecuing in swimsuits while blasting a playlist I had made so we could jump in and out of the pool before settling in to watch countless episodes of *Two and a Half Men*. That was the nature of our relationship. There were extreme highs and a lot of love, some of the tough variety, and things came at a cost. This was a relationship about extremes. Even when we were sleeping in, it was like, *Okay, nobody move or speak.* I jokingly called it "mandatory sleep camp." Rutledge is a strong personality. But I was eager to comply.

Although he and I didn't marry, we both committed to the relationship wholeheartedly. Signing on for a chapter with someone doesn't mean it's a perfect fit for the rest of your life. And if you aren't with each other till the end of time, that doesn't mean it's a *waste* of time.

Many people look at me curiously because I'm in my fifties and have never been married—though I pride myself on being a great matchmaker, having paired up married couple Fred Coury and Amy Motta! Unsure about motherhood, I entertained the thought of freezing my eggs, but when I dove deeper into what that entailed, I realized that, if my system was going haywire from Botox, if financial stress was an issue, and if I was really at the beginning of this relationship and didn't know if it was forever, then that probably wasn't the best idea. I've always had very natural maternal instincts, but between mentoring kids, being a dog and cat mom through the years, and being an aunt to Diana, Rebecca, Jeffrey, Nick, Andres, Stefano, Luca, Tristan, Sofia, and Madison... my heart was, and is, full.

Hats off to parents who can spin all the plates and commit to the level of caring and love required to *be* a parent. I don't think I could take the constant worry and heartache, as well as all the things that I'm aware come along with the joys of parenting. And I am good with that. At this stage, my life is complete. And as for the man... I joke that at this point, if I stand before God and my loved ones and say, "Till death do us part," I have a much better chance of it lasting because I'm that much closer to death!

There were ways in which I adopted things in Rutledge's routine as my own. I changed my way of starting my day with physical activity to his way of meditating—and, seeing it as a challenge, I justified it by wanting that togetherness time. I've always been open to trying new things and I am a bit of a people-pleaser, but this just didn't work for me. I am at my best when I hit the ground running, seeing people out in the world. Changing how I started my day was going against something within myself.

When I'm involved with somebody, I want to be that softest version of myself, which at times gets me in trouble. That's something I'm still working on!

At the start of our relationship, Rutledge had been working on a documentary called *3 Billion and Counting*, a passion project that took him to developing nations around the world to explore why so many people were dying of malaria, particularly babies in developing nations, who he came face-to-face with in their dying moments. He was passionate about his cause, and a typical Sunday would find us both on the couch watching what felt like a combo of a science lesson and a history lesson over and over again.

Now, before this relationship, my typical free Sunday afternoon would have found me curled up with a Julia Roberts rom-com. So it was exhausting but enlightening, and I was a supportive girlfriend in awe of his dedication to see this project through. I fulfilled a lifelong dream when I ended up co-scoring the film with Rudy after living with the temp score for so long. I was even inspired to write the closing-credits song, "Rise," which Rutledge contributed some of the lyrics for, and couldn't believe it when it was short-listed for an Academy Award nomination and I was asked to perform it on *Good Morning America*.

My relationship with Rutledge was part traditional, part unconventional, and my nephew Stefano said it best on a trip back east to introduce him to my family. Rutledge walked in wearing a black mink coat and Stefano exclaimed, "He's fancy!"

Rutledge wasn't shy about letting lyric suggestions fly from the kitchen while I was writing a song at the Liberace piano in the living room. We had this ongoing joke where I would sing:

Every day's a lesson in the house of love.

We spoke recently, and, reflecting on our time together, I said, "It can be kind of exhausting having a teacher all day in your own home."

"Kind of?" Rutledge replied, bursting out laughing.

He knows the buttons he pushed. And I have a deeper way in which I look at writing lyrics now that can be attributed to how he kept challenging me to look at things in a new light. He and my mom had that in common and often went head to head.

"Now, Diane," Rutledge said over a nice bottle of The Prisoner at our Vegas home, lovingly named the Duck House because of the lake it looked over. "All I ask is that you don't buy Deb any Brighton luggage this Christmas. I've started a collection for her. That's our thing..."

"But it's only a makeup case," Diane pushed back on December 25, Brighton gifts in hand. "It's only a garment bag!"

Rutledge was adapting too. He can look back now and confidently say he doesn't want any part of a high-output showbiz life. He didn't love that, when returning from the road after performing, I didn't always have the same kind of energy for him as I did for my audiences. Though I felt like I enjoyed giving everything I had to him and the relationship with sexy, fun date nights and travel of our own, I also wanted to just collapse with him at times and have that be okay. Ever heard of Sleeping Beauty? I couldn't be *on* everywhere I went. I require a hard reset after going full out.

It really is a shame that two people can have so much love for each other but something innately prevents it from going the distance. Rutledge suggested that I get a dachshund when it became clear a dog was in my future. Though I tried to rescue a dog named Sancho, he ended up being right about that one and I was led to my puppy soulmate Joey!

I hadn't had dogs since Rosie and Daisy had crossed the rainbow bridge, and Gleason was now happy in his new home too. So it was difficult for me—but felt right at the time—to avoid uprooting him again, as Rutledge was allergic and I was constantly on and off the road. My beloved cat seemed to be loving life with his 24/7 stay-at-home mom and his Labrador retriever brother. People say they have no regrets but, if I had to do this one all over again, I know I would have come up with another plan that saw Gleason and me reunited.

Joey appeared in my life directly from an Amish farm in Ohio and became the true emotionally supportive, loyal companion I needed. I'll never forget his first night in Vegas, arriving to all the neon. He was such a Zen puppy, even the slightest sound from the TV or the piano had him cowering in a corner. Joey has since flown all over the country with me, calming my nerves and lifting my spirits through some challenging times. He is truly my puppy soulmate.

Feeling weak and experiencing intense symptoms, I still did a show here and there for my spiritual, artistic, and financial needs. During this time, poor Buddy, Eddie, and Heather had no idea which Deb they'd be getting when I showed up for a concert performance. Doctors determined autoimmune stuff was throwing everything out of whack, and I'll never forget the day I had to be wheelchaired through an airport with a baseball hat pulled down over my head in the hopes that nobody would recognize me. If anyone did, they might well have imprinted what they saw and sent it out to the universe, and that wouldn't help me heal.

"My wires feel crossed," I kept telling those around me.

My brain wasn't functioning properly.

Once, at a stop sign in Vegas, I couldn't remember if I had to turn right or left to drive home just minutes from where I lived. At other times, I couldn't even sit at the piano for enjoyment because of my struggles trying to focus and the overwhelming fatigue. The food sensitivities didn't help; I remember taking a bite of a potato and my whole body erupting in nerve pain. Nightshades will do that when dealing with certain realms of illness. My poor body was trying to fend off this mystery disease, and every scent or toxin—be it a shampoo or a deodorant or a food item—could trigger a reaction.

Nine months of running around to doctors and practitioners resulted in me repeatedly being told it was stress, which was true, but they were treating the symptoms, not the cause. Ditto the people who, seeing me continue to lose weight, kept saying, "You have to eat."

"I'm eating fourteen times a day," I'd reply.

Please don't tell larger people to stop eating and please don't tell smaller people to eat. Nobody has any idea of how bodies react to foods or what someone is going through. I wasn't going for that heroin-chic look. Trust me, I would have given anything to be any size as long as I was strong and healthy.

"It's like my body's attacking itself—or something's invaded it."

Very big about getting to the root of things, I love traditional medicine for specific ailments, but it doesn't work for everyone and everything. There were nine months of everyone, including traditional doctors, thinking I was crazy and that I could mind-over-matter my symptoms. I love doctors who listen to what their patients are saying.

My physical structure was constantly going out of alignment and, once again, I was thrown into countless MRIs—which are triggering and exhausting in and of themselves—and once again, I had doctors telling me I needed surgery.

"I didn't get injured," I kept insisting. "This is happening from the inside out, so it must get unwound from the inside out."

I knew I needed a different realm of diagnosis and treatment, but I still hadn't found it.

On one occasion, going through security to board a plane at McCarran Airport in Las Vegas, I was so on edge because of the pain and my brain misfiring that I unwittingly cut ahead of somebody standing in line to go through the metal detector. When she said, "Hey!" in a pointed tone, I started sobbing.

"I am *so sorry*. This isn't me. I'm really sick. I don't even know who I am right now."

She gave me a much-needed hug.

It felt like *Invasion of the Body Snatchers*. I didn't know it yet, but I had literally been hijacked by something that had thrown off my neurological system.

"I feel like my body's poisoning itself," I'd say over and over, along with "I'm in here somewhere."

I looked hollow, you could see it in my eyes, and I had enough awareness to know I couldn't meditate my way out of this. It had to be treated and, determined to unwind it, I was relentless in my pursuit of answers. But I was also exhausted. Rutledge nicknamed me "Four-Hour Girl" because that's how long I could do something before needing tons of sleep.

Eventually, I was in so much pain and so tired all the time, I could barely drag myself out of bed to crawl into the living room and onto the couch. That was now my big activity for the day. Me, the Debbie Gibson you see singing and dancing all the time these days. I knew something was seriously wrong.

I was in full-on detective mode, trying to figure this all out, and saw various specialists, one being a GI doctor, Dr. Rahbar.

"It sounds like Lyme disease," he said. "Has anyone tested you for that?"

Lyme disease wasn't on the tip of everyone's tongue like it is now. But Dr. Rahbar had me tested and I was diagnosed. Off I went to Lyme-literate doctor Dr. Joseph Sciabbarrasi. And so began this very involved journey.

It's beautiful that some folks take to social media and give everyone daily updates when stepping through health challenges if that helps them garner support and ultimately is life-affirming. Everyone is different that way and what works for me may not work for you. But though I was looking to do my journey privately, that wasn't to be when I performed in Chile in April 2014.

During the flight to Santiago, unable to sit for long periods of time due to the structural issues in my back and intense nerve pain throughout my body, I had to lie on the floor of the plane, wedged in front of my and Rutledge's seats. Then, after I arrived, my gaunt look—I weighed just 108 pounds due to an inability to absorb enough nutrients—prompted some people to get nasty on social media.

"You look like a Holocaust survivor."

First of all—w*huuut?!?* Could people be more cruel or insensitive? Secondly... I'd been outed.

Onstage, I was in so much pain—and so grateful that the audience's adrenaline and high spirits helped me override it until the end of the show. Likewise, the local food—the breads, the giant local organically grown vegetables, even the wines agreed with me because they weren't processed in this beautiful country where the people are all about culture, music, and nature. That was a wake-up call—and the start of tapping into that part of me that *needs* nature, *needs* to eliminate toxic people, and thrives on real food and no medications.

Why is some illness able to take me over right now? That was the big question for me. It wasn't about the disease itself, it was about why there was such *dis-ease* in my being. And I was searching for the answer while starting to look dehydrated, with puffy white circles under my eyes and a hollow appearance.

Had I contracted the disease by running barefoot outside my sister Karen's house in New Jersey and stepping on a deer tick? Maybe I'd caught it on vacation with Rutledge in South America—or could I have gotten it in my teens on Long Island and it was only surfacing now because I was so worn down? Anything is possible, as the song goes. I never had the bullseye rash that is a common early sign of Lyme. But I did have psychological symptoms that cross over into Lyme territory.

Again, I view all disease as my body being in a state of dis-ease. Millions of people walk around with a hidden illness that never takes them over. But take me over it did during the nine months I went undiagnosed. Though there are particular protocols for Lyme, in my experience no two people dealing with this illness are the same, which makes the treatment options feel like the Wild West. There are solutions that are energetic, holistic, traditional, supplement-based, and on and on. Ultimately, finding a combo of Eastern and Western approaches, as well as unwinding how and why I got to this place where my defenses were so low, would be my unique journey.

I didn't want sympathy. I needed to reset and start anew.

Following my diagnosis, a lot of the traditional Lyme treatment paths proved to be dead ends, but I did have the support and validation I needed from those close to me to continue exploring. I even had a wonderful kinship at that time with fellow artist Avril Lavigne, who was dealing with many of the same symptoms. Comparing notes, we encouraged each other along the way. A lot of viable treatments weren't covered by insurance, as holistic doctors are devalued in the system, and I was unable to work as hard as usual. So I humbly asked practitioners to defer payments. Aware I was serious and would be accountable and pay them back, they generously helped me out. Family members and friends once again helped bridge financial gaps—and, much to their relief, with their support, I always got to the next layer of healing.

One of those people who was always there to help was Heather.

"Don't worry, I got you," she'd say. "I don't know how, but you're getting out of this."

She might have believed in me more than I believed in myself, a trait she shared with my mom. We'd joke that I could have a limb falling off and still write a song.

I'd call her in the morning, barely able to hold the phone because I was so weak, and whisper, "I'm in so much pain, I can't get out of bed."

"Okay, let's figure this out," Heather would calmly reply before arranging help from across the country.

My sisters and friends Patrick, Troy, Ron, and so many more offered emotional support by doing things like driving me to treatments. Chris Miller, Joel Schaller, Heather, her husband Colton, their son Parker, Jon Knight, and Harley Rodriguez offered their houses and apartments. And my niece Diana brought me chicken soup in NYC while on a health trip to see practitioners. Medical medium Anthony Williams even called to check up on me. If you know of someone who might be putting on a brave face but going through an unimaginable journey, the tiniest acts of kindness are so meaningful. The greatest gift you can give is to simply check up on someone.

During this time, I learned I also had Epstein-Barr virus, Lyme coinfection Babesia, Bartonella, Ehrlichia, Borrelia, and countless others. I found myself in ERs on the regular. I wish the word *hospital* didn't become the only way to be left alone to slow down. But, unfortunately, it is a language everyone understands.

These days it may look like I'm on tour and doing things all the time, but I'm actually doing only the select things that elevate my career, lift my spirit, and make an impact. Sometimes I feel like I'm running to keep up a little, but I manage it. And I always remind myself: If health issues mean less money due to a postponed show or canceled tours, I'll figure things out. Getting deathly ill taught me to never let my health suffer to that degree ever again.

I know my limits better than ever and I do occasionally push them a bit, as we all do, but hopefully never too far to not be able to swing it back. Many docs gave me fast-tracked versions of protocols. But you can't always treat someone with Lyme all that quickly, and I couldn't handle the Herx[*] reaction, which is an inflammatory response that comes from killing the spirochetes that cause the disease.

My intuition helped me find Dr. Bonnie Liakos in New York. She knew immediately what I had to do to start to heal. Her plan would mean me flying back and forth to see her over the course of nine months. "Everything's based on foods, electromagnetics, emotions, past trauma," Dr. Liakos imparted to me. "So we may have to change where you have the Wi-Fi in your house, whether or not you keep your phone in airplane mode, which feathers are in your pillows, what ingredients are in your toothpaste... Get rid of every toxic thing in your house that has a scent."

Through applied kinesiology muscle testing, a specific treatment plan is designed for each individual. Mine came with a big life overhaul. People with cancer and other diseases go through the process of trying to remove all the burden from their bodies as well as negative emotions and toxic people from their lives, to maximize their chances of turning things around. I recall feeling a bit silly and eccentric having legend in the A.K. field Dr. Michael Lebowitz teach me how to self-test for food sensitivities in the aisles of Whole Foods, but I'm now grateful to have that skill without relying on practitioners.

At one of my lowest points, told I'd need constant antibiotics and a PICC line to administer treatments, I pushed back while lying on the cold bathroom floor with debilitating pain and weakness.

"No, that doesn't make sense to me. It's not an active infection anymore, so this is all wrong. And besides, I am *not* a sick person."

The voice in my head rose to a fever pitch: *This is* not *my life.*

---

[*] *Jarisch-Herxheimer.*

It was a needle-scratch moment, stopping me in my tracks: *Deb, you must keep tuning in to that deep, deep voice and that higher power.*

I refused to be silenced or sidelined. And getting well is not always convenient. As I've mentioned, this journey's expensive and receiving financial help can be awkward for the girl who was always the breadwinner from a young age. Still, I learned to ask and to receive, and that has been one of the greatest side benefits of this traumatic time. The MusiCares Foundation—whose red-carpet event I recently attended—helped me financially with my ongoing treatments.

It's the weirdest, most unexpected gift to be a star at a charity event that once helped support you. Finding the practitioners who moved the dial forward for me, I ended up spending about half a million dollars on my healing journey between travel, treatments, and being unable to work consistently. My go-to now when I don't feel well is walking on the beach, finding a way to laugh, putting on a fun movie, playing and performing music, looking to my community, and calling on friends and family.

Shifting energy.

I constantly have to ask myself, *Am I really tired or is it stuck energy?* The unraveling for me is always like, *What can I do to control how I feel?*

I have learned that everyone's path is different, so I urge you to figure out what works best for you. The most confusing part of this illness is that there aren't straightforward treatment approaches. What works for me changes constantly. Sometimes I take supplements for support, other times homeopathic remedies, and other times I'm at my best with nothing on board. At the end of the day, it all comes down to using my own intuition and living the cleanest, most balanced lifestyle possible. I encourage you to stop at nothing to find what's best for you on your health journey.

When our health is as optimal as it possibly can be, life is sweeter.

So I listen to my body and I remind myself, *This is temporary*. It's easy to believe we're going to be stuck forever in a certain pain pattern or in discomfort while it's happening. It takes a lot of mental strength to get through these difficult chapters.

I rallied hard to get myself on set to film ABC's *Sing Your Face Off*, hosted by John Barrowman and with fellow judge Darrell Hammond, during this time, smiling through tremendous pain. I even flew cross-country to continue supporting the LGBTQIA+ community by performing at gay pride festivals, adhering to a strict, clean diet of foods I would cook myself and bring on flights, navigating terrifying physical and mental symptoms. I wasn't going to give up.

Going through these trying times has strengthened my trust in my own chemistry and what my body is capable of. I now live from the inside out and embrace the fact that my body will change and adapt internally and aesthetically to accommodate whatever it needs to help me thrive.

It's about being honest with myself and knowing my own puzzle. A lot of people go through life operating under the illusion that they must suffer to get well or to become good at something. I don't want to live like that. But I do hope reading this might help some of you avoid experiencing all the things I went through. If I traveled to the ends of the earth and learned by trial and error to save you a few steps, that would make it all worthwhile.

Chapter Twelve

ALL GOOD THINGS DISCONTINUED

Even though I wasn't feeling 100 percent healthy, an outlet I found agreeable with where I was on my journey was making movies. It is a calmer environment than concert performing with less output and less travel, which equals less wear and tear. My creative ideas that had been nurtured by David Shapira for many years were finally coming to fruition and it was exciting to venture into my favorite genre of acting: romantic comedy.

In 2015, I starred in *The Music in Me* for UP TV opposite Antonio Cupo and Gloria Reuben. And I love that little movie. It's always a good fit for me to play a music teacher, because I bridge the gap between pop star and small-town America. That would be kind of the recurring theme in my Hallmark movies.

I created *Summer of Dreams*, which was loosely based on my life, but as if it had gone horribly wrong. My character, Debbie Taylor, takes to the open road and goes to Youngstown, Ohio. Her estranged younger sister Denise, vice principal of the local high school, offers her a job filling in for the music teacher. Hallmark favorite Pascale Hutton plays Denise and Robert Gant plays the dreamy guidance counselor/love interest. It's so cool that an openly gay man was cast in this straight role. In my world he's everybody's biggest crush.

I helped craft the script with Tippi and Neal Dobrofsky, spending many hours on the phone to make sure it accurately represented the pop-music world, based on a lot of my own experiences. One of my favorite lines of dialogue that I wrote is "My business manager called and said I've been spending money I didn't know I didn't have." That's happened to *me*!

Bart Fisher let me stretch in *Summer of Dreams*. In fact, we pushed the limits so far that, after the picture was locked—meaning no more changes could be made—I found out that the opening scene of me singing my first hit, "Only in My Dreams," in an empty mattress store had been cut and replaced with the safer, more familiar stock New York City skyline shot.

This scene was based on an experience I had in the early 2000s promoting a Korean karaoke microphone in an empty Costco. It was so poignant in its self-deprecating humor and truth, it needed to happen. The same fierce little girl who'd sat on the edge of the stage and begged the producers of Atlantic's fortieth-anniversary concert to do another song at Madison Square Garden rose up once again. I remember the day. My health issues were getting the best of me, I could barely lift my head off the pillow, and I thought about just letting it go to avoid confrontation. I *hate* confrontation. But once I got the idea in my head, it had to be done. So, I conjured up the energy. Calling all the top executives, I said, "You've got to put this scene back in because an artist singing her original hit will resonate deep. I know this is new territory for you guys, but please don't be scared. Your audience is ready to see new things and will love it."

To Hallmark's credit, they reinstated the opening scene and the rest is number-one-movie history.

As I transformed into the music teacher, we removed a little of the pop edge by taking the platinum blonde down a notch, while putting me in cardigans and sweet dresses. One unexpected benefit of doing this movie was discovering that I'd inherited Mom's gift for spotting talent. This would impact my next musical chapter.

Sean Thomas showed up, cast as one of the students, when we began filming in Vancouver, Canada. Before getting the call, he'd been planning to travel to LA for the summer program at the Musicians Institute. Had that happened, it would have changed the whole trajectory of both our lives. When I saw this tall, blonde fourteen-year-old surfer-type boy on the first day of filming the music-class scenes and heard his high, pre-change voice coming from the far corner, I asked, "Do you have perfect pitch?"

"Yeah," he humbly replied in his high-pitched voice.

I sensed a special talent. As I'd come to find out, he was super-creative and tech-savvy. Having learned to play the piano at age five and the guitar shortly thereafter, mostly self-taught, he had also been a voice actor before stumbling into on-camera acting. Sean reminded me so much of me and I felt like my mom in that moment, with a crystal ball seeing the road that lay before him. Instantly, my maternal instincts kicked in and I started imparting things to him in a non-preachy way, things I'd learned that might someday save his voice and his soul.

Being around this prodigy took me back to a time when I never gave myself permission to really deal with how my life had changed or how much the intense work and travel left me depleted. Yes, I chose to make sacrifices, but that didn't mean they didn't exist. The trade-off for my success was accepting that going to the mall or a movie with friends like a normal teenager was a thing of the past. I couldn't possibly recognize it at the time, even though fans recognized *me* in a full-on disguise, complete with a brunette wig, trying to sneak into the church carnival unnoticed when fame first hit. But it was a loss I didn't realize I was mourning. I didn't want that for young Sean and I wanted to heal that trauma in young Deborah.

As a teen vocalist, I remember feeling really hoarse and run-down backstage at the Fox Theatre in St. Louis on the *Electric Youth* tour. So I called my voice teacher Guen, who talked me through breathing and vocal exercises. And I even chewed aspirin, not realizing it was dangerous because one moment of bad technique could hemorrhage a vocal cord.

I would Dr. Deb it for decades, doing whatever had to be done, and my personal experience surrounding this topic would create a firestorm during a 2016 interview on *Oprah: Where Are They Now?* The steroids I referenced back in the cruise show days are often used when singers are experiencing severe inflammation. This would end up catching up to me and affecting my adrenal health in a deep way. So when I said half of Broadway is on prednisone, it was because I felt there was very little grace being given to performers to heal naturally if they hit the wall, and doctors were often quite generous with medication, in my personal experience. I was pointing out the potential consequences that might occur down the road, because I was feeling the effects of a lifetime of "the show must go on." Weak to begin with when this all hit the fan, I was in another really debilitating Lyme moment, and this pushed me over the edge. I literally felt like I was going to die.

Prince had just passed, and when I was asked about that in the interview, it really got me thinking. As a *show-must-go-on* girl, I was pondering why I always wore pushing myself beyond healthy limits as a badge of honor. The fact is, many performers feel such a responsibility to deliver at all costs, even if it might cost them their life. Prince accidentally overdosed on the fentanyl he was taking for chronic hip pain. We fans reaped the benefit of him literally dancing his ass off onstage for decades. But we weren't with him in the privacy of his home when he was paying the price. I can't imagine the agony he must've been in or the psychological journey he must've gone on to go on with the show.

Likewise Michael Jackson, going to such lengths just to get a good night's sleep so he could keep up with the impossibly high standards he set for himself. Even beloved American treasures like Elvis Presley and Whitney Houston essentially seemed propped up onstage at a certain point, in a final attempt to deliver in the way they once had. Concerned about the slippery slope of prescription meds, I was trying to tell Oprah's audience that high-level professionals should think about protecting themselves as best they can for the long haul. And, maybe there are conversations to be had about the higher-ups protecting our most precious resource . . . people. I am all for the freedom to choose what one does with their body. It's just that so many of us entertainers have this natural reflex to over-apologize for being unable to sustain superhuman levels of performance for decades on end.

Coming from someone who doesn't like to upset anyone's apple cart, this was a polarizing point of view. The words that came out of my mouth weren't quite right in the heat of the moment, and I have since apologized for that. But, having always looked up to women like Cher, Madonna, Jane Fonda, and Eartha Kitt for being so outspoken, I took a stand. And took the heat. The people-pleasing pop princess with the pristine reputation falling from grace. Out of this painful experience, a song was born . . . "Gracefall."

I was candidly sharing, but my candor was all but getting me canceled. It was gut-wrenching to have my beloved Broadway community coming after me because they felt I was targeting them when in fact I was citing my experiences as a cautionary tale. Friends who knew my intentions and my heart came to my defense, and, realizing that how things are worded is so important, I soon took ownership of the fact that I had categorized people, which is something I've always prided myself on *not* doing. I stand by my pure intentions to protect people. But it would be a lesson I'd take with me and a great moment of evolution.

Dancing with the Stars was a big turning point. The producers offered me that show several times, but it never fit into my schedule until 2017, when I finally signed on. Career commitments or health restrictions had previously prohibited me from doing it, but even now, lying flat on the couch, I thought, *I have no business believing I can do this, and I might get kicked off in week one, but I'm gonna say yes to signal to my mind and body that it's time to get moving.*

Welcome to my roller coaster of crashes and flares. It was hard to make life plans because one minute I was full steam ahead and the next I could hardly keep my eyes open—as pupstar Joey, who was cozied up on my limp body, will attest. Still, I try to make decisions from an optimistic place, assuming my system will rev up and deliver when it's time. I'm not one to curl up in a ball and be counted out.

It kills me that I might have been a finalist or won the whole thing during a healthier time in my life, like when I was cartwheeling in high heels as Velma in *Chicago*. Instead, I accepted the offer knowing full well there was no way on God's green earth that was going to happen because I was still having many of those days when I could barely get out of bed. If a few days in a row were good, I'd be like, *I've got this in the bag. I can ace it.* But then I started to realize that wasn't my consistent state of being.

The fatigue was still so great; I was still recovering, I was still healing, I was still resetting and finding my new normal. It was unpredictable. Nevertheless, no matter the outcome, I was also determined for this to be the official start of my new chapter. I didn't want the public to cut me any slack on my skills on the dance floor, I didn't want a pity party, and I didn't want folks in the professional world to think I was limited. So, it was time to get on with it—even though, given what I knew about my health triggers, I did have certain needs. That's why, when I accepted an offer for *Dancing with the Stars*, I articulated certain requests regarding my chemical-sensitivity issues that were a component of this relentless illness:

"Please don't use carpet cleaner in my trailer. Can you please send a hair-and-makeup person to me so I'm not bombarded with hairspray all around me in the group trailer?"

These were not diva demands. I wanted to be around my fellow castmates. To be a trooper. I just knew the toxins would take me down, leaving me debilitated . . . albeit with a fabulous updo! My tipping point was delicate.

Though I loved doing the foxtrot to my very own "Lost in Your Eyes" and the quickstep, my favorite and final dance that I did was the Argentine tango to Camila Cabello's "Havana." And here's the crazy story: rhinestones and crystals were being glued onto my costume at the eleventh hour and the smell set off my body and my brain. Again, it's all these things that no one thinks about. But any little thing back then was a tipping point for my health to collapse, for my muscles not to work, for my brain wiring and nervous system to go off.

My dance partner Alan Bersten was incredibly compassionate and supportive, even traveling with me to concert destinations to rehearse, but this was his first season as a pro and I felt, *The poor guy got a bum deal having me as his partner*. I was doing my best, but I was letting him down. We were eliminated pretty early on.

After hanging up my dancing shoes, I returned to Canada for the filming of the sequel to *Summer of Dreams*, aptly titled *Wedding of*

Dreams. On set, I made a frantic call to my acting teacher Howard Fine because I was having a lot of trouble connecting in one scene in particular: "I've never been proposed to, I've never been married, and I have no idea how to react honestly in this scene."

This was one of those moments when I went, *Wow, my path has been really unconventional*. And I don't think I ever really got to the heart of it.

I have a theory that everything good gets discontinued: the French cruller at many Dunkin's nationwide, fave beauty products, a beloved movie franchise. And *Wedding of Dreams* just didn't catch fire like the first one did. It did really well but, much like *Anything Is Possible*, once you set the bar high, you're always in danger of falling short. I think people loved the juxtaposition between the funky Debbie Taylor and the more conservative Debbie, but the funky Debbie would rise again because Heather got a call from Jared Paul, acclaimed manager of New Kids on the Block.

He invited me to be a guest on the MixTape Tour with NKOTB, Salt-N-Pepa, Tiffany, and Naughty by Nature—fifty-five shows in fifty-three cities, starting in May. This put me back in a music mindset, and when the second movie was wrapped, I asked Sean, "How would you track up this song? Let's just do it as a sample."

Sean bopped back "Take the Risk"—a cute enough song from *Wedding of Dreams*, but with his production arrangement—and it sounded like a surefire pop hit.

"Okay," I said. "We have a musical kindred-spirit type vibe going on here. We need to work together."

When he sent me a short piece that he'd scored for his orchestration class, I was like, *Oh my God, this guy is James Horner meets David Foster meets Ryan Tedder. He's an orchestrator, he's a musician, he plays multiple instruments, he programs, and he's an incredible mixer.*

I was so blown away. After that, I'd send him an iPhone piano-vocal recording or a Pro Tools session with piano and vocal so he could track around that. We'd then send it back and forth or I'd call him with tweaks and ideas to incorporate.

For me, Sean's starting place was often "Wow! That's better than anything I've had inside my head!" Or: "You just *pulled* that from my head!" The same as I'd had with Fred Zarr; Sean holds on to my original vision while elevating and refining it.

I never want to be that bitter older person who thinks everything good was done yesterday or done by people who've been in the busi-

Sean Thomas, my musical kindred spirit, who I met on the set of Summer of Dreams.

ness for thirty-five years. I constantly draw inspiration from current artists and celebrate the fact that strong females like Lady Gaga, Taylor Swift, Beyoncé, Blackpink, Alicia Keys, Olivia Rodrigo, Pink, Billie Eilish, Delta Goodrem, Doechii, and Chappell Roan—to name a few—have made such an impact on pop music today based not only on their images and sound but on their mad skills.

Sean too clearly had the musical chops. If those chops had come with attitude, it never would have worked between us, but we were all joy and emojis while elevating the music at the same time.

Everything I do now is run through Sean. He touches all of my songs in some way, whether he's processing a vocal, comping a vocal, adding some keyboards, mixing, or creating an intro. There's always something. And there's also the stuff he does top to bottom.

I'm always very connected to who I was as well as who I am within the musical landscape. My melodic sensibility is always gonna be hooky and steeped in "That's a Debbie Gibson hook." My audience feels that and there's a preservation of that integrity and the connection to the old without ever sounding dated because Sean's part of the super-modern musical landscape.

He makes sure it never sounds like, *Oh, she got together with a twenty-something producer who put this on her.* The results always feel organically connected to who I am right now as well as to something from the past. Our style of communication is so great. He understands where I'm coming from in musical terms; we laugh a lot, and he is family.

In the meantime, my relationship with Rutledge was coming to an end. Though we'd had some amazing times, I was, for the first moment in my life, ready to live without having a teacher in close proximity. At this point, he was away a lot on medical missions and there was not only a physical distance between us but an emotional one. We kept going, giving it one more try. We were at home in the discomfort and dysfunction, but it became clear we didn't belong together anymore. There wasn't some big mourning period; it had been gradually unraveling. So, I moved out of our house, deciding to stay in Las Vegas in a different part of town.

The new house I found had two large primary suites and I was like, *Wow, I can make one the studio!* It seemed perfect for my needs. At this point, the *Out of the Blue* girl was out of the red and able to live my best life and I was so excited! Years earlier, when I'd moved out of my Forest Knoll Drive home in LA, I'd stored most of my belongings in a warehouse; now I was ready to retrieve them. So I made the call to Eli, the owner of the moving warehouse, and excitedly met the truck that showed up at my new home with all my stuff. Or so I thought.

There were four pallets originally sent from my house to the warehouse that I myself inventoried. At some point, I got a call saying the company was changing locations and moving all its clients' belongings to a new place across town in a different part of LA. Trusting that everything had been inventoried on this go 'round, I assumed it would be a swift and easy move.

"Ooooh . . . I can't wait to be reacquainted with all my things," I exclaimed to my close friends. "My china closet, Grandma's Swarovski collection . . ."

She had bought me crystal figurines every year for my birthday from the time I was seven years old, so I had quite a lot.

"I'm finally gonna display them properly!"

It had been almost a decade since I'd last seen my prized possessions. But after the truck pulled up in front of my new home, I noticed a leg off my childhood-home piano had gone missing as the moving men brought it in, and I knew . . .

"Where are all my kitchen items? Where's my china closet? Where's my Swarovski collection? Where's that blue rug with the white sheep on it that I got from ABC Carpet and Home in the nineties in New York?"

Anyone who knows me knows I am super-sentimental about my stuff—and that I had already said goodbye to so many of my things years earlier. Bonfire, anyone?

I still had my Liberace piano, thank God, as well as my original *Electric Youth* album-cover neon sign, my signature *EY*-era necklace I got on the UK promo trip, and half my costumes. But the other half were gone. As were original song manuscripts that had gotten transferred there when I did that TV show with the re-staged home. Looking back, it's so unfathomable that I didn't keep those personal possessions close at all times, but they needed them to shoot cutaways as I dashed for a red-eye to do an event for Nat Geo and Bobby Watman at Culture Club. Assured they would be kept safe, I clearly *wasn't* always thinking clearly and was far too trusting of others.

Suddenly, I felt for anyone who'd lost things in a fire or a robbery. This had to be a mistake. When so many items of great personal value disappear, when the universe says, *Here, I'm taking away your health, I'm taking away your money, I'm taking away your precious things— that's* when you learn what you're really made of.

I had to reframe it. Nobody had died, these were just possessions, and I'd learned a bigger lesson: *Okay, Deb, you cannot trust anyone, you must micromanage or be okay with the fact that things might go awry, and you must be more careful.*

I take full responsibility for the things I didn't keep close, but there's also a punch line to this story.

Several months ago, some girl posted on Facebook: *I've got this dresser. It's Debbie Gibson's.*

I knew it was true because of the personal photos inside it of me with Marissa Winokur.

That dresser, funnily enough, was a humbly priced piece that looked expensive but that I'd bought at Home Goods. Having walked through the dusty moving warehouse myself, looking at every freaking box to make sure something wasn't put with somebody else's stuff, I now knew somebody had taken it, somebody had auctioned it, somebody had sold it. My name and likeness were all over the things on that pallet. I couldn't make an insurance claim because it had been too long by the time I found out what had happened. And that wouldn't have brought my sentimental items back anyway.

My team and I tried to track down my missing ASCAP Songwriter of the Year award, but to no avail. Still, it's out there. And we also tried to track down the girl, but she went missing too after I attempted to make contact with her. I posted a video online saying, "I'm not mad at you, but can I have my photos? You can keep the dresser. It's not even important, but we'd love your help tracking where you got this."

ASCAP has since made me a new award, which I will receive sometime in the near future. But I still want the original. So, if any of you happen to see it...

This was a difficult period for me.

My spirits were lifted in the form of an honor given to me by the Palm Springs Walk of Stars; Crystal Miller sponsored my Gold Palm Star on behalf of the charitable organization In Our Own Quiet Way. And my Debheads turned out in full force, as did my mother with her beau, John, and bestie Liz. Friends like Bobby and Jimmy and Ray sang my praises in elegant and comical speeches; Heather, Shapira, and even Rutledge were in attendance. (We were on good terms as friends.) My longtime team member Elizabeth Neff—who is a wonderful friend and helps liaise with PR outlets, social media, fans, and promoters, and has too many other job descriptions to name—helped organize the celebration, and it was like being alive at my own funeral... or probably more like the wedding I never had. Mom gave a beautiful speech and we made some unforgettable memories.

Little did I realize how much those memories would come to mean—like the ones made at the Ladies of the '80s concert with Tiffany and Lisa Lisa in Dallas on October 18, 2018. Mom kept hemming and hawing—she wanted to fly in, she didn't want to fly in. Finally, I said, "Pack your bags, I got you a ticket. You're getting picked up at eight a.m., there's a car coming."

It would be the last headlining arena show she'd ever see me do.

I told her I was going to take a nap before sound check, but in true Diane fashion she knocked on my hotel room door, waking me up because she'd heard I'd forgotten my favorite round brush and she had one for me. She had to make her presence known, which was endearingly annoying.

Before the show, the diehards were congregating, so Heather and I told her, "Go say hi to them. They'll love it."

So many longtime supporters of mine who'd flown in from around the world had never before gotten to meet Mama Di. Many of them now have pictures with her from that night in her cozy camel shawl. The fact that it was very understated and motherly for my mom spoke volumes. It was like her goodbye. She was holding court and loving every minute of being the proud mother, taking in the love for her daughter. Having never brought her onstage before, I'm glad to say I had the sixth sense to do it on this occasion; watching her up there during "We Could Be Together," I realized we'd come full circle and she looked like a little girl, clapping and singing along.

ETERNALLY ELECTRIC

Diane loved the moment. So did I.

A month after that concert, I was perusing the Animal Foundation website. It's not that I was looking for a second dog, but when I saw this adorable dachshund staring up at me through my phone, I knew I had to go meet him. Dumped on a Vegas highway without a chip or a collar, he'd been named Chicory by the shelter, and it was love at first sight as Trouper—as he'd come to be called—was all tail wags and an air of hopefulness that spoke to me. This wasn't without its challenges, as dogs with trauma have behavioral issues, but we'd weather them together and Joey loved his new brother.

At the start of 2019, I again started to experience weird pain symptoms, which hadn't happened in ages. These weren't in my regular repertoire of bodily sensations and none of my practitioners could figure out what was going on. My search for answers had therefore taken me, once again, to NYC, where hotel manager Kelly Duke took me underwing upon seeing how fragile I was. The MixTape Tour was fast approaching and my body was, once more, a war zone. Defeated, I headed back to the West Coast to see Dr. Darrick Sahara, and, feeling despondent, I cozied up on his couch after my treatment. We are brother-and-sister-level close and he knew I wasn't in a state to be left alone. Calling my mom, I confided in her about the weird symptoms and fatigue I was experiencing . . . Cue that good ol' one-of-a-kind Diane Gibson pep talk.

"Deborah, honey. You always go through this before you start a big project. It's nerves. You have to trust that all your years of hard work and training and practice will be there for you. It's time to just relax and enjoy, because this upcoming tour is going to be big for you."

As soon as I hung up, Jimmy Van Patten called to say he'd cook me dinner and I could stay over if I wanted. Now, for starters, I never turn down homemade pasta with clam sauce courtesy of Chef JVP. And second, I wanted to give Darrick a break. So I headed over to Jimmy's townhome and tried to override my pain with great friendship and great food. That kinda worked, though I was still aware something wasn't right and I was a bit on edge.

Jimmy and I never sleep in the same bed. But this night, in the sweetest, most platonic way, akin to a couple of kids at a high school slumber party, I threw my sweats on and we giggled our way into dreamland on top of his covers, which helped me escape my pain for a little while. The next morning, I awoke to a text from Mom letting me know she had indeed gone for an aesthetic procedure I'd urged her to avoid months prior, and, although nervous, she was excited for her skin to look "as smooth as a baby's bottom."

Wasn't it already that smooth? Her skin was better than mine.

At some point, Diane had gone to a dermatologist for a routine procedure to remove a mole and that doctor clearly had a relationship with a cosmetic facility that encouraged patients to do other things. They probably had a referral deal going on and tried to convince people to go get these other procedures. It is such a comment on society that we are willing to traumatize our systems for the sake of looking better and younger and smoother. Not judging anyone here; we all do whatever we can to make ourselves feel our best. But this is a cautionary tale because there are extraordinary risks.

Mom wanted to have a laser facial, which my friends routinely do with nothing more than numbing cream. Yet in her case, they went a bit more extreme by doing sedation—without putting the patient completely under. My friends are young and healthy and not on medications, so they don't have blood pressure problems or anything that would cause issues with the procedure or the sedation.

Mom very clearly laid out for them that she had an aortic aneurysm, she had high blood pressure, and she had anxiety issues, which she was being treated for by a professional. She also divulged in writing all the medication she was regularly taking. So they knew going in that this woman in her seventies truly was not an ideal candidate for the procedure. Very clear up front that she didn't have the money to pay for it, she at one point asked if I'd be willing to exchange social media posts to promote the clinic. I'd had a huge adverse reaction to that idea because it smelled of the doc preying on my mom, and I wanted no part of it. Which is why she hid the fact that she was going in.

The doctor's medical notes stated she had her own Xanax and would take it herself. Still, she was put on some kind of drip that made her groggy, and during the procedure, she kept losing consciousness. Afterward, they couldn't fully wake her, but they still asked her how many Xanax she had taken.

"Did you take one Xanax?"

"Yes," she mumbled, kinda-sorta nodding.

"Did you take two?"

"Yes."

We'll never know.

You can't compile a medical history based on answers from someone who's under anesthesia. They should have gotten clarity *before* they started the procedure to determine exactly what she had taken, not immediately after to save their hides.

When the little silver pill case containing her medication fell out of her pocket, those so-called specialists basically ascribed everything to her being an older woman who'd taken too much Xanax. Now, keep in mind that Diane knew how to take this medication because she had been suffering from anxiety and was familiar with the correct dosing. She wasn't just popping those pills, so it's very unlikely she took enough to make her completely unconscious.

So what happened? Well, at the end of the day, when they couldn't really get her to a point where she'd safely be able to leave, they sent Mom home with a nurse to monitor her vitals throughout the night. That's incredibly unusual. In my opinion, she should have been taken straight to the ER to be evaluated. There were even ER doctors *in* the procedure room observing that day. I lived with a doctor and knew the oath "First do no harm" intimately. All this was happening, and Mom's amazing boyfriend, John—who'd thought he was simply taking her in for a routine facial akin to microdermabrasion—was left to handle it. My sisters and I didn't yet know what was going on.

Normally, Michele would have been reachable, as she was Mom's only daughter in Florida. However, the day things went sideways, she was attending the memorial service of a friend who had been murdered by her ex-husband while Michele's husband at the time, Ed, was driving that family's children to their house. You can't make this stuff up.

John kept calling Michele during the service, and as soon as it was over, she saw all the missed calls. She immediately rushed off to see my mom, who still wasn't waking up. When the nurse called the doctor, he stuck to his version of what had happened, but by seven the next morning, she was insisting that Mom should be taken to the emergency room. She even stayed beyond the time she'd been instructed to stay. When the doctor responded that said nurse could just leave, she refused.

Every now and then, Mom would open her eyes and mumble incoherently. Not a normal post-laser-facial response. Two ER doctors and the cosmetic doc had sent her home because nobody wanted to take responsibility and they'd allowed this to go on all day. Everybody just stuck to the script that she had taken too much Xanax. I still don't understand it. What were those doctors thinking?

I was driving back to Darrick's from Jimmy's place when alarming calls came in from John and my sisters telling me something had gone wrong in the procedure and Mom wasn't waking up. I could hardly believe my ears. Our poor mother.

The next day, she was evaluated in the ER. At first, the doctors there thought she'd had some kind of aneurysm. Then they realized it was a hemorrhagic stroke, a bilateral bleed that had basically been going on for twenty-four hours without anybody intervening. In Florida, doctors aren't required to carry malpractice insurance. Karen hired incredible attorneys and fought hard, but we ultimately had no case. This doctor was so well protected and Mom had signed off on all of the risks. That being said, I feel like senior women are taken advantage of and some aesthetic doctors are very cavalier about it all. Regardless, Mom was admitted to the neurology ICU.

I hopped on a flight from the West Coast and, upon arrival, *I* was immediately rushed to the ER in the same hospital that Mom was in—can you *believe* this?—because I was so viscerally affected. They couldn't give me a formal diagnosis, but I was in a full-on physical and emotional collapse. Still, I eventually regained enough strength to be released and go see Mama. All of this puts losing one's things in perspective, doesn't it?

My sisters and I were gathered around her bed day and night. Mom's face was burned beyond what I had witnessed with friends who'd had laser facials and she had about ten tubes coming out of her head. Still, she wasn't physically impacted as with a typical stroke: no drooping face or anything like that. It was all cognitive, not remembering anybody. Karen's name came back first because she's the oldest; poor Denise was "the other one." Eventually, the memory started to return, but it was a long, long road.

Chapter Thirteen

THE GIFT

Seeing this woman who'd been a superhero to all of us our entire lives in such a vulnerable state was shocking. And, though we didn't judge her decision to go and get the aesthetic procedure, it was really difficult to process that this could have been preventable. And I know Mom didn't want this to be her story. She wanted to go out in a blaze of glory as the ageless trailblazer she was, not seen as feeble or a victim. But here she was and I felt it in my bones. This was the beginning of the end. I really hated this for her.

After about ten days, Mom was transferred to a rehab facility where she relearned how to walk and write and eat. As my mom got stronger, miraculously the pain that *I'd* been experiencing for months started to lift. It was like I'd had a bodily premonition that something bad was going to happen. Spiritually insightful people told me this was an "un-twinning." That's how close my mother and I were.

Aunt Linda, my sisters, and I started a text thread called "The Real Sisters... and Aunt Linda" during Mom's ongoing ordeal. Not that we were by any means estranged; this event just brought us all closer. Leave it to Diane to do whatever she had to do to get her daughters to call and text each other every day. This support would come in handy when I hit the road, which felt weird to do with my mother in her current situation. My family reassured me that Mom, of all people, would be happier than anyone to know that I was out there doing my thing. And in time, she was able to convey this herself.

In anticipation of the MixTape Tour, I got a call from NKOTB's captain himself, Donnie Wahlberg, inviting me to play a hot teacher in the "Boys in the Band" video. I had an absolute blast strutting down the hall, leading a team of high school cheerleaders... an eternally electric moment indeed! On that same call, Donnie asked if he could share my number with Joey McIntyre because Joe had a creative idea to ask me about. I immediately flashed back to meeting Joey for the first time when New Kids on the Block were performing at Westbury Music Fair and he was sitting on his sister's lap in the dressing room. Although he was only two years younger than me, as a teenager, I felt like the cool senior to his sophomore. Worlds apart, we were about to be close in an unexpected way.

"How would you like to do 'Lost in Your Eyes' as a duet with me on the tour?" he asked.

Aware I was getting about twelve minutes of stage time, performing medleys of my hits, I thought, *Dang, that takes some cojones to ask me to share my biggest song.* Then, within a split second, I was like, *Oh, I get it. He's brilliant. Sign me up!*

What resulted was an incredible reimagining of the song in front of an audience, everything I thought it could be and more. When Joey

ETERNALLY ELECTRIC

opened his mouth to sing, grown women were weeping . . . and I was one of them.

I was the only person on that tour who had the privilege of playing an instrument because everything was live to track. It was about being wowed by the visuals; they poured all the money into that. But I didn't need anyone going to bat for me like Lance back in the *NSYNC tour days. This time, no one begrudged me my moment to shine at the piano. So Naughty by Nature would be going, "Heyyy-hohhh, heyyy-hohhh," with hands in the air and the audience in a frenzy, and then my piano would come up out of the stage while I was getting into character for "Foolish Beat." It was a fun moment in how wildly different their song was to mine. I would then rise from my seat as the same intro that I'd heard back in my club days would kick in for "Only in My Dreams" and segue into "Lost in Your Eyes."

I'll never forget opening night because nobody knew what was coming and there was a collective gasp from the audience when Joe walked onstage. This happened many nights because the Blockheads, as fans of NKOTB call themselves, often purposely stayed away from social media to avoid spoilers.

I get weak in a glance
Isn't this what's called romance.[*]

Joe would lean into *this* with that resonant theater-honed tone, and his sweet falsetto was perfection on *what's called romance*.

"You were born to sing this song," I'd always tell him. It was such a perfect fit.

---

[*] "Lost in Your Eyes" by Deborah Gibson. Copyright © 1987 by Music Sales Corporation (ASCAP). International Copyright Secured. Used by permission. All rights reserved.

I still recall, when we were prepping for the tour in our own parts of the world, Joe texted me, *I have an idea for the end of the song.*

Next I saw this picture pop up of Barbra Streisand and Neil Diamond for "You Don't Bring Me Flowers" from a performance they did together at the Grammys with her hand on his face.

Wow, he's going deep, I thought. *That is such an avant-garde reference.*

Joe has a unique, eccentric, very cool universal vibe. And he knows himself. He was well aware that if we paused at the end and did a face touch that made it look like we were gonna kiss, every woman in the audience would be living vicariously through me. I'd like to think that's because I've never been threatening—and I prefer it that way. It was more like, *Awww, shucks . . . I guess I'll take one for the team!*

After everything it took to get back on a tour bus and back in the mix, having this peer of mine pour himself into a song I wrote on my childhood piano . . . You can see the expression on my face in the videos that live online. My heart was so full in this moment each and every night. And guys, listen: In addition to Joe being a peer and a friend, I played those cassettes on my Walkman on repeat, and I too had Joe on my wall.

I really want to take a moment here to commend Joe's awesome wife, Barrett, for being secure enough to share Joe with all of us. We all know what a loyal husband he is. Joey has the utmost respect for that marital circle of trust. He's really an upstanding guy that way. And his gal clearly supports the freedom he enjoys when engaging with his audience, particularly all of his Joe Girls.

One Joe Girl who wasn't going to miss this reimagining of a song she'd been such a huge part of the first time around was Diane Gibson. Although she'd lost a lot of weight and was looking gaunt, Mom had miraculously been able to attend the final show of the MixTape Tour.

It's such a gift that she got to see me one last time in that arena mania. Joey, Jordan, Tiffany, Danny, Jon, and Donnie went up to her backstage with the utmost respect because they knew the path she'd forged and knew that she was so much a part of why I was onstage with them that night. They all relayed that in their own way, and I looked on proudly as she received it. It lives on as such a beautiful memory. This was all so incredibly layered for me.

Also layered was the reconnection with my fans who had stayed on this journey with me through thick and thin. This tour validated us all in a weird way. Not that we needed it. But I know that my community of supporters are always out there in the world, singing my praises. That is why I have really grown to love the one-on-one time I get to spend at meet 'n' greets. The VIP experience, to me, is not an assembly line. I try to give each person a unique moment and, in so doing, there's the reciprocal gift in getting to know them as well. Some may have waited their whole life to tell me a particular story or this may be one of many times I've met them, but that moment of connection helps fuel their spirit, and none of this is wasted on me.

Depending on where I fit (or not) into the pop-culture landscape at any given moment, my Debheads are met with an array of reactions. Now, once again, there was a bigger understanding and acceptance of who I was as an artist.

This was also the time when I really started owning my sexuality and fashionista side. Though it had often been suggested I move into that lane in my earlier days, I'd come to it on my own. You have to remember I grew up in the days of women wearing power suits because the hot girl couldn't possibly be the CEO of her own company. I realized the core power of being a woman is to be able to remain outwardly playful and sexy while having the chops to get things done behind the scenes.

I loved knowing that people in the crowd were also aligned with this journey of coming into their own: a mix of early fans who had lost track of me since the '80s, casual fans who were now reignited, and my diehards who bought tickets to everything I did over the years, from my appearances with the Learning Annex to *Chicago* in Beverly, Massachusetts, and beyond. They weren't only there for the hits; they were there to celebrate this victorious moment with me and our entire Debhead community.

It was the beginning of me getting to know the people behind the faces more intimately through not only the meet 'n' greet experiences, but our communication on social media. It was the true start to my second act. And I was overcome with emotion, reflecting on the little girl with big dreams. *Wow.* Here we were together more than three decades later.

Please say you'll stay, say you might
*Then say we are, staying together.**

I was napping on the bus one day before sound check at the Hollywood Bowl when—*ding-ding-ding*—my phone started blowing up with texts. It was Iris.

Hey, Deb, remember Doug Cohn?

I did, from a near-romantic setup in 1985 when he and my junior high bestie were on a teen tour together. Though he liked boys back then—and still does today—we ended up having a professional relationship when he worked at Atlantic and VH1.

He would love to come to the show tonight and say hi.

---

* "Staying Together" by Deborah Gibson. Copyright © 1987 by Music Sales Corporation (ASCAP). International Copyright Secured. Used by permission. All rights reserved.

With one eye open, I replied, *Sure!*

Inundated with requests for the Hollywood Bowl tickets, I was like, *Jeez, should I just ignore this? I'm so tired, I need to keep napping.*

I'm glad I managed to pry my eyes open to honor this one last ticket request. When Doug saw me backstage, he said, "Okay, you're amazing and we need to work together on a new project of mine. Want to be a mentor/judge on *America's Most Musical Family* with Ciara and David Dobrik?"

Did I ever! Nick Lachey was the host and it was an amazing show that made me realize the holy grail is being a mentor/judge on TV. It's such a natural fit for me to nurture dreams, and because showing up to create a fabulous look is not rocket science and is a lot of fun, it was a breath that I didn't know I needed after the rigorous road schedule. I got to be the show's seasoned blonde Barbie with longtime glam guru and friend Jon Lieckfelt, who, incidentally, also dolled me up for this book cover. Playing dress-up in fabulous clothes, I imparted words of wisdom from my years of experience in the most non-preachy way possible to these up-and-coming entertainers—some kids, some adults—and it was a dream come true, foreshadowed by my stint on *American Juniors* and honed at my own camps. I was so thrilled to crown the Melisizwe Brothers the winning act and even went on to write songs with them after the show was a distant memory.

I grew up singing harmony with my sisters and singing with my dad. So, being invested and deeply connected made it all the more disappointing when the show wasn't picked up for a second season. It obviously didn't do what Nickelodeon had hoped it would. TV is a very tough landscape.

The money I made from the MixTape Tour was not as much as you might think, just because of all the people I had helping me, so it was good to earn a little money from the reality show; it enabled me to tell Heather, "I'm gonna take a jaunt across the pond to vacation in the UK."

I found peace and joy in the freezing-cold London winter, treating myself to a hot cocoa and buying Christmas gifts at Harvey Nichols and Harrods. I also took in Matt Goss's holiday concert with two of my favorite Tims, one on either arm: Tim Vincent, who I became friends with when he worked as a host on *Access Hollywood* and who covered my skating show by doing a segment where we skated together in NYC, and Sir Tim Rice, who is one of the nicest, most supportive creative geniuses you will ever meet.

On the plane back, I caught a winter bug that felt like every respiratory infection I'd ever had, except ten times worse. Then I started hearing rumblings about some virus that was spreading like wildfire, prompting me to assume I was one of the first COVID cases or had something in the SARS realm. Given my compromised immune system, I quite literally thought I was going to die. But I rose to the occasion and soon I was filming a coveted guest-starring role on the acclaimed show *Lucifer* at the request of the devilishly talented Tom Ellis, as well as making a music video for my song "Girls Night Out" that Sean produced, I wrote, and DJ Tracy Young ended up remixing to perfection.

We'd use her version as the single and it went to #4 on the *Billboard* dance chart. The video, directed brilliantly by John Asher and choreographed to perfection by Buddy and Eddie, was filmed down the street here in Vegas at Planet Hollywood. It featured a carousel horse that found its way into my piano room as a fiftieth-birthday present from the folks at Caesars Entertainment. Showcasing the talents of incredible drag queens cast by Vegas drag legend Frankie Marino, divas like a then relatively unknown Elliott with 2 T's—who has gone on to international stardom—graced this celebratory music video that put me back on the map. It was the tip of the iceberg to this new pop-music chapter we'd been working toward for nearly a decade.

On the set, having barely recovered from that incredible mystery virus, I was warned to not shake hands as some illness of epic proportions was going around. Welcome to the world of COVID. The much-needed break I was planning to take as we were plotting my next career move wasn't to be. The pandemic hit and artists were in demand because we were able to spread joy through music and lift people out of their funk.

I was among the first artists on a Zoom concert that would become the groundbreaking *Quarantunes*, which would go on to raise over thirty million dollars for charity. Long before a creative like me knew about Zoom, I was doing something I do best—snuggling with my napping dogs on the couch—when my phone started going *ding-ding-ding*. Who was incessantly texting me? Enter my dear friend Richard Weitz, the cochairman of WME who's the mayor of all things LA. His daughter Demi was bummed out that nobody could celebrate her sixteenth birthday in person because of the pandemic safety restrictions, so Richard had decided to get some friends together, including DJ D-Nice and John Mayer.

Under the persistent urging of Richard, I got up off the couch, went to the piano, and clicked the link to find the best vibes and John Mayer joining me on guitar and vocals for a rendition of "Only in My Dreams." After Demi suggested they tie the event to charity by providing a link, the event grew and grew till every hit artist lent their time and talents to this marathon weekly Woodstock-style musical extravaganza.

I recall one day when I was particularly depressed, isolating at home like the rest of the world, and got the inspired thought to throw on a pair of nice heels and a cute outfit and pull my trash bins from the side of the house . . . while singing the theme song to *Mister Rogers' Neighborhood*.

> *It's a beautiful day in this neighborhood*
> *A beautiful day for a neighbor.**

The world of COVID for someone like me, who was deemed immunocompromised, was supposed to be a scary place. But I felt like if I let fear bring me down, then yes, surely I *would* get deathly ill.

It helped that my assistant JT, who was living in my house on and off during this time, nudged me to get my pandemic baby, another dachshund who I named Levi. Even though I advocate for adoption, I stumbled upon Levi at a pet store where I was buying bones for Trouper and Joey. There for way too long, Levi had seemingly come from a puppy mill, so I scooped him up—jokingly (but not) saying I "rescued him" from the pet store. He was the crazy, charactery kid brother juxtaposed with my Zen master healer Joey and wise ol' Trouper—and would help take the edge off things when they got too serious.

Though I did get the virus a few times, not being able to pop in and out to check on Mom during this time was even harder on my health. Now, remember, she had been put into a rehab to regain her motor skills and I was aware that I most likely wouldn't be able to visit her for a long time. I knew the lack of social interaction, especially with her loved ones, was contributing to her decline.

I am, for sure, super-tied to my emotions. I could feel the stress about the pandemic and what was going on with my mother begin-

---

* "Won't You Be My Neighbor" © Fred M. Rogers, 1963. Courtesy of Fred Rogers Productions. All rights reserved.

ning to take hold in the form of shooting pains down my arm, which eventually led to a frozen shoulder.

I was one of the many people, most of them women, experiencing this very painful condition. But even being holed up in my home with limited range of motion couldn't stop me from taking the opportunity to put my hat in the ring for a prize acting role on *Girls5eva*, created by Meredith Scardino, who co-executive produced the series with Tina Fey and so many other high-level creative luminaries. A pro at hiding pain, I had my comedic chops on full display. However, the role of Summer went to its rightful owner, the brilliant Busy Philipps.

One of the fun things about straddling the music and acting worlds is that I break the rules a bit. Take, for instance, the request from casting to have actors film against a plain backdrop. I took so many liberties on this self-tape because I'm an actual pop artist and I was *playing* an actual pop artist. I figured what would I have to lose by going outside the box and giving them my full-on authentic personality and rock 'n' roll spirit? I had a blast, in isolation, re-creating *Behind the Music*–type segments and music videos to insert into my scene work. At first, the producers were open to all ethnic backgrounds for the role of Wickie, so I read for that part as well. In fact, there's an Instagram post where I'm wearing a wig and remove it; that's a clip from my self-tape audition!

It's fun when expectations are low to none, which was the case with this audition. So, the fact that I went all the way to the end to read opposite A-list actors and comedians who were also not cast but were in the running, down to the wire like me, was a thrill. I did feel like it was a *Hello, Universe* kind of moment because doing this show would have been a detour from making music.

It was so wild turning fifty during the pandemic, but weirdly I preferred it. Not one for overblown social affairs where someone gets offended if they're left off the invite list, it was showbiz-fabulous in an intimate way. Nischelle Turner and Kevin Frazier sent their *Entertainment Tonight* crew to telecast the moment I received balloons. I also had a fabulously memorable Zoom party hosted by Richard Weitz, with friends Matt Goss and Jackie Romeo serenading me.

Mom and the nurses at her facility were fumbling, trying to figure out how to log her into Zoom. I therefore FaceTimed her so that she could be a part of the celebration. I took comfort in seeing her face and her fiery red hair on what she always fondly referred to as *her* birthday. She had acquiesced to letting it go to its natural shade of white for a while, but I knew it wasn't her vibe and sent a car and driver to take her to salon appointments twice a month.

Anyone who was separated from loved ones during lockdown knows how weird it was not having them around for milestone moments. Sugar to the rescue when, at the end of the night, I was treated to a beautiful cake, courtesy of Heather, delivered by my pet-sitter neighbor Julie. It was a unique celebration, which I ultimately embraced. The night ended with my fur babies and me snuggling and decadently eating that cake in bed!

With that monumental moment behind me, I dove back into my art. Known for being prolific, I was writing songs at a steady pace. It felt like the Merrick days all over again and I was excited. Producer Kerry Brown helped fine-tune my Pro Tools home setup to up my game during this virtual time while we were still being quarantined, and he'd say, "Play me some stuff you've been writing."

We never actually collaborated, but he instigated, and one of the first songs I played him was called "Baby, It's You," which was a sort of John Legend–type piano ballad. I experimented with all different styles, though I was leaning heavily into the ballads. So, to perk things up a bit, I reached out to Tracy Young again since we'd worked so well together on "Girls Night Out," though I had yet to hear her work as a writer.

She sent me a bunch of tracks that didn't grab me right away. Because I can write a song top to bottom, anything I collaborate on must feel like an extension of me. Nothing was resonating. But I knew she had something magical up her sleeve, and that gem would come via inspiration on a trip she took to Paris on a track that would become "One Step Closer."

Holy crap, this is genius!
I immediately began writing to it.

You lit me up when baby
You called me crazy
But, man you saved me
Now I'm one step closer to love.[*]

There's a thing in writing called toplining. If I sit at the piano and I'm writing the chords and the melody, it's my creation. However, sometimes creatives like Tracy will put together a track—beats, chords, and an arrangement. In the case of my collab on "Freedom" with Dirty Werk's Steve Smooth, I added the chorus chords that became the hook to his stellar creation. When Sean then sent me the track for "Runway," I was like, "Were you born in the eighties?"

What I love is that I don't have anything to prove anymore in the way of writing. I know if someone sends me a track, it's gonna inspire me and trigger an idea I otherwise never would have had. I love expanding my world to include more people and more ideas, and it makes me happy to share the credit. Artists make songs their own. I doubt anyone thought "One Step Closer" was diluted with somebody

---

[*] *"One Step Closer" by Deborah Ann Gibson and Tracy Young. Copyright © 2021 by Birdsong Publishing (ASCAP) and Ferosh Publishing (ASCAP). Used by permission. All rights reserved.*

else's energy. It all becomes *my* artist statement—and I'm open to that now in a way that really fits this ever-expanding version of who I am.

Writing more upbeat songs, I told Heather, "This feels like a dance EP that's formulating."

It became clear that I had a full album organically coming to life with the addition of songs like "Legendary," "Red Carpet Ready," "Strings," "Me Not Loving You," and the title track, "The Body Remembers," all written solely by me. Suddenly, it was not only an aggressive upbeat dance-pop-rock album with touches of my signature chant/rap/spoken-word hybrid, but it contained just enough ballads to give the listener an emotional reprieve. And not only was it an album, it was my message—the message in the music that I'd waited twenty years for.

In the midst of recording, I put on my business hat and joined the Zoom strategy meetings, and, under Heather's fierce guidance, we embarked on a highly ambitious campaign to once again get the music to the people on our very own Stargirl records.

Heather had been quietly looking for new team members who'd help usher in this musical era; she assembled an A-list group of people, including attorney Monika Tashman; Missi Callazzo, our distribution partner; Rebecca Shapiro; Josh Page of Shore Fire Media; my acting agent Matt Jackson, who championed me while casting *The Suite Life of Zack and Cody*[*]; and booking agent Jeff Howard, along with our longtime business management team of Michael Ullman and Erik Moreno and OG Team Deb's Elizabeth Neff.

The players were ready to play after hearing and falling in love with the new music. It always has and always will begin and end with the music.

---

[*] *I was among the final three actresses considered for the role of Carey Martin.*

ETERNALLY ELECTRIC

Boss babes at play! Heather and I take a moment away from our joint creative ventures to celebrate in Las Vegas.

I feel like *The Body Remembers* is *Electric Youth*, part two: hooky dance-pop songs mixed with ballads and live elements. The aggressiveness of the tracks and the beats was the energy shift I needed during the pandemic while dealing with some residual love angst that I chose not to publicize or write about. I felt in this case it was more powerful to let the music do the talking. And in order to hear all that I was trying to convey, I went deep in the way of details.

It takes me back to being that teen in the home studio, but this time it's me in my nightgown waking up in the middle of the night and going out to the driveway to do the car-speaker test. This was to make sure every emotion, every frequency, every little thing I set out to make the listener feel was in play.

The attention to every little nuance on this album is extraordinary. I own that. This wasn't something I was ever going to phone in. It had been twenty years since I'd done an original pop album and I was gonna make sure it was a piece of work I was extremely proud of. I even used all the pronouns—he, she, they—each time the hook of the song "Freedom" was repeated. Everyone is fully represented.

The title *The Body Remembers* speaks to all the things we absorb throughout our lives. We hold the physical blueprint to our experiences. The body remembers pain, trauma, love, where you were when you heard a certain song . . . all of it. And the song itself encapsulates *newstalgia*, speaking of that great young love who stays with us, even now.

Around this time, I told my team, "I want to start a new fan club, like a modern-day DGIF, called the Diamond Debheads. I think there are people out there who want to commune through my music."

I'm pretty sure the pandemic triggered that thought from doing Instagram Lives and feeling the sense of community out there. Even though I hadn't released all of the new music yet, my fans were already conveying they wanted to be a part of a community. And I now realized I could take this to a whole new level. So I promised them a welcome video, and on the first day of filming a video at home in Vegas with JT, we were psyched to see about two hundred sign-ups in the first go-round. It was so cool.

I enjoyed knowing I was going to be getting even closer to my people and I'd stop calling them fans because they were so much more and

I wanted to get to know them on a whole new level. It's been a huge part of this current chapter. The Diamonds even appeared in my "Love Don't Care" video, starring my younger-man love interest, consummate professional, and friend Charlie Gillespie. He, Anthony Michael Hall, and I starred in a cool indie film released in 2022, *The Class*.

My favorite thing about my community is that they've formed relationships and unbreakable bonds separate and apart from me because of me and my music. I peer in from the outside on social media to watch them take care of and support each other. That's a huge part of my legacy and something from which I derive an extraordinary amount of gratification.

All the Debheads waited with bated breath for the new record. Upon its release in August 2021, their posts and videos made it clear they were taken aback and genuinely blown away. I don't think they expected something so relevant and modern-sounding. And that was due in part to Sean, but also to DJ Tracy Young, Steve Smooth of Dirty Werk, Josh Gudwin, ASHBA—my Vegas neighbor and dear friend who positively lit it up with his layered, rockin', nuanced guitar work—Lars Halvor Nelson, and Cinderella drummer and producer/arranger Fred Coury, an old friend who I was so thrilled to have aboard this project.

Photographer Nick Spanos captured the essence of this music perfectly on the album artwork on a shoot for which he flew himself to Vegas to show me what he could do on spec. And we've been connected creatively and as friends ever since.

So many more incredibly talented people were a part of this project—too many to name, but please, check out the credits online! I was out to up my game and I always knew I could write a hook that would ensure it sounded like that classic Debbie Gibson song that people grew up with, but with a modern flair. I never want to get stuck in the past. It's the quickest way to age yourself out.

During the pandemic, I had called Joey Mac and said, "I think it's time to rerecord 'Lost in Your Eyes.'"

He always says that call was a lifeline for him when the entire country was under lockdown. We both needed it, and I think our fans needed it. I cut my vocal in my home studio while suffering from another round of COVID. I was a bit nervous about cutting the vocal while sick, but I'd recorded "Foolish Beat" with a fever and we all know how that turned out! After Joe and I recorded our vocals, Sean expertly produced the track and he had a very hard job. The "Lost in Your Eyes" intro was iconic and creating something a little more JP Saxe and not dated—that was spacious and had just a hint of the original—brought it into a new era. Giving the track its own identity without offending the purists was no easy task, but Sean did just that.

Joe and I shot the video, directed by Pat Anthony, which featured us in the recording studio. It currently has well over two million views on YouTube.

Another favorite call from Joe: "You know, as we're doing all this, why don't I come out your way so we can do some shows?"

It was a personal and professional highlight and I love that our audiences cross over. People loved investing to see their "idol" and their "crush" together onstage. I'd like to do it again. We need our own variety show because our banter in Vegas was off the rails!

One day, Joe called and said, "Let's open the show with 'All Coming Back to Me Now.'"

"The Céline Dion song? Have you met me? I'm not that kind of vocalist. You want me to do Céline in Vegas where she's been headlining for fourteen thousand years?"

"Yeah. You can do it. The pandemic's virtually over and we're reemerging into the world."

He always has an artistic vision that's hard to dispute. "Okay, I'm gonna try it." I dug in with my magical new voice teacher Erik Landry.

Vocally, I really went there. Some nights I mastered it, some nights I didn't, but it was fun—even though Joe had me do my least favorite thing, which was open the show with a ballad. That's my nightmare because I'm always a little jittery, but we did it, and then I came up with the idea of us going into Dua Lipa's "Levitating." Also performing "You're the One That I Want" and "Islands in the Stream/Ghetto Superstar," we had a great time.

I love that camaraderie Joe and I have onstage. I vividly recall a moment when I forgot a step during "Islands" and he looked at me, good-naturedly shaking his head as if to say, "Ohhh, Deb." It probably was too subtle for the audience to see, but the connection we share is palpable. This was first-rate fun, from the costumes to the choreography by Buddy and Eddie and sharing a band.

I laugh because I was championing Sean, this young unknown, to be our musical director and keyboard player, and Joe was getting sick of hearing about him because I was pushing so hard.

"You have to meet this kid," I told him. "It's my one stipulation."

We were on a Zoom call and I was exhausting him.

"Okay, okay, I know I need to meet him, Deb. I *hear* you!"

Cut to the Solo Joe tour with Sean as now the only other musician on his stage. He's even Joe's collaborator on his recent album *Freedom*. He's also done preproduction for NKOTB and New Edition, and there have been times when it's like Joe and Sean are sailing off into the sunset while I can barely get either of them on the phone . . . I kid. They both show up for me constantly—and it makes so much sense and makes me so happy. Joe knows that.

Heather was with us for that whole run. Every night while I did a quick change in my dressing room directly off to the side of the stage,

Joe would run through it to make his entrance, prompting my manager to say, "Hey, buddy, you're cutting it a little close!" Well, one night he ran through while I was stark naked. Moments later, Joe was onstage telling the audience what he had seen. He did an imitation, making it look like I had my back arched and was doing the bend-and-snap from *Legally Blonde*. That was so not true! I'm laughing as I write this.

"Oh my God!" I shouted.

"I didn't see anything! I didn't see anything! I didn't see anything!" Joe shouted back.

Onstage for our next song together, we were looking at each other, and again, this is the chemistry you can't buy in a bottle.

"I saw everything," he admitted on mic. "She's as gorgeous as you think she is . . . as *I* think she is . . . I'm stuttering!"

I live for that kind of walking-on-a-high-wire live experience, as does the audience. At one point, I walked into the wings and then came back and lay down flat on the ground because I didn't even know where to go with this. But I was also playing it up. Joe and I are the king and queen of unrestrained banter; nobody would ever script a Deb and Joe show. That night was a free-for-all and one of the most fun times I've ever had on a stage.

I also brought in my longtime soundman whom I met during the finale of *DWTS*. He's mixed live tours for everyone from Whitney to Michael Jackson to Prince and now Ne-Yo. Doreonne has been such an amazing confidence booster when I most need it, as my ongoing health journey unexpectedly affects my voice. Reassuring me that you cannot hide star power, he likens me to a 1961 Ferrari 250 GT similar to the one in *Ferris Bueller's Day Off*. We have many laughs over the idea that you can't put spinners on a luxury car—and that if anyone tries to devalue me, it's time to cut them loose!

Mom was sad she couldn't be in the audience for my Vegas run, but

Joey, Trouper, Levi, and I would FaceTime her. She called my boys her *granddogs* and the phone was the only way we had to connect, being in different states, isolating through these trying times. But even the joy of the video calls was short-lived as she started suffering hallucinations and suicidal ideation. Mom had to go to a psych ward and get an evaluation. Big surprise: She contracted COVID in there.

Supposed to be in for seventy-two hours, she was forced to stay for months because, despite no longer having any symptoms, she kept testing positive. Understandably agitated, she was put on sedatives, which resulted in her putting on weight. Alone in her room, doing a whole lot of nothing for weeks on end, she'd call me on the phone in the hallway and say, "Deborah, I feel like I'm in a scene from *One Flew Over the Cuckoo's Nest*. Somebody's gotta come get me outta here!"

I felt so helpless because in another time and place I would have gone and busted her out. But, during the pandemic, we were all at the mercy of the rules, and Mom couldn't fully comprehend restrictions even in normal times, let alone in lockdown. Already disoriented, she needed her family around her, but unable to get the vaccine for a long time, I couldn't go near her because of my health issues. Michele was the one who'd take her out and bring her to the house for dinner . . . until she got into a boating accident, severely injuring her back, and couldn't help out anymore.

Things took a very dark turn during those months in the psychiatric unit, where Mom became almost non-functioning. Wanting her to be around the most family members, we transferred her from Boca Raton to the Actors Fund Home in Englewood, New Jersey. Of course she fought us on that, but John was getting worn out and he loved knowing she was nearby—as long as he had some support.

A nurse would drive Mom to and from Karen's house twice a week, but by now she was suffering from congestive heart failure and definitely had mobility issues. Cognitively, she was also slowing down—good long-term memory, not so good short-term—but she was still very communicative. And she was certainly happy to be around Karen, Denise, and the grandchildren.

Nigar, our eccentric little Turkish housekeeper from the House That Pop Music Built days, lived in the next town over from the Actors Fund Home, and, although no longer working for us, she was very attached to my mom. It was like the weird love-hate relationship with the relative you can never quite get rid of. Well, she pretty much muscled her way into the home outside of visiting hours. Which just goes to show that, despite complaining about being in New Jersey, my mother had plenty of love coming at her during her final chapter.

When Christmas 2021 arrived, all four of her daughters were with her along with many of the grandkids. She and I were fighting a little bit at this point because she wanted to go back to Florida. No way was that about to happen; she could no longer get on a plane, and besides, there was nobody to help her in Florida. Remembering it from when she was independent, she wanted to resume her life there—just not her recent life.

"I never get to see all of my girls here," Mom lamented.

"Everyone was just together with you for Christmas," Karen reminded her a few hours later.

"*Nobody* was here for Christmas," Mom replied, having already forgotten.

Karen showed her some photos that proved otherwise.

I went to say goodbye the next day because I was returning to the city before flying back to the West Coast—and my dear mother really didn't want me to leave. She longingly pleaded with me to stay. But it was time to go pack and head back to the West Coast. Staying as long as I could, I made a conscious shift at some point to not do the whole martyr syndrome thing that, being Italian, we all grew up with: You sleep on the bed and you *stay*. Who cares if you also go into a full-on collapse. I knew no one was going to take care of me but me, so I did what I could and I was at peace with that.

We were all attached to Mom in our own ways. I'd had her connected at the hip for a lot of my career, so I admittedly had my limits and boundaries—and visiting hours were coming to an end that day. She was very sad, almost like she knew something, which she often intuitively did. Yet there was no indication of any significant medical issue. Assuming she wasn't going anywhere anytime soon, I planned to return once a month to see her in Jersey; in fact, I vowed I'd actually get back twelve times in the next twelve months. But it would be too late.

When I arrived back in Vegas after what turned out to be our final Christmas with Mom, it was nearly New Year's Eve. With all the many invites one has on the Vegas Strip for big see-and-be-seen parties, I opted to stay in with my doxie crew and once again FaceTime with my mother. Ordering a pizza, I ended up serenading her at the piano and I think I may have been having a premonition of what was to come. This would be the last intimate, meaningful hang and musical exchange between me and Mama—and it profoundly brought about the song "Cheers," which I had been humming pieces of a month or so prior to this night. Magically and mysteriously coming together, it's one of the most inspired pieces of music I have ever had the honor of delivering to all of you.

> *Here's to the end and the beginning*
> *What a year*
> *Cheers!**

---

* "Cheers" by Deborah Ann Gibson. Copyright © 2022 by Birdsong Publishing (ASCAP). Used by permission. All rights reserved.

Chapter Fourteen

ANYTHING IS POSSIBLE

It was late January and Darrick Sahara invited me to a belated fiftieth-birthday celebration weekend in Laguna Beach and I was a bit run-down, but because it was Darrick, I wouldn't miss it for the world. After checking into La Casa del Camino, I got myself dolled up, went to the rooftop restaurant, and had an incredible time with the intimate group that was gathered to celebrate our beloved friend.

We met up the next morning for coffee, and when "Mama Said" by the Shirelles came over the speakers, I started singing along and even made a video, immediately posting it up. I love that song. We had a nice hang and decided to walk back to the hotel when, all of a sudden, a young couple who we'd seen in the coffee place pulled up beside us in their car and handed me a Bible, quoting the Book of John. *John?* Like *Mama's* John?? Okay, Universe . . .

Leaving my friend, I went into my room and proceeded to have a wrestling match with my bathing suit. It's this contraption that has asymmetrical straps and is different shades of orange. It's funny what we remember. I was planning to go down to the beach when the phone rang. It was Karen.

"Hey, what's up?" It wasn't totally unusual for my big sis to be calling, but I sensed something.

"I just got a call from the Actors Fund Home," she said in that hushed, intense tone, like when Mom called me on 9/11. "Mom was eating lunch and the nurse, Deborah, walked back in twenty minutes later and found her unresponsive."

Unresponsive? Not entirely sure what this meant while deeply aware what it meant, I walked down to the beach. I don't know how many of you have lost a parent, but I kind of went into a numb state. It was a zone I had never been in before, even without the news being delivered as of yet.

I was awaiting another phone call from Karen when my cell rang right on cue. It was the news I'd been hoping wouldn't come. Arriving at the home, Karen had discovered Mom was gone. She had passed. Karen relayed that she didn't look distressed, as her expression was peaceful, but our mother's worst fear had been realized: She had died alone. Not in terms of the number of people who loved her, but circumstances had dictated she needed to be in a facility, and while we'd never know whether her death was due to a stroke or her heart just giving out, that didn't matter to us.

Diane's journey on earth had come to an end. I asked Karen to hit FaceTime so I could see Mom's face one last time and have that closure. To see this woman who had filled every room lying there lifeless . . . there are no words. Karen asked me to call Dad, and he had an awkward kind of reaction. He was obviously sad, but I don't think he knew exactly how to feel—and I felt for him, telling him in this moment I was so grateful to have him as my dad and what an amazing job he'd done. Endearingly, this always surprised him to hear. So even if you assume people know how you feel, *tell them*.

I immediately called many people whom Mom and I were close to. I needed my loved ones in this moment. This was the cathartic way I dealt with the initial shock. I got the first plane out to New Jersey to start planning everything with my sisters, sorting through photographs and jewelry, consoling one another.

It was the night of the viewing and I wasn't sure if Denise wanted to see Mom one last time. I generally prefer to remember people in their living state, but I'd vowed that whatever Denise wanted was what I'd do. I could stay outside the viewing room with her so she wasn't the only one not going in or I could accompany her in. At this point, it was just the body, but when you've spent so much time connected at the hip, it is its own kind of letting go. She opted to go in, and Karen asked if I could play my song "The Gift." I was so moved by this request; it was quite a moment.

> *'Cause your love is what I'll miss*
> *Your love is December's kiss*
> *I just tore up my list*
> *'Cause your love is the gift.*[*]

I lay in bed the next morning, as I knew my mom's request to be cremated was happening at a certain time. For Diane, who placed great importance on the physical body, this was a very profound and traumatic moment. That trip was beautiful, making angels in the snow at Karen and Jeff's house and just being with family and friends. So

---

[*] *"The Gift" by Deborah Ann Gibson. Copyright © 2022 by Birdsong Publishing (ASCAP). Used by permission. All rights reserved.*

many people attended Diane's memorial by Zoom, and Richard Weitz exclaimed that he wanted to sign Uncle Carl because his tribute was so funny and poignant and in the moment—unforgettable. Denise didn't want to speak and each of us who did speak had our own style and our own unique relationship with our mom. That made every tribute unique and reminded me that, even though we share the universal experience of losing a loved one as a point of connection, everyone's experience is also vastly different.

I know my mom was so proud at the end; she had come full circle. And I know I speak a lot about our complicated relationship, but I love Diane eternally, and if I had it to do all over again, I would pick her all over again to be my mommy. I couldn't imagine my life without that passionate, loving, loyal, colorful woman.

Not quite ready to launch myself back into things, I needed more time to grieve. But I always took comfort in making music. And to make music was to honor Mom.

I'd been quietly moving forward with the recording of my first-ever holiday album. The unconventionally out-of-order girl was ready to throw her hat in the holiday ring. I finally had the new material that, like *The Body Remembers*, made a statement. And I felt that upon writing "The Gift" at Ray Garcia's wedding in Texas to longtime love Daran Norris—on the back of the emergency-drill instructions printout at the motel where I stayed. Likewise "Christmas Star," which feels new yet familiar. Howard Fine always said that was the sign of a hit *anything*.

Upon hearing my Virgo sister Sylvia's gem "I Wish Everyday Was Christmas," I begged her to let me adopt it as my own, making it only the second new original I'd ever recorded that I hadn't written or cowritten. An instant classic! I also wrote my first-ever original Hanukkah song, "Illuminate," making this an inclusive album full of universal messages. I consulted with Jonathan on the details of this beautiful holiday. The theme: When we don't think we have enough, it will be provided if one has faith.

Adding some timeless covers, I enlisted the help of David Andrews Rogers, aka DAR, as well as a magical virtual orchestra from Russia, found online by Heather. Getting to witness their greatness in real time and being able to produce them from another country was something I was so grateful for, since in-person recording sessions weren't happening.

While Ira was back on guitar, Fred Coury rocked production and drums on "Cheers" and encouraged me to play a live glockenspiel part, hearkening back to my days in the fifth-grade marching band at Camp Avenue Elementary. Credited as the "Diamond Choir," my Diamond Debheads sang on the song "Cheers!" and I love that they are immortalized on my album forever.

Releasing two albums independently within fourteen months was highly ambitious, as was offering *Winterlicious* in different colors of vinyl, but Heather and I were on a mission and gaining momentum. So, to say the least, we really appreciated the grace given to us when the record plant pressing the vinyl mixed up which color went with which cover. Again, you can't make this stuff up. Being able to offer these options on my own label—helped by Team Deb's Jourdyn, Elizabeth, and Hidhe, with Heather and me at the helm, executing the wild ideas—was so much fun! We even submitted *TBR* and *Winterlicious* for Grammy consideration, and, though I haven't yet received one—or an American Music Award—in my long career, there's always this next stretch!

Last summer I helped create a movie with screenwriter Rick Garmen for Hallmark, once again with executive Bart Fisher. Hallmark had come a long way in terms of inclusiveness, and there was a moment in time when they'd received backlash for airing an ad for a wedding-planning site featuring a lesbian couple. In my family, the first wedding among all the nieces and nephews was my niece Diana's marriage to her wife, Anna; they are the most extraordinarily loving couple you will ever meet. It was so important to know that a network I was on was celebrating my beloved LGBTQIA+ community.

Notes of Autumn follows two romantic storylines, a heterosexual couple and a same-sex couple, within a fun house-swap premise. Originally, I was supposed to star as Ellie, ultimately played beautifully by Ashley Williams. Indeed, the character was custom-tailored for me and by me, but Hallmark had other casting ideas at the eleventh hour and I had a tour to do, so once again I looked on the bright side and pivoted. It was my call as to whether I wanted to scrap the entire movie or see it to fruition. Getting this movie made was bigger than me and my on-camera ego.

The goal of this creative moment was representation, so it was my distinct honor to be a part of shifting the consciousness and imparting to the public that calling a network a "family network" as a way to avoid including *all* families wasn't acceptable anymore. Was it ever? Families are about love and support and come in all sorts of configurations. I'm therefore so thrilled this story got to be respectfully told and that there was this incredible, groundbreaking, split-screen *Gone with the Wind* moment at the end of the film when the two couples share their kiss.

While my vision was coming to life on the small screen, I hit the road once more in my RV, Big Al.

My Fleetwood Flair is like a mini–tour bus and I've put over thirty thousand miles on it in the past two years doing concert tours, a welcome change after spending so many of them in hotels and on expensive tour buses as a teen touring artist. Having always loved the open road and curious about RVs, one day in January 2022 I decided on a whim to test-drive one. The first vehicles I drove were kind of generic and lacked personality, so I kept searching and documenting my adventures in this quest on social media, leading me to one owned by *TBR* engineer Luca Pretolesi.

Here was my dream RV. It *spoke* to me. And I was instantly hooked on all the things it offered, including a built-in recording studio. The high price tag normally wouldn't have been a problem for my type A risk-taking personality: *I'll go on tour and make plenty of money*. But since Mom's passing was so fresh, I was a little bit gun-shy about committing to a heavy workload by splashing the cash on this shiny new object. I'd had to run to keep up with things too many times.

Fortunately, Karen saw things differently and was right there, giving me the friendly nudge that Mom had always given me: "Deb, this is going to be such an adventure for you, I can feel it. Losing Mom has taught us that anything can happen at any time. You're a savorer of life and I know you want this, so take the leap."

That's exactly what I did—and I now don't know how I fathomed living this chapter of my life without this incredible new vehicle for change, evolution, and adventure. The RV became my mode of transportation for *The Body Remembers* tour, driven by Kurt Buckardt, who was a perfect tour sidekick. We shared the same mentality of winging it and leaning into joy as well as spontaneity every chance we got, even hitting lemonade stands, antique stores, and Michael Jackson's childhood home.

Not wanting me to be the damsel in distress, Kurt taught me to do my own oil change in 117-degree Nevada heat and had me document it on social media so that other women might be inspired to do the same. Yep, all this from the girl who wrote "Shake Your Love."

Firing up the RV for *The Body Remembers*, *Winterlicious*, and *The Body Remembers* Encore tours has been one of the great joys of my life. What's more, the fact that we've done these tours without a big promoter is astounding. And exhausting. And meaningful on all levels. I have been blown away by my community's show of support, which even found longtime DG connoisseur and Diamond Tim Chang offering to drive our crew in his RV and hold it down at the merch table with Kurt.

During *The Body Remembers* Encore Tour, I was awoken on the RV presumably by Diane, as I quite literally felt a tap on the shoulder to see a giant sign. On it was the name of a town that holds a lot of meaning for me. Yup, there it was: the last name of *The Boy*, big as anything, right before me.

That prompted me to send my old friend a DM and so began over two years of texts, voice notes, and, eventually, an in-person friendship. We never miss a day of communicating. My life wouldn't be the same without his daily energy. It hasn't had its own moment in time to see what it could be as a fully realized relationship, but there has been *a thing that's not a thing that was a thing that could be a thing* . . .

Once I stepped into his world of kids and family and friends, it was hard to unknow that feeling of familiarity and comfort mixed with the excitement of something new. I am not one to push anyone to be where they are not or to feel what they don't, but the chemistry and connection is undeniable and I have learned just how patient and unwavering I can be. Turns out I can carry a torch for a long time.

> *If I come complete, how do you complete me?*
> *Had gone unseen, but oh how you see me*
> *It burns the whole night through*

Ain't nothin' I won't do
The Torch it burns for you.*

I often jokingly look up and ask Mama if she's just sending me song inspiration.

I will always remember that summer
When I opened my heart again.**

But this time I go on record: I want the song *and . . . The Boy.*

Living somewhere between letting go and hanging on to hope is a difficult place to be. I've not quite figured out how to navigate that one, but I'm working on it. And I am aware that maybe we won't end up being the right fit for each other. In the meantime, I'm faced with that age-old juggling act of putting my feelings aside to show up as a friend. I want what's best for everyone. I'm working on not bleeding out energy on things I can't control. Having my heart opened for the first time in a long time, I'm often left feeling vulnerable to an extreme degree. This doesn't go unnoticed by people close to me.

Richard Weitz, who you may recall presided over my birthday Zoom, has always had that respect and a full understanding of who I am, on and off the stage, since I was one of his first clients when he was just a baby agent during the *Think with Your Heart* era. He invited me to attend Clive Davis's pre-Grammy party—the one I wore that pink-and-white low-cut gown to—and I thoroughly enjoyed the evening,

---

* "The Torch" by Deborah Ann Gibson. Copyright © 2025 by Birdsong Publishing (ASCAP). Used by permission. All rights reserved.
** "That Summer" by Deborah Ann Gibson. Copyright © 2025 by Birdsong Publishing (ASCAP). Used by permission. All rights reserved.

but he could instantly see I was a bit preoccupied during his postshow gathering at the Polo Lounge.

"What's going on with you tonight?" he asked as a brass band serenaded us at the table.

"Well, I'm a bit of a Diane Keaton movie these days," I replied, alluding to me laughing one minute and crying the next.

"I get it. I mean, you're alone in that trailer park..."

Huh? Where did *that* come from? "That dig is very Diane Gibson," I shot back, feeling hurt and like I was about to cry right there in front of Richard, the band, and Adrien Brody, who had sauntered over to say hello.

Richard knew my mom. Seeing I was hurt, his sharp tone shifted to a caring one. "No, what I meant was I picture you in the back of your RV and it can be overwhelmingly lonely."

Richard certainly knew a thing or two about that. And how I was ongoingly affected by *The Boy*.

Constantly traveling the world, he was surrounded by people all day, every day, while spending nights alone in the quiet of his own mind. *From chaos to crickets*; this intense transition from day to night and from show to postshow can be overwhelming and bring up all sorts of radical feelings. So he tapped in to what I call "Girl in back of RV with feelings": those moments when I have too much time and space to entertain my emotions... which usually aren't so entertaining.

These days, between the Mom grief and the newly discovered feelings for this guy, consumed with longing for something that may or may not become the thing I picture, while rebuilding my health and my touring career... it's the stuff of life. And it's a *lot*.

Some people think, *Oh, it's Deb, she's tough like one of the boys and she can take it*, because I do have that side to me. But I also can be a little fragile within the solitary existence that's required to stay the course in my career. I'm not immune to anything. Unwilling to flippantly or gratuitously date, I also often fly solo in terms of love. The thought of my sans-plus-one self hitting the road back to Malibu while *The Boy* is out there in the world tonight—when I wish he was with me—brought my feelings to the surface. Even when the traveling band accompanied Tiffany Haddish in a singalong that found me gleefully duetting on "New York, New York."

I hugged Richard, thanked the lovely Clive Davis, returned home alone, and shed the Cinderella gown to once more become "Girl in back of RV with feelings." There's something about my bohemian beach lifestyle that oddly nourishes and connects me to important parts of myself. I mean, who would've known that I got ready in an RV to go to Clive's party? And who can keep up the Cinderella thing 24/7 anyway?

Those glass slippers—on that night, Swarovski-crystal Louboutins—hurt my feet after a while, hence me kicking them off, both on- and offstage. This isn't just a bit, but should it be perceived as such, make no mistake: All good bits come from someplace real . . . albeit someplace slightly painful.

My core audience will tell you I'm known for kicking off my shoes and deconstructing as the show goes on. They also know I give my all, all the time, so if ever I am a bit under, they immediately turn into a family of people who care about my well-being first and the public persona second. That is priceless in the *fair-weather-friend* world of showbiz—and how we all operate in our organization.

Heather and I are boss babes who have our morning strategy meetings and who engage and collaborate with our high-level teammates. But it's now *my* turn to do what Heather has done for over a decade. And that is to support her on her own health journey.

A cancer diagnosis was not what any of us were expecting in the fall of 2023—especially for Heather, who has endless stamina and runs circles around me. Our team leader needs to know she is supported above all else and it is up to me to wear more hats, navigate, and find that delicate balance between keeping things as normal as possible and not leaning on her in ways that take the energy she needs for her own healing process. She won't always tell me. I just need to know.

Always one to quip "All you need is a good wig and a great attitude," she's added layers to her hero status and I am more in awe of her than ever. As is her otherworldly artist Jackie Romeo, who she signed to management after discovering her at my 2017 recording workshop hosted by yours truly on Long Island. It's a bit of a girls club around here, where men are welcome but powerful female energy and loyalty abounds.

I was recently reminded that being a powerful female also means sometimes you must surrender. I hadn't missed a solo concert in decades, but in winter 2024 I had an all-out collapse that forced me to cancel one of my LA *Winterlicious* shows. Followed by a challenging time vocally, this was all a humbling reminder that the superwoman cape needs to get hung up now and again.

Sitting in the chair in the basement of the Bourbon Room, I was unable to move and uncertain about the fate of the rest of the tour. As my team went upstairs to break the news to the ticket holders who were growing restless that the show would be canceled, I felt utterly defeated. My tour manager Danny, Eddie, and Buddy ran up and down the steep stairwell and packed up my Kia Sportage. Sylvia, there to attend the concert, was a pillar of grounded strength as she reassured me that these things happen and the focus needed to be on my getting well, *period*. Word came back that the crowd was disappointed, of course, but more concerned with my well-being than anything.

I'm crying writing this because, at the end of the day, what matters is that level of caring and investment we have in each other as human beings. And, after so many years of being a commodity, to know this depth of love is astounding. Despite my weakness and pain, I felt oddly present and so proud of this community built on all things that uplift.

This story ends where we began: *Electric Youth* celebrating its thirty-fifth anniversary is a wrap and the gang and I went from Asia to New York City for a total of eleven shows. I wore the original costumes so the audience could see the then-and-now of it all from 1989 on the big screens right in front of them. I then hit the road for *Acoustic Youth*, performing sixteen concerts that featured stripped-down versions of songs from the *Electric Youth* era to honor the thirty-fifth as we kept the celebration going. I closed out the year by getting back on the reindeer, finishing out the remaining shows of my *Winterlicious* holiday run!

The new year began on a high, as I entertained over fifty million people worldwide at the Rose Parade, a career highlight. I was living for rockin' the classical piano intro to "Electric Youth" in the dramatic rose-covered cape, and embraced getting up at midnight to rehearse on the dark cold streets of Pasadena with Betty Who and hundreds of wonderful young dancers. But the biggest highlight? Debbie Allen appearing in *my* number. My *Fame* moment, full circle. *Divine*.

Today I'm overseeing musical arrangements, wardrobe, and visuals for my next tour, being dog mom to Joey and Levi after losing Trouper in late 2023, putting the finishing touches on this book with my dream collaborator Richard Buskin, managing my health, rehabbing my voice, and protecting my heart. As we know, I'm an indefatigable cat who always lands on her feet. But not without support and diligence.

After going for a little playtime with my dogs, I turn on Troye Sivan's "One of Your Girls" while getting dolled up to make shout-out videos for my Diamonds. I'll soon be donning the black Capezio leotard I wore in the "Love Don't Care" video, lovingly nicknamed

Leotardo DiCaprio—and, perched atop my neon Debbie sign, I'll be creating a personal video for each one of my nearly four hundred Diamonds. Because while love may not care, *they* do. And *I* do.

Even though my OG hat is long gone, I have a fresh, bigger, more bohemian black hat that I pack for my upcoming shows. Nothing is ever really lost, just reimagined. And this reminds me to share one parting story before I go. It's about my newfound love affair with Malibu.

As many of you know, many parts of Malibu and areas in Southern California, including a post–Rose Parade Pasadena, suffered an immense tragedy at the start of 2025 when so many people lost irreplaceable things in the fires. Maybe it's because I'm so grateful to be healthy and strong and alive; maybe it's because I, too, suffered over the loss of personal sentimental items. But I felt a calling to go help.

So, firing up Big Al for his maiden voyage after an engine replacement, I brought in nephews Stefano and Tristan, as well as my part-time assistant Hidhe Gonzalez, who stepped up big-time for this effort. Then we hit the road with thousands of dollars' worth of goods, courtesy of money raised by my Debhead community, ASHBA, and me. Then, out of nowhere, there was smoke, the RV started swerving, and I felt a loss of control that had me really worried. Fortunately, we coasted to safety on the side of the I-5, and after many calls and six hours of waiting, we unpacked the RV, which got towed back to Vegas, repacked everything into a U-Haul, and were on our way again.

Four of us across a three-seater with me at the wheel driving a U-Haul for the first time kept us focused on our mission to arrive at the LA Dream Center, where we'd be greeted by iHeart DJ JoJo Wright, my Diamonds, Pastor Matthew, and thirty male residents in recovery,[*] who proceeded to unload all the goods in three minutes flat.

---

[*] *From drug and alcohol addictions, depression, and abuse.*

The whole time, I kept thinking, *Though I'm tired and this pushes up against deadlines, what I feel is nothing compared to the people directly affected and on the front lines.*

It took me a minute to recover from this journey, but recover I did, and I jetted off on my first-ever *Love Songs* tour in honor of Valentine's season. Upon my return to Vegas, I relished being the Nevada Ballet's choice for Woman of the Year, an honor I was deeply moved to receive. A bit "always the bridesmaid, never the bride," I graduated to Queen status and it felt slightly new and uncomfortable. The fact that there was an empty seat at my table with a place card for *The Boy* might have made me feel unworthy. But I really heard my friend Tony Orlando when, in his beautiful off-the-cuff tribute, he deemed me . . . *worthy.*

Overcoming the element of disappointment, I soaked in every ounce of joy the night had to offer. It's an art. And it takes practice. Focusing on who *was* at that table, I strutted into that grand ballroom, microphone in hand, on the arms of my beloved Bookend Baldies. Taking no prisoners and leaning into joy, I showed us all that I can indeed do it *with* a broken heart. I can do it *without* a broken heart. Baby, *I can do it*!

My point? I believe resilience is available to everybody, but it is also a mindset. My mindset and that discipline have been tested as of late between grieving the loss of my mom, reframing the romantic picture I had in my storyline, financial unpredictability, and wondering, *Are we there yet?* Wherever *there* is. So I continue to make intentional decisions and I continue to get out of bed every day to figure out how I can dig deeper, how I can be better, and how I can block out anything that's bringing me down, depressing me, triggering me.

It's constant work that we all must do.

As I don't have the security of somebody writing me a paycheck or a partner to lean on, everything relies on my energy, my health, my mental strength. I savor my freedom, but how much I move a dial forward day to day to day is on me. I also do have people I employ and a team relying on me whom I feel a huge sense of responsibility to . . . including those who put forth their time, energy, and hard-earned money to buy a ticket and see me perform live. I have this tremendous drive to keep giving to my audience—not because I'm obligated, but because I *want* to. It's my calling. And, as far as love goes, Miley Cyrus sings, "I can buy myself flowers"—but just because I can doesn't mean I want to. I'm content, but also hopeful.

I carry that hope for animals as well, advocating for them and visualizing an animal rescue or sanctuary in my future. I begin every day by looking at my dogs and saying, "I'm here and *you're* here!" Everything else is icing on the cake! I find *only good vibes* in the simplest of pleasures.

When you've experienced being unable to move your body at all, a stroll on the beach becomes a gift. I am always optimistic about there being love on the horizon, be it in the way I script it or an unexpected surprise. And I remain open to everything because, indeed, *anything is possible* and I'll continue to face challenges head-on while cartwheeling my way into the unknown, leaning into joy every chance I get. *Only good vibes* is a frequency, and if I can tune in, so can you.

Anything is possible . . . if you just put your mind to it.[*]

I love that, though the world has kicked my *arse* a bit, I'm not bitter. I still view that world with fresh eyes. It's fun to be playful and hun-

---

[*] "Anything Is Possible" by Deborah Ann Gibson and Lamont Dozier. Copyright © 1990 by Music Sales Corporation (ASCAP) and Beau Di O Do Music Inc (BMI). International Copyright Secured. Used by permission. All rights reserved.

gry and to feel like I'm always on the verge of something. It reminds me every day that I want to experience new things. You can either get busy living or get busy dying, as the saying goes. That's my innate spirit. But it's also a choice.

As I write this, I'm getting ready to fly off to New York City tomorrow to be in my element. I was born to do this, so I'm visualizing the concert energy that lies ahead. It is mania and magic and there is meaning in the music and the connection, with *newstalgic* vibes and everyone reconnecting with the past while looking with newfound vitality to what lies ahead for all of us. Because the future is, after all . . . *Eternally Electric*!

Thank you, Singapore!
EY35 Tour with Adam, Buddy, Stepp, Joey, and Eddie!

ACKNOWLEDGMENTS

First and foremost, I would like to thank my extraordinary collaborator, Richard Buskin. I am someone who is at my best when partnering with the right person, and from day one I knew that you, Richard, had that unspoken insight into who I am and the story I wanted to tell. You challenged me to go deeper while protecting my vision and helping channel my voice. I am not precious, so it is no wonder that I chose a "tell it like it is" Brit with a sharp sense of humor to help guide me in this process, and I could not be more grateful for your friendship, wisdom, and commitment to me and my memoir!

With my Eternally Electric *collaborator Richard Buskin in Las Vegas, bringing magic to the page over almond croissants and coffee!*

ACKNOWLEDGMENTS

To my literary agent, Yfat Reiss Gendell, thank you for your patience and expertise. I knew when you said in our first meeting that I am your spirit animal that this experience was safe in your hands.

A big heartfelt thank-you to Monika Tashman for connecting all of these dots and being such an instrumental part of ushering in this new chapter. (Pun intended!) Here's to you and all the creative endeavors that are yet to come.

So grateful to you, VP and executive editor at Gallery, Natasha Simons. I was so thrilled when the stars aligned to work on this monumental project together. Your connection to me, my music, and my audience have been evident in this process, and I cannot thank you enough for the support that you and your team have shown me.

Speaking of your team... THANK YOU:

SVP and publisher: Jennifer Bergstrom
VP and deputy publisher: Jennifer Long
Associate publisher: Eliza Hanson
VP and editorial director: Aimée Bell
VP and director of publicity and marketing: Sally Marvin
Publicist: Lauren Carr
Publicity assistant: Abby DeGasperis
Marketing director: Mackenzie Hickey
Assistant editor: Clara Linhoff
Senior managing editor: Caroline Pallotta
Managing editors: Emily Arzeno and Angel Musyimi
Copyeditor: Tracy Roe
Production editor: Jamie Selzer
Design director: Jaime Putorti
Senior art director: Lisa Litwack
Jacket designer: John Vairo Jr.

ACKNOWLEDGMENTS

Jacket photographer: Nick Spanos
SVP, sales: Kim Shannon
VP, director of subsidiary rights: Paul O'Halloran
Simon & Schuster CEO and president: Jonathan Karp
Publicity for Ms. Gibson: Rebecca Shapiro and Josh Page, Shore Fire Media
YRG Partners team rights director: Ashley Napier
YRG Partners finance team: Lisa Tilman
Agent to Mr. Buskin: Frank Weimann, Folio Literary Management
Photo retouching: Richard Buskin, Nick Spanos, and Todd Warner
Photo shoot team:
Lighting: Adam Torgerson
Lighting: Braden Moran
DigiTech: Steve Kay
BTS photos: Jill Augusto
Studio: EDGE LA
Hair and makeup artist: Jon Lieckfelt
Stylist: Elizabeth Margulis
Assistant to Ms. Gibson: Sarah Drissi
Nutritionist to Ms. Gibson: Lisa Giannini
Emotional Support Dog: Joey Gibson

I would not be me without the millions of you out there who embraced the music over the years. We have grown and evolved together and I would not be the artist I am without you all!

A very special thank-you to my Debhead community and my Diamonds! The pride that every one of you takes in each shared victory, and the love and inclusiveness you bring to me and each member of our family is my legacy beyond anything the little girl who wrote "Only in My Dreams" could have dreamt up!

ACKNOWLEDGMENTS

Elizabeth Neff: I am so grateful for your dedication and friendship since 2006.

Jourdyn Kelly: Thank you for your loyalty and creative spirit!

Kurt Buckardt, Tim Chang, and all who keep the bus rolling along... literally and figuratively! Couldn't do it without each of your unique contributions!

Missi Callazzo: My record distributor. A million thanks!

A big thank-you to my current touring family: Joey Finger, Adam Tese, Kirk Powers, Ariel Bellvalaire, Danny Stanton, Doreonne Stramler, Ronda Grinds, Devon Marie, Stepp Stewart, and all who have graced my stage, especially:

Buddy Casimano: You were there from high school to the first note in the first club. It is so meaningful to write about all of our experiences in this book. I am beyond grateful for you!

Eddie Bennett: You have left an immeasurable imprint on my art and in my heart!

My dream musical collaborator Sean Thomas—my electric kindred spirit.

Aunt Linda, Uncle Carl, Karen, Michele, and Denise—thank you for your contributions to this book and to my life. Love you all!

Daddy Joe—I would pick you all over again. The best dad and bowling buddy a girl could ask for!

To my entire extended family, friends, teachers, castmates, and mentors who contribute every day in every way to my life and my art... I am eternally grateful for your love.

To the incomparable Nick Spanos, who captured my *Eternally Electric* spirit in this cover photo so brilliantly. Your work and our friendship are treasures beyond words!

To my Pop Soulmate, Joey McIntyre. There was no one else to write the foreword to this book. You have been such a loyal friend and

ACKNOWLEDGMENTS

unexpected gift of this era. Thank you for your beautiful words and investment in me. When your wonderful observant self speaks from the heart, it is perfection. Love you, my friend.

And the grand finale: Heather Moore...

Your loyalty, fierce vision, and unwavering belief have allowed me to thrive creatively in this modern artistic landscape. You approach all you do with a boldness and focus that go unparalleled. You respect my soul, spirit, well-being, art, and my audience in a way that makes me know our partnership was written in the stars! Here is to our next grand adventure. Thank you for being a sounding board, confidant, and fearless leader on this monumental and meaningful project! Love you, sister!

A girl in her Vegas home studio. The EY sign made it!

PHOTO CREDITS

Throughout

Page v. Diane and Debbie Gibson. Courtesy of M. Christine Torrington.

Page 67. Anthony Sanfilippo, Debbie, Larry Yasgar, and Bruce Carbone. Courtesy of David Salidor.

Page 68. Debbie in the recording studio. Courtesy of Newsday LLC/Newsday via Getty Images.

Page 162. Debbie on the set of "Didn't Have the Heart." Courtesy of Kevin Mazur.

Page 193. Handwritten lyrics for "We Could Be Together" by Deborah Gibson. Copyright © 1988 by Music Sales Corporation (ASCAP). International Copyright Secured. Used by permission. All rights reserved.

Page 199. Debbie and Ahmet. Courtesy of Kevin Mazur.

Page 249. Debbie and Sean. From Ms. Gibson's personal collection.

Page 275. Heather and Debbie. From Ms. Gibson's personal collection.

Page 301. Adam, Buddy, Debbie, Stepp, Joey, and Eddie. Courtesy of Eddie Sung.

Page 303. Richard Buskin and Debbie. From Ms. Gibson's personal collection.

Page 307. Debbie in front of her *Electric Youth* sign. Courtesy of Nick Spanos.

PHOTO CREDITS

Insert

Page 1. Karen, Denise, Debbie, and Michele. From Ms. Gibson's personal collection.

Page 1. Christmas dinner. From Ms. Gibson's personal collection.

Page 1. Debbie as a toddler at the beach. From Ms. Gibson's personal collection.

Page 2. Debbie and Placido Domingo. From Ms. Gibson's personal collection.

Page 2. Debbie and musical collaborator Fred Zarr. From Ms. Gibson's personal collection.

Page 2. Club kids Buddy, Debbie, and Robert Alvarez. Courtesy of David Salidor.

Page 3. Debbie and the BEAR. From Ms. Gibson's personal collection.

Page 3. Debbie and Tiffany. From Ms. Gibson's personal collection.

Page 4. Debbie with NKOTB's Donnie and Joey. From Ms. Gibson's personal collection.

Page 4. Doug Morris, Debbie, and Diane. Courtesy of David Elkouby.

Page 5. Bobby and Debbie, 2024. From Ms. Gibson's personal collection.

Page 5. Brian Bloom, Debbie, and Michael Damian. From Ms. Gibson's personal collection.

Page 5. Debbie at South Street Seaport. Courtesy of David Salidor.

Page 6. Debbie writing songs. From Ms. Gibson's personal collection.

Page 6. Debbie and Iris. From Ms. Gibson's personal collection.

Page 6. Lisa, Bernie, Debbie, Elton, Diane, Mike, and David. Courtesy of David Salidor.

PHOTO CREDITS

Page 7. Mackenzie, Stepp, Debbie, Denise, Buddy, and Scott. From Ms. Gibson's personal collection.

Page 7. Billy Joel, Debbie, and Elton John. From Ms. Gibson's personal collection.

Page 7. High school friends. From Ms. Gibson's personal collection.

Page 8. Debbie and Michael Jackson. Courtesy of David Salidor.

Page 8. Uncle Carl, Debbie, and Aunt Linda. Courtesy of Anthony Billante, Cashman Photo Enterprises.

Page 8. Brian Bloom and Debbie. From Ms. Gibson's personal collection.

Page 9. Debbie as Éponine. Courtesy of Kevin Mazur.

Page 9. Chris Bruno and Debbie. From Ms. Gibson's personal collection.

Page 9. Craig McLachlan and Debbie. From Ms. Gibson's personal collection.

Page 10. Debbie in her dressing room. From Ms. Gibson's personal collection.

Page 10. Debbie and the Elephant Girls. From Ms. Gibson's personal collection.

Page 10. Betty Buckley and Debbie. Courtesy of Joan Marcus.

Page 11. Rutledge and Debbie. From Ms. Gibson's personal collection.

Page 11. Marissa, Diane, and Stepp. From Ms. Gibson's personal collection.

Page 11. Lamont Dozier, Debbie, Jellybean Benitez, and Taylor Dayne. Courtesy of Kevin Mazur.

Page 12. Debbie and NSYNC. From Ms. Gibson's personal collection.

Page 12. Team Deb. From Ms. Gibson's personal collection.

PHOTO CREDITS

Page 12. Joey McIntyre and Debbie. From Ms. Gibson's personal collection.

Page 13. Debbie, Ray Garcia, and Sylvia MacCalla. Courtesy of Ray Garcia.

Page 13. Eddie, Debbie, and Buddy. Courtesy of Nick Spanos.

Page 13. Daddy Joe and Debbie. From Ms. Gibson's personal collection.

Page 14. Debbie at the *TBR* photo shoot. Courtesy of Nick Spanos.

Page 14. Orfeh and Debbie. From Ms. Gibson's personal collection.

Page 14. Jimmy Van Patten and Debbie. From Ms. Gibson's personal collection.

Page 15. Ron and Debbie. From Ms. Gibson's personal collection.

Page 15. Nick, Debbie, Eddie, and Buddy at the "LDC" video shoot. Courtesy of Denise Truscello.

Page 15. Richard Weitz, Debbie, and Richard Jay-Alexander. From Ms. Gibson's personal collection.

Page 16. Debbie with Levi, Joey, and Trouper. Courtesy of Nick Spanos.

Page 16. Debbie and Joey on the open road. From Ms. Gibson's personal collection.

Page 16. Debbie and the Diamonds. From Ms. Gibson's personal collection.